5 STEPS TO A 5™

AP European History

2017

5 STEPS TO A 5™

AP European History

2017

Jeffrey Brautigam, PhD

McGraw Hill Education

New York   Chicago   San Francisco   Athens   London   Madrid
Mexico City   Milan   New Delhi   Singapore   Sydney   Toronto

1 2 3 4 5 6 7 8 9   RHR   21 20 19 18 17 16

ISBN: 978-1-259-58676-7
MHID: 1-259-58676-6
ISSN: 2150-6388

e-ISBN: 978-1-259-58677-4
e-MHID: 1-259-58677-4

Trademarks: McGraw-Hill Education, the McGraw-Hill Education logo, *5 Steps to a 5*, and related trade dress are trademarks or registered trademarks of McGraw-Hill Education and/or its affiliates in the United States and other countries and may not be used without written permission. All other trademarks are the property of their respective owners. McGraw-Hill Education is not associated with any product or vendor mentioned in this book.

AP Advanced Placement Program and *College Board* are registered trademarks of the College Board, which was not involved in the production of, and does not endorse, this product.

The series editor was Grace Freedson, and the project editor was Del Franz.

Series design by Jane Tenenbaum.

McGraw-Hill Education products are available at special quantity discounts to use as premiums and sales promotions or for use in corporate training programs. To contact a representative, please e-mail us at bulksales@mheducation.com.

ABOUT THE AUTHOR

Jeffrey Brautigam is Professor of History and Division Coordinator for the Humanities at Hanover College in Hanover, Indiana, where he evaluates all requests for AP college credit and placement in history. A recipient of a PhD in history from the University of Florida, he has taught European history at the college level for 20 years. The coauthor of *A Student Introduction to Charles Darwin* (Kendall/Hunt, 1999, ISBN 0-7872-6311-7), Professor Brautigam is a historian who writes for students and general audiences.

CONTENTS

STEP 5

Build Your Test-Taking Confidence

PREFACE

Welcome to the world of Advanced Placement (AP) European history. Whether you are, or have been, enrolled in an AP European history course at your school or are preparing on your own, this guide will help you to move smoothly and confidently from your individual starting point through a five-step process that will bring you the level of preparation you desire. Along the way, you will be evaluating your current level of preparation, evaluating your learning strategies, reading widely, analyzing primary documents, taking practice multiple-choice tests, and writing practice essays. As you go, you will be developing the strategies and confidence you need to score a 5 on the AP European History Exam.

The five-step process is described in detail in the Introduction. Here, I simply want to urge you to enter into your preparation with enthusiasm. The intricate story of European history is dramatic, fascinating, and extremely relevant to the world in which you live. The information, understanding, and skills that you will learn by working through this guide will help you to do well on the AP European History Exam, but they will also help you to excel in college and to become a well-informed, critically thinking human being.

As you begin, it is important that you not think of this guide as some large book to "get through." This guide is a tool and, like many tools, it can be used in a number of different ways. You can follow it through from beginning to end, or you can jump around, using the information and exercises contained in it in any way that suits you best. So take some time to familiarize yourself with the contents of this guide; get a feel for how it "works." Then, when you are ready, read Chapters 1 and 2; they will help you to choose the mode of preparation that is right for you.

Good luck, and enjoy your journey!

ACKNOWLEDGMENTS

I would like to thank Eric Dodge for putting me in touch with Grace Freedson, and Grace Freedson for connecting me with McGraw-Hill Education. I would also like to thank all those who assisted me in the preparation of this book: Del Franz for superior editing, Robyn Ryle for her critical reading and support, and my daughter, Grace Brautigam, for her patience.

INTRODUCTION: THE FIVE-STEP PROGRAM

The Basics

If you are looking at this book, it is because you are considering taking the AP European History Exam. Maybe you are enrolled in an AP European History class in your high school, or maybe you are planning a course of study on your own. Either way, you need some help, and you have come to a bookstore or are shopping online to find it. Right now, there are a number of guides either on the shelf or on the screen in front of you, and you are wondering about the differences between them. The fact is, all the guides in front of you are similar in a number of ways: each is written by an experienced history instructor who is intimately familiar with the AP European History Exam; each contains a concise review of the material you will need to master in order to do well on the exam; and each contains a number of practice exams and exercises to assist you in that preparation. There is, however, one crucial difference: this book is based upon the highly successful 5 Steps to a 5 program. If you are like the thousands of students who have used the 5 Steps to a 5 program to successfully prepare for AP Exams, it is a difference worth exploring.

Introducing the Five-Step Program

This book is organized as a five-step program to prepare you for success on the AP European History Exam. These steps are designed to provide you with the skills and strategies vital to the exam and the practice that can lead you to that perfect 5. Here are the five steps:

Step 1. Set Up Your Study Program

In this step you'll learn the information you need to know about the AP European History Exam itself and be guided through a process to help determine which of the following preparation programs is right for you:

- Full school year: September through May
- One semester: January through May
- Six weeks: Basic training for the exam

Step 2. Understand the Skills That Will Be Tested

In Step 2 you will learn about the various ways in which historians think and discover the historical skills that the AP European History Exam seeks to test, including the following:

- Reasoning chronologically
- Putting information in context
- Arguing from evidence

Step 3. Develop Strategies for Success

Here you'll find the strategies that will help you do your best on the exam. These strategies cover all four types of questions asked on the exam. In the four chapters included in Step 3, you will learn the following:

- How to read and answer multiple-choice questions, including whether or not to guess
- How to read and answer short-answer questions
- How to read and answer the document-based question
- How to read and answer the long-essay question

Step 4. Review the Knowledge You Need to Score High

In this step you will learn or review the major themes of modern European history that you will need to know for the exam. You will learn or review the key concepts you will need to know on the exam.

Step 5. Build Your Test-Taking Confidence

In the final step you will complete your preparation by testing yourself on a practice exam. This guide contains a complete exam in European history, with full answers and explanations for each multiple-choice and short-answer question, as well as suggestions and possible outlines for answers to the document-based question and the long-essay question. Be aware that these practice exams are *not* reproduced questions from actual AP European History Exams, but they mirror both the material tested by AP and the way in which it is tested.

Introduction to the Graphics Used in this Book

To emphasize particular concepts, strategies, tips, and practice exercises and make them easy to find, several icons are used throughout this book. An icon in the margin will alert you that you should pay particular attention to the accompanying text. The three icons used include the following:

This icon indicates an important concept, fact, or explanation that you should not pass over.

This icon calls your attention to a step-by-step approach you might want to try when attempting to answer a particular type of question.

This icon indicates a suggestion or other helpful information you can use when you prepare for or take the exam.

5 STEPS TO A 5™

AP European History

2017

STEP **1**

Set Up Your Study Program

CHAPTER 1

What You Need to Know About the AP European History Exam

IN THIS CHAPTER

Summary: The AP European History program allows students who score well on the AP exam to earn college credits while still in high school. This chapter describes the AP European History program and exam and answers frequently asked questions, including what's on the exam and how it is scored.

KEY IDEA

Key Ideas:

✪ The exam consists of multiple-choice questions, short-answer questions, a document-based question, and a longer essay question.

✪ The exam is scored on a scale of 1 to 5; most schools will give you college credit for a score of 4 or 5, and some will give credit for a 3.

Background Information

The Advanced Placement (AP) Program is overseen by an organization known as the College Board, which is involved in many facets of the college admissions process. The program offers highly motivated high school students the opportunity to take college-level courses while still in high school and the opportunity to earn credit or advanced standing at a college or university by taking the Advanced Placement exams.

Frequently Asked Questions About the AP European History Exam

Why Take the AP European History Exam?

Most students take the exam with the hope of earning college credit. Most schools will give you college credit for a score of 4 or 5, and some will give credit for a 3. However, the policies of individual colleges and universities vary, so you should check with the schools you are interested in attending for their specific policies.

One advantage of having college credit in European history is that you are one class closer to graduation, but there are a couple of other good reasons to take the exam:

- First, getting college credit for AP European history means that you will be able to opt out of either a required introductory course in European history or an elective course. Either way, you will have greater flexibility in choosing your courses, and you will be able move on to the more advanced and specific courses (either in history or in some other field) that interest you.
- Second, having AP credit on your transcript can increase your chances of getting into the school you want because it tells college admissions officers that you are a serious student who has some experience with college-level work.

Do I Have to Take an AP European History Class to Take the Exam?

No. Taking an AP European History class at your high school is a great way to prepare for the exam, but it is not required. The College Board simply urges students to study the kinds of skills and subjects outlined in the AP European History Course Description. The Course Description is available online from the College Board (www.collegeboard .org). The McGraw-Hill Education five-step program is based on both the College Board Course Description for AP European History and on the Exam Guidelines, so working through this guide will help you to develop the relevant skills and to familiarize yourself with the relevant subject material.

Who Writes and Grades the AP European History Exam?

The exam is written by a team of college and high school history instructors called the AP European History Test Development Committee. The Committee is constantly evaluating the test and field-testing potential questions. The exam is graded by a much larger group of college and high school teachers who meet at a central location in early June to evaluate and score exams that were completed by students the previous month.

What Is on the Exam?

Beginning in May 2016, the AP European History Exam will adopt a new format. The new format of the AP European History exam is shown in Table 1.1.

Table 1.1   AP European History Exam Format as of May 2016

SECTION	TEST ITEMS	TIME LIMIT	PERCENTAGE OF TOTAL GRADE
I. Multiple-Choice	55 questions	55 minutes	40%
II. Short-Answer	4 questions	50 minutes	20%
III. Document-Based	1 question	55 minutes	25%
IV. Long-Essay	1 question	35 minutes	15%

Each section of the exam has a set of objectives that fit into the overall scheme of the exam. We will discuss strategies for doing well on the multiple-choice section in Chapter 9, the short-answer questions in Chapter 10, the document-based question in Chapter 11, and the long-essay question in Chapter 12.

How Is the Exam Evaluated and Scored?

The multiple-choice section is scored by computer. The other sections are all scored by "readers" (the college and high school teachers who are hired to do the job), who have been trained to score the responses in accordance with a set of guidelines. The scoring guidelines for each question are drawn up by a team of the most experienced readers. (We will discuss what kinds of things the guidelines tell the readers to look for in Chapters 10 through 12.) Evaluation and scoring are monitored by the Chief Reader and Table Leaders, and scoring is periodically analyzed for consistency.

The scores from all sections are combined into a composite score on the AP five-point scale:

- 5 is the highest possible grade; it indicates that you are extremely well qualified to receive college credit.
- 4 indicates that you are well qualified to receive college credit.
- 3 indicates that you are qualified to receive college credit.
- 2 indicates that you are possibly qualified to receive college credit.
- 1 indicates that you are not qualified to receive college credit.

How Do I Register?

Whether you are enrolled in a high school AP course or preparing for the test on your own, the best thing to do is see your guidance counselor. He or she will direct you to the AP Coordinator for your school. You will need to contact the coordinator because it is this person who will collect your money and give you information about the exact location and date of the test. If for some reason your school does not have an AP Coordinator, you can test through another school. To find out which schools in your area offer the test and to find a coordinator, you can check the College Board's website (www.collegeboard.org). You should visit the site, even if your school has an AP coordinator, as it will always have the latest and most up-to-date information.

In 2016, it cost $92 to take the AP European History Exam. Students who demonstrate financial need may receive a $29 refund to help offset the cost of testing. There are also several optional fees that must be paid if you want your scores rushed to you or if you wish to receive multiple grade reports.

What Should I Bring to the AP Exam?

There are several things that are either required or a good idea to have with you at the exam. They include the following:

- A good supply of #2 pencils with erasers that don't smudge (for the multiple-choice section)
- Several black- or blue-colored ink pens (for the other sections)
- A watch so that you can monitor your time. You never know if the exam room will have a clock, and you won't have a cellphone or other electronic devices (be sure to turn any alarms or chimes off).
- Your photo ID and social security number

What Should I NOT Bring to the Exam?

There are a number of things that you are not allowed to use during the exam. Prohibited items you should *not* bring include the following:

- Reference books of any kind, including notebooks, dictionaries, and encyclopedias
- A laptop computer
- Electronic devices, like cellphones, personal digital assistants (PDAs), pagers, and walkie-talkies
- Portable music devices of any kind, including CD players, MP3 players, and iPods
- Mom, dad, and friends (there is no room for them, and you don't need the distraction)

How to Plan Your Time

IN THIS CHAPTER

Summary: To do your best on the AP European History Exam, you will need to prepare. Your preparation plan will depend on the time you have available and the way you like to study. This chapter maps out three alternative plans; choose the one that you can most easily adapt to your needs.

Key Idea:

✪ Create a preparation plan adapted to your needs.

Three Approaches to Preparing for AP Exams

What kind of preparation program for the AP exam should you follow? The answer depends on two things: how much time you have and what kind of student you are. Obviously, if you only have one semester or four to six weeks before you intend to take the exam, you can't choose the full-year program. So first decide how much time you have. Then consider what kind of preparation works best for you. No one knows your study habits and learning style better than you do. Consider the three profiles below to see which one most closely describes you and your situation. Then, choose one of the three programs of preparation.

Full-Year Preparation: Approach A

You are a full-year prep student (and should follow Approach A) if:

1. You are leaning strongly toward history as a college major.
2. You like detailed planning and preparation.
3. You feel more comfortable and confident when you feel thoroughly prepared.
4. You can't wait to get started.
5. You have been successful with this approach in the past.

One-Semester Preparation: Approach B

You are a one-semester prep student (and should follow Approach B) if:

1. You are fairly interested in history.
2. You like to plan but feel there is such a thing as being over prepared.
3. You feel comfortable and confident when you feel you have prepared sufficiently.
4. You have more than one exam you are preparing for and feel one semester is enough time to prepare.
5. You have been successful with this approach in the past.

Four-to-Six-Week Preparation: Approach C

You are a four-to-six-week prep student (and should follow Approach C) if:

1. You are only fairly interested in history, or you are interested only in the exam.
2. You feel like you get stale if you prepare too far in advance.
3. You feel well prepared already and are just looking to sharpen your focus.
4. You are prepping for several exams, and this one is your lowest priority.
5. You have been successful with this approach in the past.

Detailed Calendar for Each Plan

Calendar for Approach A: Full-School-Year Preparation

September to October (Check off the activities as you complete them.)

_____ Read the Introduction and become familiar with the 5-Step Program.

_____ Read Chapter 1 and become familiar with the AP European History Exam and procedures.

_____ Become familiar with the College Board AP website.

_____ Read Chapter 2 and confer with your AP European History teacher about your preparation program.

_____ Read Chapter 3 and get into the habit of thinking historically.

November

____ Read Chapters 4–7, and learn strategies for success for each of the four types of questions asked on the AP European History Exam.

____ Complete the "Further Practice" sections in each of these chapters.

December

____ Read Chapters 8–11, along with relevant outside readings and course materials, and become familiar with the events, processes, and key concepts of modern European history covered in those chapters.

____ Complete the Review Questions at the end of each chapter.

January

____ Read Chapters 12–15, along with relevant outside readings and course materials, and become familiar with the events, processes, and key concepts of modern European history covered in those chapters.

____ Complete the Review Questions at the end of each chapter.

February

____ Read Chapters 16–19, along with relevant outside readings and course materials, and become familiar with the events, processes, and key concepts of modern European history, covered in those chapters.

____ Complete the Review Questions at the end of each chapter.

March

____ Read Chapters 20–23, along with relevant outside readings and course materials, and become familiar with the events, processes, and key concepts of modern European history covered in those chapters.

____ Complete the Review Questions at the end of each chapter.

April

____ Review Chapters 3–23.

____ Take the Practice Test included in this guide.

____ Evaluate your strengths and weaknesses based on your performance on the Practice Test.

____ Study the appropriate chapters and readings to address the areas you still feel shaky on.

May (First Two Weeks)

____ Make a list of topics you still feel shaky about and ask your instructor or study group to help you focus on them.

____ Answer additional practice questions offered online.

____ Evaluate your performance.

____ Review your incorrect answers.

____ Get a good night's sleep before the exam.

____ Go to the exam feeling confident; you have prepared well.

Calendar for Approach B: One-Semester Preparation

January (Check off the activities as you complete them.)

____ Read the Introduction and become familiar with the 5-Step Program.

____ Read Chapter 1 and become familiar with the AP European History Exam and procedures.

____ Become familiar with the College Board AP website.

____ Read Chapter 2 and confer with your AP European History teacher about your preparation program.

____ Read Chapter 3 and get into the habit of thinking historically.

February–March

____ Read Chapters 4–7, and learn strategies for success for each of the four types of questions asked on the AP European History Exam.

____ Complete the "Further Practice" sections in each of these chapters.

____ Read Chapters 8–23, along with relevant outside readings and course materials, and become familiar with the events, processes, and key concepts of modern European history covered in those chapters.

____ Complete the Review Questions at the end of each chapter.

April

____ Review Chapters 3–23.

____ Take the Practice Test included in this guide.

____ Evaluate your strengths and weaknesses based on your performance on the Practice Test.

____ Study the appropriate chapters and readings to address the areas you still feel shaky on.

May (First Two Weeks)

____ Make a list of topics you still feel shaky about and ask your instructor or study group to help you focus on them.

____ Answer additional practice questions offered online.

____ Evaluate your performance.

____ Review your incorrect answers.

____ Get a good night's sleep before the exam.

____ Go to the exam feeling confident; you have prepared well.

Calendar for Approach C: Four-to-Six-Week Preparation

April (Check off the activities as you complete them.)

____ Read Chapters 1–23.

____ Take the Practice Test included in this guide.

____ Evaluate your performance and review as needed.

May (First Two Weeks)

____ Answer additional practice questions offered online.

____ Evaluate your performance.

____ Review your incorrect answers.

____ Get a good night's sleep before the exam.

____ Go to the exam feeling confident; you have prepared well.

STEP 2

Understand the Skills That Will Be Tested

CHAPTER 3

The Ways Historians Think

IN THIS CHAPTER

Summary: The AP European History Exam requires you to apply the thinking skills historians use. This chapter covers the skills you will need to be proficient in this type of thinking in order to do well on the exam.

Key Idea:

○ The skills you will need to be proficient in applying can be grouped into three basic categories: (1) Reasoning chronologically, (2) Putting information in context, and (3) Arguing from evidence.

Introduction

The AP European History Curriculum identifies interrelated sets of "Historical Thinking Skills" and requires students to apply one or more of them in each section of the exam. Your first task is to familiarize yourself with these skills and to understand how historians use them in creating a historical understanding of change over time.

There are many ways in which one might describe and categorize the intellectual skills employed by the historian. The simplest and clearest way for our purposes is to think of them as making up three interrelated thought processes: (1) Reasoning chronologically, (2) Putting information in context, and (3) Arguing from evidence.

Reasoning Chronologically

Chronology is the placing of events in the order in which they occurred. Once an accurate chronology has been constructed, reasoning based on that construction can begin.

Chronology and Causation

All historians seek, in one way or another, to explain change over time. One way to begin to do that is to create a chronology of events and then ponder cause and effect. For example, suppose we know the order of three events that occurred during the first year of World War I (WWI): the Russian Army invaded East Prussia (August 17, 1914); the German Army on the Eastern Front was put under new command and launched an attack against Russian forces (August 23–30, 1914); and Erich von Falkenhayn replaced Helmuth von Moltke as Chief of Staff of the German Army (September 14, 1914). Because we know the chronological order of these events, certain cause-and-effect relationships suggest themselves, whereas others are logically impossible. For example, because the change in command of the German forces on the Eastern Front and the German attack on Russian forces there occurred roughly a week after the Russian Army invaded East Prussia, it is a logical possibility that the Russian attack caused the Germans to react by changing command and counterattacking. Conversely, because the German decisions came roughly a week after the Russian attack, it is simply impossible for the German decisions to have caused the Russian attack.

Notice that, in our example, it is both the order in which the two events occurred and the close proximity of the two events (both occurred in the same geographical area, and less than a week elapsed between the two events) that make the possibility of a cause-and-effect relationship between the two seem likely. Conversely, while it is possible that the first two events in our example caused the third (the change in overall command of the German Army from von Moltke to von Falkenhayn), the logical argument for a cause-and-effect relationship is weaker because of a lack of close proximity: the general commander was in charge of the entire war, and nearly a month had passed since those two events had occurred on the Eastern Front.

Correlation vs. Causation

Being able to show that a series of events happened in close proximity to one another (both chronologically and geographically) is to show that those events were correlated. However, it is important to understand that correlation does not necessarily imply causation. The fact that two events happened in close geographical or chronological proximity makes a cause-and-effect relationship *possible*, but not *necessary*; the close proximity could have been merely a coincidence. To establish a cause-and-effect relationship between two events, the historian must identify and use evidence. The use of evidence is part of the third set of skills identified by the AP European History Exam and is discussed below.

Multiple Causation

The sophisticated student of history understands that significant events in history usually have many causes. Accordingly, one looks for multiple causes in order to explain events. For example, if the historian discovers evidence (such as correspondence between high-ranking German Army officials) that supports the logical assertion that successful Russian incursions into East Prussia caused both a change in command for the Eastern Front and the decision to launch a counterattack, he or she still asks additional questions and looks for evidence of other contributing causes. What else was happening on the Eastern Front at that time? What did the overall German war effort look like at that time? What other considerations may have gone into those decisions?

Continuity

The historian recognizes that change does not come easily to people or to civilizations. Accordingly, the historian is sensitive to the persistence of certain forms of human activity (social structures, political systems, etc.). Sensitivity to the power of continuity forces the historian to ask questions about the forces that were strong enough to bring about change. For example, sensitivity to the power and importance of continuity in the way in which people live and work reminds the historian that a change from a localized and agriculturally oriented economy to an interconnected, commercial economy was neither inevitable nor even particularly likely. That realization sets the historian looking for the powerful forces that fostered those changes.

Comparison

When seeking to explain change over time, the historian often looks for patterns. Some patterns can be detected by asking basic questions, such as who, what, where, and when. For example, when seeking to understand the gradual and persistent shift from an agricultural economy to a commercial economy in Europe between the fourteenth and eighteenth centuries, the historian asks: What kinds of people tended to be in the vanguard of such change? Which type of work tended to change first? Did the changes occur simultaneously or follow a geographical progression? What type of economic activity changed first? The next step is to make comparisons. For example, the historian compares the nature of the changes that occurred in Britain to those that occurred in France and in the economies further to the east. The comparisons reveal both similarities and differences, which the historian then explores, hoping to establish patterns of both change and continuity.

Contingency

Finally, the historian seeking to understand the cause-and-effect nature of historical events understands the role that contingency can play in human events. An event is said to be "contingent" if its occurrence is possible but not certain. The sophisticated student of history understands that there is a profound sense in which all significant events in history are contingent, because their occurrence depends on the action of human beings. For example, one of the most significant events in the history of the French Revolution is the storming of the Bastille on July 14, 1789. On that day, a crowd stormed the notorious fortress in the heart of Paris, killed the guards who defended it, and paraded the severed heads of those guards around the city. Historians seeking to explain this event point to powerful forces, such as the politicization of the urban working people of Paris and their tremendous fear that the armies of their king, Louis XVI, would descend upon the city at any moment. But those same historians know that it was possible that the day could have gone very differently. They know that the crowd believed that there were many prisoners and an enormous amount of weapons inside the Bastille. They also know the crowd was mistaken; the only prisoner was the Marquis de Sade (and he was imprisoned for moral depravity, not political activity), and there were virtually no weapons inside the Bastille. These historians know, therefore, that the situation could have been defused; the guards could simply have abandoned the Bastille (the King's cause would not have been harmed nor the Revolution's helped). But the guards were young, inexperienced, and insecure; they panicked and fired into the crowd. Those completely unpredictable actions of the guards are the contingent causes of the storming of the Bastille.

Putting Information in Context

The historian must put every piece of information he or she encounters into its "proper context." That means connecting that information to all of the relevant events or processes occurring at the time and place in which the source of the information was produced.

Constructing a Context for Past Events and Actions

The art of contextualization sounds complicated in the abstract, but in practice, it is really about asking additional, logical questions about a given event or action in the past. For example, one of the most notorious episodes in the history of conflict between England and Ireland is the massacring of the inhabitants of two Irish towns, Drogheda and Wexford, in September and October 1649, respectively. In the context of the English Civil War (1642–1649), Oliver Cromwell and his anti-Royalist army were sent to Ireland by the English Parliament to put down an anti-English rebellion that had been simmering there since 1641. From September 2–11, 1649, Cromwell and his army laid siege to the town of Drogheda. During the four days *following* Drogheda's surrender, Cromwell oversaw the killing of some 4,000 of its people. Similarly, 2,000 more people were killed *after* the fall and surrender of the town of Wexford in October. Understandably, these events have earned Cromwell a reputation for a level of impulsive cruelty that is practically unintelligible.

But making such actions intelligible (constructing an understanding of how such a thing could occur) is precisely the task of the historian. To do it, the historian has to "put the events in their context," or, more precisely, the historian has to construct a context around the event by asking further questions. In the case of Cromwell, historians have asked: Of the many other towns that Cromwell forced to surrender in his nine-month march through Ireland, how many times did he massacre a town's inhabitants? The answer, interestingly, is none. Did Cromwell view the Irish who resisted merely as military enemies? No, Cromwell was among those within the Parliamentarian faction of the English Civil War who viewed themselves as "Saints," whose mission was to purify the realm of false religions. Accordingly, Cromwell viewed the Catholic Irish not only as rebellious subjects, but as heretics. Was it unusual to kill large numbers of people after a successful siege? The rules of war at the time called for the inhabitants of a town to be spared, *provided* the governor of the town surrendered without a fight. Conversely, if the governor of a town decided to resist, he knew that he was putting the inhabitants at risk of retribution.

The historian uses the knowledge gained from asking and answering these contextual questions not to condone Cromwell's actions, but to make sense of them. Once the Drogheda and Wexford massacres are put into context, they remain ghastly, but they are no longer unintelligible. Cromwell may indeed have been impulsive and cruel, but he was not insane; there was a rationale behind his actions. He committed no more massacres in Ireland in 1649 because he did not need to. The governors of the other towns had seen the cruel consequences of resistance and surrendered without a fight.

Contextualization of Sources

Another aspect of historical thinking in which contextualization is important is in the use of sources. Historians build their understanding of past events and processes on the use of primary sources: all manner of artifacts that have come down to us from the times and places we wish to study. In order to gain an understanding of those sources—and to use them later as part of an interpretive argument—the historian must first put the sources in context. The process is similar to the one discussed above. The historian begins by asking a number of questions about the sources; the sum total of the answers to those questions makes up the context in which the sources must be interpreted.

For example, in the writing of her remarkable account of the English Civil War, the historian Diane Purkiss uncovered multiple primary sources offering eyewitness testimony to the events that occurred at Barthomley Church in Cheshire, England, in 1643. During the course of the English Civil War, Royalist troops arrived in the town of Barthomley, whose inhabitants were sympathetic to the Parliamentary side. One source that Purkiss uncovered asserts that the Royalist party encircled the church, where about 20 towns-people had taken refuge in the steeple. When the people would not come out, the source asserts, the Royalists set fire to the church, and when the people finally came out to escape the smoke and flames, the Royalists stripped them naked, abused them, and killed them. Another source confirms the report and asserts that it was one of many such instances in the area.

So, Purkiss has primary-source accounts that seem to corroborate each other, but Purkiss knows that even corroborating reports have to be put in context. Both sources, though produced independently of one another, are what is known as "newsbooks." Such newsbooks were penned by Parliamentary sympathizers who were supplying "news" about the conflict. In short, Purkiss knows that such newsbooks were essentially Parliamentary propaganda, and that they cannot, therefore, be counted on as reliable accounts of what happened.

Arguing from Evidence

The process of putting sources in context leads the historian directly to the art of arguing from evidence. For example, a historian would initially be tempted to argue that the existence of multiple primary sources asserting that an unprovoked massacre had been carried out by Royalist troops at Barthomley was proof that such a thing had occurred. However, by contextualizing those sources, Purkiss shows that such an argument will not hold up; the preponderance of evidence that shows that the contents of such newsbooks served as Parliamentary propaganda casts too much doubt on the reliability of those accounts.

But rather than give up on those sources, Purkiss asked herself what the historian *could* reliably learn from Parliamentary propaganda. Purkiss knew that the purpose of propaganda was to cultivate outrage at, and hatred of, the enemy. She knew, in other words, that propaganda aimed to play on the worst fears of its readers. So in order to learn something from those sources, Purkiss changed her question. Rather than asking, "What happened at Barthomley?" she asked, "What do the sources tell us about the fears of Parliamentary readers?" Because all of the newsbook accounts of the incident at Barthomley stressed setting fire to the church, stripping and abusing the people taken prisoner, and the murdering of those people, she concluded that it might be reasonable to assume that the greatest fears of people in that region during the conflict were the desecration of their holy places and the suffering and death of their loved ones at the hands of marauding soldiers. Finally, she went on to show that that those fears did, in fact, mirror the major themes of atrocity stories in a large number of Parliamentary newsbooks.

Arguing from Evidence in an Essay

Let's look at an example of how one argues from evidence. Suppose you were faced with the following question:

Explain ONE lasting effect of the Revolutions of 1848 on European political culture.

You might choose to answer with the following assertion:

The ultimate failure of the attempt, in the Revolutions of 1848, to bring about liberal, democratic reform in continental Europe caused a large portion of the European population to put their faith in conservative, rather than liberal, leaders.

Next, you would need to argue from evidence; that is, you would need to support and illustrate the assertion you have made by presenting and explaining events that serve as specific examples of what you have asserted. The result would look something like this:

In February 1848, the decision by King Louis Philippe to ban liberal reformers from holding public meetings led to massive street demonstrations in Paris. Demonstrations soon escalated into revolution, forcing Louis Philippe to abdicate and a new French republic (known as the Second Republic) to be established. The Assembly of the new republic attempted to establish a liberal, democratic constitution for the French Republic. However, in June of the same year, the French Army reestablished conservative control of Paris. An election in December swept the conservative Louis-Napoleon Bonaparte, nephew of Napoleon, to power. Three years later, he staged his own coup d'état, putting an end to the Second Republic.

Similarly, violence broke out in the major cities of the German kingdoms in the first half of 1848. In Berlin, Frederick William IV was forced to order the army out of the city and to agree to the formation of a parliament. In the wake of that victory, liberal leaders from all over Germany formed the Frankfurt Assembly and proclaimed that they would write a liberal, democratic constitution for a united Germany. But in the second half of 1848, Frederick William IV refused the Frankfurt Assembly's offer to be the constitutional monarch of a united, democratic Germany, and instead used military troops to disperse the Assembly and to reassert conservative control in the cities. When, in November, troops moved back into Berlin, they faced little resistance. In the subsequent decades, popular support for German unification was given to Frederick William IV and his conservative chancellor, Otto von Bismarck, rather than to the liberals.

Rapid Review

The AP European History Curriculum identifies interrelated sets of "Historical Thinking Skills." Those skills can be categorized as follows:

- Reasoning chronologically
- Putting information in context
- Arguing from evidence

Reasoning chronologically is the practice of placing events in the order in which they occurred and then making reasonable inferences from that order about cause and effect. Putting information in context means connecting historical sources to all of the relevant events or processes occurring at the time and place in which the source was produced. Arguing from evidence is the art of making inferences and constructing a logical argument with specific examples.

STEP 3

Develop Strategies for Success

CHAPTER 4

The Multiple-Choice Questions

IN THIS CHAPTER

Summary: The multiple-choice questions of the new AP European History Exam are all based on a "visual stimulus," making them a little different from the multiple-choice questions you're used to. This chapter will help you learn what to expect and develop a strategy to successfully approach these questions.

Key Ideas:

✪ Use the process of elimination to find the best answer.
✪ If you can't eliminate all but one answer choice, take a guess. In fact, don't leave any multiple-choice answers blank; there's always a chance you will guess correctly.

Introduction

Section I, Part A, of the AP European History Exam consists of 55 multiple-choice questions to be completed within 55 minutes. The questions come in sets of two to five questions, which are tied to a "visual stimulus." The visual stimulus presents a primary or secondary source, a historian's argument, or a historical problem. We will look at an example in a minute, but first let's remind ourselves of what we already know about multiple-choice questions.

Passive Knowledge and the Process of Elimination

All multiple-choice exams test passive knowledge. The multiple-choice section of the AP European History Exam will test your passive knowledge of European history from roughly 1450 to the present. That is, it will test your ability to recognize the *best* answer out of a group of possible answers to a specific historical question. The word *best* is important. It means that all multiple-choice questions are answered through a process of elimination; you begin by eliminating the one that is most clearly not the "best" and continue until you have a "survivor."

Putting Your Historical Thinking Skills to Use

Remember that the point of each section of the AP European History Exam is to test your ability to use the thinking skills of the historian. Recall that the three main categories of historical thinking skills are reasoning chronologically, putting information in context, and arguing from evidence. Although you won't create your own argument from evidence in the multiple-choice section, you will be asked to identify which answer choice is supported by the evidence in the visual stimulus. That means that you will find the best answers to the questions by using all three of these types of historical thinking skills. Let's look at an example and see how that would work.

Here is a set of multiple-choice questions similar to the ones you will encounter on the AP European History Exam, followed by an explanation of how you would arrive at the best answer.

Questions 1 and 2 relate to the following passage:

I do not feel obliged to believe that the same God who has endowed us with senses, reason and intellect has intended us to forgo their use and by some other means to give us knowledge which we can attain by them. . . . From these things it follows as a necessary consequence that, since the Holy Ghost did not intend to teach us whether heaven moves or stands still, whether its shape is spherical or like a discus or extended in a plane, nor whether the earth is located at its center or off to one side. . . . I would say here something that was heard from an ecclesiastic of the most eminent degree: "That the intention of the Holy Ghost is to teach us how one goes to heaven, not how heaven goes."

Galileo Galilei, *Letter to Christina, Grand Duchess of Tuscany,* 1615

1. Based on this excerpt, it can be inferred that Galileo was participating in what intellectual and cultural development?

   A. The consolidation of political power in the sixteenth and seventeenth centuries

   B. The rise of natural philosophy and the Scientific Revolution

   C. The Great Voyages of Exploration and early colonization

   D. The Industrial Revolution

Read the passage (the visual stimulus), and scan the four possible answers. *It is possible that you recognize that the correct answer is B, because you know that the historical context with which Galileo is associated is the rise of natural philosophy and the Scientific Revolution.* But suppose for a moment that you were taking the exam and drew a blank on Galileo. You could still answer the question fairly quickly by asking yourself a series of chronological and contextual questions about the possible answers. First, you notice that the passage is dated 1615. Can you eliminate any of the answers based on that chronology? Yes, D can be eliminated because you know the Industrial Revolution was a late eighteenth- and early nineteenth-century phenomenon. C also is improbable because most of the Great Voyages occurred earlier than 1615. Now examine the contexts of the remaining answers. Does the passage seem to have anything to do with the context of sea voyages? No, so C can definitely be eliminated. Does the passage seem to have anything to do with the consolidation of political power? No, so A can be eliminated. Finally, contextual reference to the conflict between the authority of the church and concern for how the heavens move confirms that the context for this passage is the rise of natural philosophy and the Scientific Revolution.

2. Based on the document, you can infer that Galileo's natural philosophy has brought him into conflict with

   A. the King of France

   B. the barons of industry

   C. the Holy Roman Emperor

   D. the authority of the Catholic Church in Rome

Here again, you may know that natural philosophers like Galileo came into conflict with the Catholic Church in Rome. Conversely, the other choices can be eliminated through a combination of chronological reasoning (industrialization, and therefore, the creation of barons of industry, is a nineteenth-century phenomenon) and contextualization (arguments about the movement of the heavens have no contextual relationship to political rulers like the King of France or the Holy Roman Emperor).

About Guessing

Should you guess? Total scores on the multiple-choice section are based solely on the number of questions you answer correctly. Points are not deducted for incorrect answers, and no points are awarded for unanswered questions. In other words, there is no guessing penalty. If you are unsure of an answer, take a guess.

Further Practice with Multiple-Choice Questions

In this book you'll find test-like multiple-choice questions at the end of each content review chapter in Step 4. Use these to practice your strategy for attacking the multiple-choice section of the AP European History Exam. Use the explanations provided to help you understand any questions you get wrong. It's a good idea to read the explanations, not only for the questions you missed, but also for any that you were unsure of or didn't understand one of the answer choices for. Additional practice for the multiple-choice questions can be found in the practice test in Step 5. To gain more practice and become more proficient, access the sample multiple-choice questions provided online at the College Board website (www.collegeboard.org).

CHAPTER 5

The Short-Answer Questions

IN THIS CHAPTER

Summary: The AP European History Exam contains a section composed of short-answer questions. This chapter will help you learn what to expect and develop a strategy to successfully approach these questions.

Key Ideas:

✪ A good answer to a short-answer question is only one paragraph, or, in the case of a question that asks for two things, two short paragraphs.

✪ For each paragraph, create a topic sentence that answers the question and four or five more sentences that support and illustrate your assertions.

Introduction

On the AP European History Exam, you will encounter four short-answer questions and have 50 minutes to respond. Some of the questions may be accompanied by a visual stimulus.

Putting Your Knowledge and Historical Thinking Skills to Use

The short-answer questions test two things: your knowledge of modern European history and your historical thinking skills. Recall that the three main categories of historical thinking skills are reasoning chronologically, putting information in context, and arguing from evidence. The short-answer questions do not require you to make an argument from evidence, so that means that you will answer the question by using your knowledge, reasoning chronologically, and contextualizing. Let's look at an example to see how that would work.

Question 1: Using your knowledge of European history, answer parts A and B below.

A) Briefly explain two significant consequences of the development of market-based agriculture in the eighteenth century.

B) Briefly explain how the traditional population and productivity cycles of Western Europe were broken in the eighteenth century.

Begin by making sure you know what the question is asking. In the short-answer questions, that will be straightforward. In the example above, you are to briefly explain two related events: the development of market-based agriculture and the breaking of the population and productivity cycles. Organize your thoughts by locating the two events chronologically, thereby activating your knowledge of the appropriate era and events. These eighteenth-century developments are covered in Chapter 14 of this text: "Economic Change and the Expansion of the State."

A good answer to the short-answer questions is typically one paragraph, or, in the case of a question that asks for two things, two short paragraphs. So what you need is a topic sentence that answers the question and four or five more sentences that support and illustrate your assertions.

Part A of the Short-Answer Question

Here again is part A of the question, followed by an example of a good response:

A) Briefly explain two significant consequences of the development of market-based agriculture in the eighteenth century.

Topic sentence (an assertion that answers the question): Two significant consequences of the development of market-based agriculture in the eighteenth century were the advent of the enclosure movement and a wave of technical innovation that increased production.

Body of paragraph 1 (supports and illustrates the first assertion of the topic sentence): The shift to cash crops that characterized market-based agriculture in the eighteenth century created a demand for larger amounts of high-profit crops. Accordingly, traditional landowning elites abandoned their feudal obligations to the peasantry and adopted the attitude of the merchant class. Specifically, they instituted a process known as "enclosure," in which hedges, fences, and walls were built to deny the peasantry access to the commons, which were now converted to fields for cash crops. Later, the land owners extended enclosure into other arable lands, breaking traditional feudal agreements and gradually transforming much of the peasantry into wage labor.

Body of paragraph 2 (supports and illustrates the second assertion of the topic sentence): The demand for larger amounts of high-profit crops also engendered a wave of technical innovation that produced higher yields. The old three-field system, which left roughly one-third of the land fallow, was replaced with new crops such as clover, turnips, and potatoes, which replenished the soil while producing foodstuffs that could be used to feed livestock in winter. As the century progressed, more highly technical innovations, such as the cotton gin (invented in 1793 by the American Eli Whitney), which efficiently removed seed from raw cotton, increased the speed with which agricultural products could be processed and sent to market.

Part B of the Short-Answer Question

Here again is part B of the question, followed by an example of a good response:

B) Briefly explain how the traditional population and productivity cycles of Western Europe were broken in the eighteenth century.

Topic sentence (an assertion that answers the question): A combination of market-based agriculture and rural manufacturing broke the traditional cycles of population and productivity by subverting the traditional limits to both.

Body of the paragraph (supports and illustrates the assertion of the topic sentence): Natural limits to both population and economic productivity created a traditional cycle in which population and productivity initially rose together, as an increase in the number of people working in an agricultural economy increased the agricultural yield. Eventually, the agricultural yield reached the maximum amount that could be produced given the land available and the methods in use. For a while, population would continue to rise, but eventually, as the number of people far outstripped the agricultural yield, food became scarce and expensive. Scarcity and high prices eventually caused the population to decline. When the population was safely below the possible productivity, the cycle began again. The advent of market-based agriculture shifted the agricultural system from farming for local consumption to a reliance on imported food sold at markets. The introduction of rural manufacture, where people were paid in currency to work at textile production, put money in people's pockets, allowing them to buy food and making them less dependent on land and agricultural cycles, thereby breaking the natural check on population growth.

Further Practice with Short-Answer Questions

In this book you'll find a test-like short-answer question at the end of each content review chapter in Step 4. Use these to practice the skills necessary to do well on the short-answer section of the AP European History Exam. Compare your work to the answer and explanation provided. Additional practice for the short-answer questions can be found in the practice test in Step 5. To gain more practice and become more proficient, access the sample short-answer questions provided online at the College Board website (www.collegeboard.org).

CHAPTER 6

The Document-Based Question

IN THIS CHAPTER

Summary: The AP European History Exam contains an essay question called the "document-based question" (DBQ), which involves using historical documents of various types. In this chapter you'll find out what to expect and develop a strategy to do well on this task.

Key Idea:

✪ The key to doing well on the DBQ is being able to write a history essay of high quality—one that answers the question, makes an argument, and supports the argument with evidence.

Introduction

 Your task for both the document-based question and the long-essay question (see Chapter 7) is to write a history essay of high quality. I have seen a lot of gibberish written about how to "crack" AP essay questions that dwells far too much on "what the graders are looking for" and gives misguided advice, such as "throw in a few big words." In reality, those who grade the AP essay exams are "looking for" the thing that all history instructors look for, and, I dare say, hope for when they read student essays: a reasonably well-written essay that answers the question, makes an argument, and supports the argument with evidence. In short, the key to "cracking" the AP essay questions is to know how to write a short history essay of high quality. Learn that skill now, and you will not only do well on the AP Exam, but you will do well in your history classes in college. And, yes, in this chapter, I *do* discuss the guidelines that are given to those who grade the AP European History Exam essays, but only for you to get a sense of the purpose of the questions and an understanding of how they are scored.

The High-Quality History Essay

There are three basic components to a short history essay of high quality:

- A clear thesis that answers the question
- Three to five topic sentences that, taken together, add up logically to the thesis
- Evidence that supports and illustrates each of the topic sentences

The Thesis

In a short history essay, the thesis is a sentence that makes a clear assertion in response to the question. It is, therefore, also a statement of what your reader will believe if your essay is persuasive.

Topic Sentences

Topic sentences should appear at the beginning of clearly marked paragraphs. Each topic sentence makes a clear assertion that you will illustrate and support in the body of the paragraph. All of your topic sentences together should add up logically to your thesis. That is, if you were to successfully persuade your reader of the truth (or at least plausibility) of your topic sentences, the reader would have no choice but to admit the plausibility of your thesis.

Evidence

This is the part that makes your essay historical. In a history essay, the evidence is made up of specific examples, explained to support and illustrate you claim.

Five Steps for Creating an Outline for Your Essay

 Before you begin writing a history essay, you should always make an outline. You probably know that, but when you keep the three components of the high-quality history essay in mind, you can produce an outline quickly and efficiently by following a very simple five-step process:

Step 1. Find the Action Words in the Question and Determine What the Question Wants You to Do

Too many essays respond to the topic instead of the question. In order to answer a question, you must do what it asks. To determine, specifically, what a question is asking you to do, you must pay attention to the action words—the words that give you a specific task. Look at the following question, notice the action words, and go to Step 2.

Sample Question: Compare and contrast the roles played by the various social classes in the unification of Italy and Germany in the 1860s and 1870s.

Step 2. Compose a Thesis that Responds to the Question and Gives You Something Specific to Support and Illustrate

Compare the following two attempts at a thesis in response to the question:

A. The German and Italian unifications have a lot in common but also many differences.
B. The unifications of both Italy and Germany were engineered by the aristocracy.

Alas, attempts at a thesis statement that resemble example A are all too common. Notice how example A merely makes a vague claim about the topic and gives the author nothing specific to do next. Example B, in contrast, makes a specific assertion about the role of a social class in the unifications of Italy and Germany; it is responding directly to the question. Moreover, example B is a thesis because it tells its readers what they will accept if the essay is persuasive. Finally, example B gives the author something specific to do, namely, build and support an argument that explains why we should conclude that the unifications of Italy and Germany were engineered by the aristocracy.

Step 3. Compose Your Topic Sentences and Make Sure That They Add Up Logically to Support Your Thesis

In response to the sample question, three good topic sentences might be the following:

A. The architects of both Italian and German unification were conservative, northern aristocrats.
B. The middle classes played virtually no role in Italian unification, and in the south of Germany, the middle classes initially opposed the unification of Germany.
C. The working classes and the peasantry followed the lead of the aristocracy in both the unification of Italy and Germany.

Notice how the topic sentences add up logically to the thesis, and how each gives you something specific to support in the body of the paragraph.

Step 4. Support and Illustrate Your Topic Sentences with Specific Examples

The sentences that follow a topic sentence should present specific examples that illustrate and support its point. That means that each paragraph is made up of two things: factual information and your explanation of how that factual information supports the topic sentence. When making your outline, you can list the examples you want to use. For our question, the outline would look something like this:

Thesis: The unifications of both Italy and Germany were engineered by the aristocracy.

Topic Sentence A: The architects of both Italian and German unification were conservative, northern aristocrats.

Specific Examples: Cavour, conservative aristocrat from Piedmont; Bismarck, conservative aristocrat from Prussia. Both took leadership roles and devised unification strategies.

Topic Sentence B: The middle classes played virtually no role in Italian unification, and in the south of Germany, the middle classes initially opposed the unification of Germany.

Specific Examples: Italy: mid-century Risorgimento, a middle-class movement, failed and played virtually no role in subsequent events. Germany: middle-class liberals in the Frankfort Parliament were ineffective. Middle-class liberals in southern Germany were initially wary of Prussian domination; they rallied to the cause only when Bismarck engineered the Franco-Prussian War.

Topic Sentence C: The working classes and the peasantry followed the lead of the aristocracy in both the unification of Italy and Germany.

Specific Examples: In Italy, the working classes played no role in the north. The peasantry of the south followed Garibaldi but shifted without resistance to support Cavour and the king at the crucial moment. The working classes in Germany supported Bismarck and Kaiser William I of Prussia. The socialists, supposedly a working-class party, rallied to the cause of war.

Step 5. *If You Have Time,* Compose a One-Paragraph Conclusion that Restates Your Thesis

A conclusion is *not* necessary, and you will get little or no credit for one. If you have time remaining, and you are happy with all the other aspects of your essay, then you can write a one-paragraph conclusion that restates your thesis.

Pitfalls to Avoid

There are some things that sabotage an otherwise promising essay and should be avoided. They include the following:

- **Avoid long sentences with multiple clauses.** Your goal is to write the clearest sentence possible; most often the clearest sentence is a relatively short sentence.
- **Do not get caught up in digressions.** No matter how fascinating or insightful you find some idea or fact, if it doesn't directly support or illustrate your thesis, don't put it in.
- **Skip the mystery.** Do not ask a lot of rhetorical questions, and do not go for a surprise ending. The readers are looking for your thesis, your argument, and your evidence; give it to them in a clear, straightforward manner.

Characteristics of the DBQ

The document-based question is simply an essay question about primary sources. It asks you to respond to a question by interpreting a set of excerpts from primary-source documents (typically five to seven) that were written in a particular historical period. The DBQ is the third section of the AP European History Exam. It is administered after the short break that follows the multiple-choice and short-answer sections of the exam. Because the DBQ involves reading and organizing short excerpts from documents, it begins with a 15-minute reading period. Following the reading period, you will have 45 minutes to write your essay.

In their present form, the directions you will encounter are lengthy and complex; don't let that worry you.

Directions: The following question is based on the accompanying Documents 1–7. (The documents have been slightly edited for use with this exercise.) The purpose of this question is to assess how well you are able to apply several historical thinking skills simultaneously. These skills include the ability to understand and use arguments based on historical interpretation, the ability to assess and use evidence from history, the ability to understand historical context, and the ability to synthesize historical knowledge. In writing your response, base your ideas on your analysis of the documents and on whatever outside knowledge of the topic you may have. Your essay should do the following:

- Present a thesis that addresses all parts of the question

- Support that thesis with evidence from all of the documents (or all but one of them) AND your own knowledge of European history

- Analyze and interpret the documents in terms of their intended audience, the author's purpose and point of view, any limitations in the author's perspective, and the historical context within which the document was created

- Place your thesis within the context of broader national, regional, or global historical trends

That is a lot of instructions, but the good news is that, basically, it boils down to writing a quality essay and being conscious of demonstrating your knowledge and skill. The only instruction not automatically taken care of by writing a quality essay is to make sure that you use all or all but one of the documents.

Applying the Principles of the High-Quality History Essay to the DBQ

Keeping in mind the need to use all, or all but one, of the sources, the five steps to outlining a history essay explained above can easily be modified for the DBQ. Here are the five steps adapted for the DBQ:

Step 1. As you read the documents, determine what they have in common and how you can group them.

Step 2. Compose a thesis that explains how these documents are linked in the way you have chosen.

Step 3. Compose your topic sentences, and make sure that they add up logically to your thesis.

Step 4. Support and illustrate your thesis with specific examples that contextualize the documents.

Step 5. *If you have time,* compose a one-paragraph conclusion that restates your thesis.

A Sample DBQ

Let's look at a question similar to the one you might see on the AP European History Exam and see how you could approach it.

Question: Discuss the changing attitudes and arguments regarding the basis for knowledge of the natural world in the following documents.

Document 1
Source: Giambattista della Porta, *Natural Magick*, 1584.

"There are two sorts of Magick, the one is infamous, and unhappy, because it has to do with foul spirits and consists of incantations and wicked curiosity; and this is called sorcery. . . . The other Magick is natural; which all excellent, wise men do admit and embrace, and worship with great applause; neither is there anything more highly esteemed, or better thought of, by men of learning. . . . Others have named it the practical part of natural philosophy, which produces her effects by the mutual and fit application of one natural thing to another. Magick is nothing else but the survey of the whole course of nature."

Document 2
Source: Galileo Galilei, "Letter to the Grand Duchess Christina of Tuscany," 1615.

"[Copernicus] stands always upon physical conclusions pertaining to the celestial motions, and deals with them by astronomical and geometrical demonstrations, founded primarily on sense experiences and very exact observations. . . . I think that in discussions of physical problems we ought to begin not from the authority of scriptural passages, but from sense-experiences and necessary demonstrations. . . . Nature . . . is inexorable and immutable; she never transgresses the laws imposed upon her, or cares a whit whether her abstruse reasons and methods of operation are understandable to men."

Document 3
Source: Robert Bellarmine, "Letter on Galileo's Theories," 1615.

"For to say that, assuming the earth moves and the sun stands still, all the appearances are saved better than with eccentrics and epicycles, is to speak well; there is no danger in this, and it is sufficient for mathematicians. But to want to affirm that the sun really is fixed in the center of the heavens . . . is a very dangerous thing, not only by irritating all the philosophers and scholastic theologians, but also by injuring our holy faith and rendering the Holy Scripture false."

Document 4
Source: Francis Bacon, *Novum Organum*, 1620.

"There are two ways, and can only be two, of seeking and finding truth. The one, from sense and reason, takes a flight to the most general axioms, and from these principles and their truth, settled once for all, invents and judges of all intermediate axioms. The other method collects axioms from sense and particulars, ascending continuously and by degrees so that in the end it arrives at the most general axioms. This latter is the only true one, but never hitherto tried."

Document 5

Source: William Harvey, *On the Motion of the Heart and Blood in Animals*, 1628.

"The heart, it is vulgarly said, is the fountain and workshop of the vital spirits, the centre from which life is dispensed to the several parts of the body. Yet it is denied that the right ventricle makes spirits, which is rather held to supply the nourishment to the lungs. ... Why, I ask, when we see that the structure of both ventricles is almost identical, there being the same apparatus of fibres, and braces, and valves, and vessels, and auricles, and both in the same way in our dissections are found to be filled up with blood similarly black in colour, and coagulated—why, I say, should their uses be imagined to be different, when the action, motion, and pulse of both are the same?"

Document 6

Source: Johannes Agricola, *Treatise on Gold*, 1638.

"All true chymists and philosophers write that common corporeal gold is of not much use in man's body if it is only ingested as such, for no metallic body can be of use if it is not previously dissolved and reduced to the *prima materia*. We have an example in corals. The virtue of corals is not in the stone or the body but in their red color. If the corals are to release their power, a separation must first occur through a dissolution, and the redness must be separated from the body. . . . Consequently, whoever wants to do something useful in medicine must see to it that he first dissolve and open his metallic body, then extract its soul and essence, and the work will then not result in no fruit."

Document 7

Source: Isaac Newton, *Principia Mathematica*, 1687.

"Rule I. We are to admit no more causes of natural things than such as are both true and sufficient to explain their appearances.
"Rule II. Therefore to the same natural effects we must, as far as possible, assign the same causes.
"Rule III. The qualities of bodies, which admit neither intension nor remission of degrees, and which are found to belong to all bodies within reach of our experiments, are to be esteemed as universal qualities of all bodies whatsoever."

Getting Started

Remember the first step to a history essay of high quality adapted to the DBQ:

Step 1. As you read the documents, determine what they have in common and how you can group them.

For this question, the documents display a wide array of positions, so a good strategy would be to try to identify a central dividing issue. In these documents, you can notice that some seem to take some sort of position on the senses and observation: some believe that all knowledge of nature must start with direct sense experience, whereas others argue that starting with sense experience is a mistake. Focus your essay on that central divide and then see if you can form a few groups based on the similarities and differences between the approaches used in these pieces.

Creating the Outline for the DBQ

Recall that the next steps in creating your essay in response to the DBQ include the following:

Step 2. Compose a thesis that explains how these documents are linked in the way you have chosen.

Step 3. Compose your topic sentences and make sure that they add up logically to your thesis.

Step 4. Support and illustrate your thesis with specific examples that contextualize the documents.

An outline for your essay in response to this DBQ could look like this:

Thesis: These documents show that arguments regarding the basis for knowledge of the natural world have often hinged on assumptions about the reliability of sense experience.

Topic Sentence A: Documents 1 and 6 illustrate the faith in direct, trial-and-error experience that developed in the "alchemy" and "natural magic" traditions.

    Specific Examples: della Porta's emphasis on "practical application"; Agricola's emphasis on handling the materials, making "dissolutions" and "combinations" and recording results carefully

Topic Sentence B: Documents 4 and 5 illustrate the emphasis on observation as the correct starting place for knowledge of the natural world.

    Specific Examples: Bacon outlines two approaches and argues for the superiority of the one that begins with observed particulars; Harvey illustrates how the method should work

Topic Sentence C: Documents 2 and 7 refine the process to include the goal of finding general laws.

    Specific Examples: Galileo: sense experiences and very exact observations. Begin not from the authority of scriptural passages, but from sense-experiences and necessary demonstrations. Nature never transgresses the laws imposed upon her. Newton codifies the approach into "rules."

Topic Sentence D: Document 3 dissents from the view that sense experience is a valid foundation for knowledge of the natural world.

    Specific Examples: Bellarmine: the dangers of contradicting scholastic and church authority

Now you are ready to write your essay based on this outline. If you have time, you can go on to step 5, but remember a conclusion isn't actually necessary. Here's a sample topic sentence for a short concluding paragraph:

Conclusion: The variety of attitudes and positions regarding knowledge about the natural world depended upon the amount of faith one put in the reliability of sense experience.

Scoring the DBQ

Although I encourage you not to get too concerned with how the graders go about scoring the exams (writing a quality essay is the best way to ensure a good score), it is worth mentioning that the scoring of essays on the AP European History Exam is now done with an "analytical rubric" as opposed to a "holistic rubric." What that means is that instead of awarding a single score for the overall quality of the essay, the high school and college instructors scoring your essay will be awarding points for particular aspects of a response. That is, they will be awarding points for each of the historical thinking skills you demonstrate. So it is worth remembering that, in their most basic forms, the historical thinking skills are reasoning chronologically, contextualizing, and arguing from evidence. Accordingly, you can look at the essay you have constructed and ask yourself if you have done all three of those things. If you have constructed a good thesis, created a good argument, and supported the argument with evidence, you will have automatically demonstrated the three categories of historical thinking.

Further Practice for the DBQ

To practice creating an outline and writing a response to a DBQ question, you can use the practice exam provided in Step 5 of this book. Give yourself 55 minutes to create your essay for the DBQ. Then compare your work to the answer and explanation provided. To gain more practice responding to a DBQ, go to the College Board website (www.collegeboard.org).

CHAPTER 7

The Long-Essay Question

IN THIS CHAPTER

Summary: The AP European History Exam contains a long-essay question that involves using your European history knowledge to create a historical argument. In this chapter you'll find out what to expect and develop a strategy to do well on this task.

Key Idea:

✪ The key to doing well on the DBQ is being able to write a history essay of high quality—one that answers the question, makes an argument, and supports the argument with evidence.

Introduction

The long-essay question tests your ability to use your knowledge of European history to create a historical argument. On the AP European History Exam, you will choose one of two available long-essay questions and have 35 minutes to respond. The keys to success are choosing properly and following the five steps to writing a history essay of high quality.

Choosing Your Topic

You can choose which one of two topics you want to write about. The key to choosing properly is to understand that you are *not* looking for the "easiest" question to answer; each of the questions you encounter on the exam will take equal amounts of knowledge and effort. The key is to recognize the question for which you are best prepared to respond. Keep in mind the five-step process to writing a history essay of high quality. That means that you should look at each question and ask yourself, "For which of these questions can I most quickly write a clear thesis and three topic sentences that I can illustrate and support with several specific examples?" Then choose your topic based on this analysis.

Applying the Five Steps to a High-Quality History Essay

Once you have chosen your question, simply follow the five-step formula to constructing a history essay of high quality:

Step 1. Find the action words in the question, and determine what the question wants you to do.

Step 2. Compose a thesis that responds to the question and gives you something specific to support and illustrate.

Step 3. Compose your topic sentences, and make sure that they add up logically to support your thesis.

Step 4. Support and illustrate your topic sentences with specific examples.

Step 5. *If you have time,* compose a one-paragraph conclusion that restates your thesis.

Also, remember the pitfalls to avoid:

- **Avoid long sentences with multiple clauses.** Your goal is to write the clearest sentence possible; most often the clearest sentence is a relatively short sentence.
- **Do not get caught up in digressions.** No matter how fascinating or insightful you find some idea or fact, if it doesn't directly support or illustrate your thesis, don't put it in.
- **Skip the mystery.** Do not ask a lot of rhetorical questions, and do not go for a surprise ending. The readers are looking for your thesis, your argument, and your evidence; give it to them in a clear, straightforward manner.

Sample Question

Let's look at a question similar to the one you'll encounter on the AP European History Exam and see how you could approach it.

Question: Discuss the relative successes and failures of seventeenth-century monarchs' attempts to consolidate political power within their kingdoms.

Outlining Your Essay

Formulate a thesis statement such as the one below:

Thesis: The success or failure of seventeenth-century monarchs to consolidate political power within their kingdoms rested on their ability to form an alliance with a rising commercial class.

Then you outline between three and five topic sentences that build a logical case for your thesis. Note specific examples you will use to support and illustrate the points asserted in the topic sentences:

Topic Sentence A: The French monarchy built the most absolutist government by cementing an alliance with both the clergy and middle class, and by using the great administrative expertise of both to build a powerful centralized bureaucracy.

Specific Examples: Richelieu's division of France into 30 administrative districts, each under the control of an *intendent*, an administrative bureaucrat, usually chosen from the middle class.

Topic Sentence B: In England, the Parliament successfully resisted the absolutist designs of the Stuart monarchy because the English Parliament of the seventeenth century was a pre-existing alliance of nobles and well-to-do members of a thriving merchant and professional class that saw itself as a voice of the "English people."

Specific Examples: Social composition of the two camps in the English Civil War: traditional landed nobility and the high church sided with the king; the newer, commercial-based nobles and the merchant class fought for Parliament.

Topic Sentence C: In those areas where the commercial class was less developed, a political standoff between monarch and landed nobility was the norm.

Specific Examples: Brandenburg-Prussia, the independent German states, Austria, and Poland all lacked a well-developed commercial class, and all were characterized by a political compromise between monarchy and traditional elites.

Now you write your essay, beginning with the thesis and starting a new paragraph for each topic sentence. As you write the body of each paragraph, make sure to identify the example you are using and explain why it supports and illustrates your topic sentence. If you have time, you can write a concluding paragraph, but this isn't actually necessary.

Scoring of the Essays

Like the DBQs, the long-essay questions are scored on a point system, but, again, there are no tricks to the scoring, and the best way to get the highest score is to simply write a history essay of high quality. If your essay answers the question with a clear thesis, and develops and supports your thesis with paragraphs made up of clear topic sentences and specific examples, you will get the maximum number of points.

Further Practice for the Long-Essay Question

To practice creating an outline and writing a response to a long-essay question, you can use the practice exam provided in Step 5 of this book. Give yourself 35 minutes. Then compare your work to the answer and explanation provided. To gain more practice responding to this type of question, go to the College Board website (www.collegeboard.org).

STEP 4

Review the Knowledge You Need to Score High

CHAPTER 8

Major Themes of Modern European History

IN THIS CHAPTER

Summary: The AP History course is focused on five broad themes of European history. All of the questions on the AP European History Exam involve one or more of these themes. In this chapter you'll learn more about those five themes.

Key Idea:

The five themes of the AP European History course and exam are as follows:
- ✪ Interacting in a Larger World
- ✪ Changes in Wealth and Who Had It
- ✪ Changes in Knowledge Systems and World View
- ✪ Changes in Society and Its Institutions
- ✪ Changes in Political Power and Its Institutions

Introduction

The AP European History Exam identifies five main themes in modern European history. These themes are explored throughout the curriculum of AP European history courses. In fact, *all* of the various kinds of questions posed on the AP European History Exam refer to one or more of these themes. The particulars of each theme will be discussed in detail in Chapters 9 through 23. For now, just become familiar with these broad themes, as such familiarity will allow you to take the first step in contextualizing the visual prompts from each question on the exam.

Interacting in a Larger World

By the fifteenth century, increased wealth flowing into the economies of Western European kingdoms from reviving trade with Eastern civilizations made both the monarchies and the merchant class of Western Europe very wealthy. Beginning in the fifteenth century, the combined investment of those monarchies and merchant classes funded great voyages of exploration across the globe, establishing new trade routes and bringing European civilization into contact with civilizations previously unknown to Europeans. The effects of this exploration and interaction on both the civilization of Western Europe and on those they encountered were profound.

Changes in Wealth and Who Had It

From the fifteenth through the nineteenth centuries, the economies of Western European civilization expanded and changed. The new wealth that flowed into those economies from their trading empires and colonies fostered a shift in the very nature of wealth and in who possessed it. At the outset of the fifteenth century, wealth was land, and it was literally in the hands of those who had the military ability to hold and protect it. Gradually, over the next four centuries, wealth became capital (money in all of its forms), whereas land became simply one form of capital—one more thing that could be bought and sold. The wealthy, those who had and controlled capital, became a larger and slightly more diverse segment of society, ranging from traditional landholders who were savvy enough to transform their traditional holdings into capital-producing concerns, to the class of merchants, bankers, and entrepreneurs who are often referred to as the bourgeoisie.

Changes in Knowledge Systems and World View

Throughout the course of modern European history, intellectuals were engaged in the pursuit of knowledge. In traditional or medieval European society, knowledge was produced by church scholars whose abilities to read and write allowed them access to ancient texts. From those texts, they chose information and a world view that seemed compatible with Christian notions of revealed knowledge and a hierarchical order. Accordingly, traditional

Christian scholars found knowledge in texts they believed to be divinely inspired and which presented a world view in which humans sat in the middle (literally and figuratively) of a cosmos created especially for them by a loving God.

Beginning in the sixteenth century, increased wealth allowed European elites to create secular spaces for intellectual pursuits. This development bred a new type of secular scholar who stressed the use of observation and reason in the creation of knowledge, and who, in due course, successfully challenged the notion of a human-centered universe. This change resulted in a large variety of cultural responses.

Changes in Society and Its Institutions

Beginning in the fifteenth century, the expansion and increasing complexity of the European economy and a corresponding growth in the size of its populations put great stress upon the traditional social structures and institutions of European society. Changes in the means of production and exchange both fostered and benefitted from dramatic changes in where and how the population lived and worked.

Changes in Political Power and Its Institutions

The economic and social changes occurring from the fifteenth through the twentieth centuries created demands for corresponding changes in the nature of political power and to the institutions through which that power was exercised. From the sixteenth through the eighteenth centuries, traditional European elites found themselves contending with newer, commercial elites for political power. In the nineteenth century, industrial and urban workers began to agitate for access to, and sometimes participation in, the wielding of political power.

The Organization of the AP Course into Units

To organize the content relating to these major themes of European history, the College Board has defined four "units," or time periods. These units form the basic structure of the AP course—but don't worry, you won't have to memorize these time periods. They are only a behind-the-scenes organizational structure for the course and won't be part of the AP exam. It may be useful, however, to see what these four units are and to know how they correspond to the review chapters in this book, especially if, besides using this book, you are also using the College Board website to review for the AP exam. The table below provides this information.

UNIT	TIME PERIOD	CHAPTERS IN THIS BOOK
Unit 1	1450–1648	Chapter 9 The Challenge of the Renaissance
		Chapter 10 The Rise of Natural Philosophy and the Scientific Revolution
		Chapter 11 The Reformation and the Fracturing of Christianity
		Chapter 12 The Great Voyages of Exploration and Early Colonization
		Chapter 13 Economic Change and Political Consolidation
Unit 2	1648–1815	Chapter 14 Economic Change and the Expansion of the State
		Chapter 15 The Enlightenment
		Chapter 16 The French Revolution and Empire
Unit 3	1815–1914	Chapter 17 The Industrial Revolution
		Chapter 18 Cultural Responses to Revolution and Industrialization
		Chapter 19 Mass Politics and Nationalism
		Chapter 20 Mass Politics and Imperialism
Unit 4	1914–Present	Chapter 21 Politics of the Extreme and World War I
		Chapter 22 The Interwar Years and World War II
		Chapter 23 The Cold War, Integration, and Globalization

CHAPTER 9

The Challenge of the Renaissance

IN THIS CHAPTER

Summary: The Renaissance refers to the revival of commerce, the renewal of interest in the classical world, and the growing belief in the potential of human achievement that occurred on the Italian peninsula between 1350 and 1550. This chapter describes the society, values, and artistic achievement of the Italian Renaissance and its spread to northern Europe.

Key Terms:

- ☺ **Guilds** Exclusive organizations that monopolized the skilled trades in Europe from the medieval period until broken by the development of cottage industries in the eighteenth century.
- ☺ **Humanism** In the Renaissance, both a belief in the value of human achievement and an educational program based on classical Greek and Roman languages and values.
- ☺ *Studia humanitas* The educational program of the Renaissance, founded on knowledge of the classical Latin and Greek languages.
- ☺ *Oration on the Dignity of Man* One of the best articulations (1486) of the belief in the dignity and potential of humans that characterized Renaissance humanism, authored by Giovanni Pico della Mirandola.
- ☺ *The Prince* The book by Niccolo Machiavelli (1513), which marks the shift from a "civic ideal" to a "princely ideal" in Renaissance humanism. The princely ideal is focused on the qualities and strategies necessary for attaining and holding social and political power.

- ✪ **Neoplatonism** In the Renaissance and Early Modern period, a philosophy based on that of Plato, which contended that reality was located in a changeless world of forms and which, accordingly, spurred the study of mathematics.
- ✪ **Florentine Academy** An informal gathering of humanists devoted to the revival of the teachings of Plato, founded in 1462 under the leadership of Marsilio Ficino and the patronage of Cosimo de Medici.
- ✪ **Frescos** Paintings done either on wet or dry plaster; an important medium of art during the Renaissance.
- ✪ **Michelangelo's *David*** Sculpted by Michelangelo Buonarroti (1504), this sculpture of the biblical hero is characteristic of the last and most heroic phase of Renaissance art. Sculpted from a single piece of marble, it is larger than life and offers a vision of the human body and spirit that is more dramatic than real life, an effect that Michelangelo produced by making the head and hands deliberately too large for the torso.
- ✪ **Treaty of Lodi** The treaty (1454–1455) that established an internal balance of power by bringing Milan, Naples, and Florence into an alliance to check the power of Venice and its frequent ally, the Papal States. The balance of power was shattered in 1494, when Naples, supported by both Florence and the pope, prepared to attack Milan.
- ✪ ***Colloquies*** Dialogues written (beginning in 1519) by the most important and influential of the northern humanists, Desiderius Erasmus, for the purpose of teaching his students both the Latin language and how to live a good life.
- ✪ **Lay piety** A tradition in the smaller, independent German provinces, flourishing in the fifteenth and sixteenth centuries, whereby organized groups promoted pious behavior and learning outside the bureaucracy of the church.

Introduction

The word *Renaissance* means rebirth. Historically, it refers to a time in Western civilization (1350–1550) that was characterized by the revival of three things: commerce, interest in the classical world, and the belief in the potential of human achievement. For reasons that are both geographical and social, the Renaissance began in Italy, where renewed trade with the East flowed into Europe via the Mediterranean Sea and, therefore, through the Italian peninsula. The Renaissance flowered for approximately a century, and then, as a result of invasions from France and Great Britain, it flowed north into the rest of Western Europe.

Italian Society of the Renaissance

The society of the Italian peninsula between 1350 and 1550 was unique in Western civilization. The most outstanding characteristic of Italian society was the degree to which it was urban. By 1500, seven of the ten largest cities in Europe were in Italy. Whereas most of Western Europe was characterized by large kingdoms with powerful monarchs and increasingly centralized bureaucracies, the Italian peninsula was made up of numerous independent city-states, such as

Milan, Florence, Padua, and Genoa. These city-states were, by virtue of their location, flourishing centers of commerce in control of reviving networks of trade with Eastern empires.

Social status within these city-states was determined primarily by occupation, rather than by birth or the ownership of land, as was common in the rest of Europe during this period. The trades were controlled by government-protected monopolies called guilds. Members of the manufacturing guilds, such as clothiers and metalworkers, sat at the top of the social hierarchy. The next most prestigious were the professional groups that included bankers, administrators, and merchants. They were followed by skilled laborers, such as the stone masons.

Because the city-states of Italy developed as commercial centers, wealth was not based on the control of land as it was in the rest of Europe during this period. Instead, wealth was in the form of capital, and power was the ability to lend it. Accordingly, the traditional landed aristocracy of the Italian peninsula was not as politically powerful as their other European counterparts. Rather, powerful merchant families dominated socially and politically. Their status as the holders of capital also made the commercial elites of Italy powerful throughout Europe, as the monarchs of the more traditional kingdoms had to come to them when seeking loans to finance their wars of territorial expansion.

The city-states of Renaissance Italy were set up according to a variety of models. Some, like Naples, were ruled by hereditary monarchs; others were ruled by powerful families, such as the Medicis of Florence; still others, like Venice, were controlled by a military strong man known as a *doge*.

Renaissance Values

Prior to the Renaissance, the values of European civilization were based on the codes of honor and chivalry that reflected the social relations of the traditional feudal hierarchy. During the Renaissance, these traditional values were transformed to reflect both the ambition and pride of the commercial class that dominated Renaissance Italian society. In contrast to traditional European noblemen, who competed for prestige on the battlefield or in jousting and fencing tournaments, successful Renaissance men competed via displays of civic duty, which included patronage of philosophy and the arts.

At the center of the Renaissance system of values was humanism. Renaissance humanism combined an admiration for classical Greek and Roman literature with a newfound confidence in what modern men could achieve. Accordingly, Renaissance humanism was characterized by the *studia humanitas*, an educational program founded on knowledge of the classical Latin and Greek languages. Once these languages had been mastered, the Renaissance humanist could read deeply in the classical works of the ancient Greek and Roman authors, absorbing what the philosophers of the last great Western civilization had to teach them about how to succeed in life and how to live a good life.

To the Renaissance humanist, the ancient Greek and Roman philosophers were guides, but guides whose achievements could be equaled and eventually improved upon. The ultimate goal of the Renaissance humanist program was the truly well-rounded citizen, one who excelled in grammar, rhetoric, poetry, history, politics, and moral philosophy. These scholarly achievements were valued in their own right, as a testament to the dignity and ability of man, but also for the way in which they contributed to the glory of the city-state.

Prime examples of early Renaissance humanism were Petrarch, who celebrated the glory of ancient Rome in his *Letters to the Ancient Dead*, and Boccaccio, who compiled an encyclopedia of Greek and Roman mythology. The best articulation of the belief in the dignity and potential of man that characterized Renaissance humanism was Pico della Mirandola's *Oration on the Dignity of Man* (1486). In the *Oration*, Pico argued that ‹ God endowed man with the ability to shape his own being and that man has the obligation to become all that he can be.

By the late Renaissance, humanism lost some of its ideal character, where scholarly achievements were valued for their own sake, and took on a more cynical quality that promoted only individual success. This shift is sometimes characterized as a shift from a "civic ideal" to a "princely ideal," as texts like Castiglione's *The Book of the Courtier* (1513–1518) and Machiavelli's *The Prince* (1513) focused on the qualities and strategies necessary for attaining and holding social and political power.

Artistic Achievement of the Renaissance

The unique structure of Renaissance society and the corresponding system of Renaissance values combined to give birth to one of the most amazing bursts of artistic creativity in the history of Western civilization. The wealthy and powerful elites of Renaissance society patronized the arts for the fame and prestige that it brought them. The competitive spirit of the elites both within and among the Italian city-states meant that artists and craftsmen were in almost constant demand.

For example, Lorenzo de Medici, who led the ruling family of Florence from 1469 until his death in 1492, commissioned work by almost all of the great Renaissance artists. As an art patron, he was rivaled by Pope Julius II, whose patronage of the arts during his papacy (1503–1513), including the construction of St. Peter's Basilica, transformed Rome into one of Europe's most beautiful cities.

The artists themselves usually hailed not from the elite class but from the class of guild craftsmen. Young men with skill were identified and apprenticed to guild shops run by master craftsmen. Accordingly, there was no separation between the "artistic" and "commercial" sides of the Renaissance art world. All works were commissioned, and the artist was expected to give the patron what he ordered. The Renaissance artist demonstrated his creativity within the bounds of explicit contracts that specified all details of the work.

Another aspect of the guild culture that contributed to the brilliant innovations of the Renaissance period was the fact that the various media, such as sculpture, painting, and architecture, were not viewed as separate disciplines; instead, the Renaissance apprentice was expected to master the techniques of each of these art forms. As a result, mature Renaissance artists were able to work with a variety of materials and to apply ideas and techniques learned in one medium to projects in another.

Whereas medieval art had been characterized by religious subject matter, the Renaissance style took the human being and the human form as its subject. The transition can be seen in the series of frescos painted by Giotto in the fourteenth century. Although he still focused on religious subject matter (i.e., the life of St. Francis), Giotto depicted the human characters in realistic detail and with a concern for their psychological reaction to the events of St. Francis's life. The Renaissance artist's concern for the human form in all its complexity is illustrated by two great sculptures, each nominally depicting the biblical character of David:

- One is Donatello's version (completed in 1432), which was the first life-size, free-standing nude sculpture since antiquity, and which depicts David in a completely naturalistic way and casts him as a young Florentine gentleman.
- The second version was sculpted by Michelangelo Buonarroti (completed in 1504) and is characteristic of the last and most heroic phase of Renaissance art. Sculpted from a single piece of marble, Michelangelo's *David* is larger than life and offers a vision of the

human body and spirit that is more dramatic than real life, an effect that Michelangelo produced by making the head and hands deliberately too large for the torso. Upon its completion, the rulers of Florence originally placed Michelangelo's *David* at the entrance to the city hall as a symbol of Florentine strength.

The Spread of the Renaissance

In the late fifteenth century and throughout the sixteenth century, the Renaissance spread to France, Germany, England, and Spain. The catalyst for this spread was the breakup of the equilibrium that characterized the politics of the Italian peninsula. An internal balance of power had been established by the Treaty of Lodi (1454–1455), which brought Milan, Naples, and Florence into an alliance to check the power of Venice and its frequent ally, the Papal States. The balance of power was shattered in 1494, when Naples, supported by both Florence and the pope, prepared to attack Milan. The Milanese despot, Ludovico il Moro, appealed to the French king, Charles VIII of France, for help, inviting him to lead French troops into Italy and to revive his old dynastic claims to Naples, which the French had ruled from 1266 to 1435. French troops invaded the Italian peninsula in 1494 and forced Florence, Naples, and the Papal States to make major concessions. In response, the pope and the Venetians persuaded the Holy Roman Emperor, King Ferdinand of Aragon, to bring troops to Italy to help resist French aggression. From the late 1490s through most of the sixteenth century, Italy became a battleground in a war for supremacy between European monarchs.

Once the isolation of the Italian peninsula was shattered, the ideals and values of the Renaissance spread through a variety of agents:

- Teachers migrating out of Italy
- Students who came to study in Italy and then returned home
- European merchants whose interests now penetrated the peninsula
- Various lay groups seeking to spread their message of piety

However, the major cause of the spread of Renaissance ideals and values was the printing press. Invented by Johannes Gutenberg in the German city of Mainz in about 1445 in response to increased demand for books from an increasingly literate public, the moveable-type printing press allowed for faster, cheaper, mass-produced books to be created and distributed throughout Europe. By 1500, between fifteen and twenty million books were in circulation. Among the ideas that spread with the books were the thoughts and philosophies of the Renaissance humanists, which were both adopted and transformed in northern Europe.

The most important and influential of the northern humanists was Desiderius Erasmus, sometimes referred to as "the prince of the humanists." Spreading the Renaissance belief in the value of education, Erasmus made his living as an educator. He taught his students both the Latin language and lessons on how to live a good life from Latin dialogues that he wrote himself. Published under the title of *Colloquies*, Erasmus's dialogues also displayed the humanist's faith in both the power of learning and the ability of man by satirizing the old scholastic notions that the truth about God and nature could be discerned only by priests. Erasmus argued instead that, by mastering ancient languages, any man could teach himself to read both the Bible and the works of an array of ancient philosophers, thereby learning the truth about God and nature for himself.

In France, England, and Spain, the existence of strong monarchies meant that the Renaissance would be centered in the royal courts. In the smaller, independent German provinces, the characteristics of the Renaissance were absorbed into a tradition of lay piety, where organized groups, such as the Brethren of Common Life, promoted pious behavior and learning outside the bureaucracy of the church. In that context, German scholars, such as Martin Luther, who were educated in a context that combined the humanistic and lay piety traditions, would be prominent in the creation of the Reformation.

Review Questions

Multiple Choice

Questions 1 through 3 refer to the following passage:

[Considering the origin of] grace, I find one universal rule concerning it, which seems to me worth more in this matter than any other in all things human that are done or said: and that is to avoid affectation to the uttermost and as it were a very sharp and dangerous rock; and, to use possibly a new word, to practice in everything a certain nonchalance [*sprezzatura*] that shall conceal design and show that what is done and said is done without effort and almost without thought. From this I believe grace is in large measure derived, because everyone knows the difficulty of those things that are rare and done well, and therefore facility in them excites the highest admiration.

[And] I wish to discuss another matter, which I deem of great importance and therefore think our Courtier ought by no means to omit: and this is to know how to draw and to have acquaintance with the very art of painting. . . . And truly he who does not esteem this art, seems to me very unreasonable; . . . [For] the ancients greatly prized both the art and the artists, which thus attained the summit of highest excellence; very sure proof of which may be found in the antique marble and bronze statues that yet are seen. . . .

Baldesar Castiglione, *The Book of the Courtier*, 1508–1513

1. The passage is indicative of the "princely ideal" of the late Renaissance, because
   A. it promotes individual achievement
   B. it is by the author of *The Prince*
   C. it describes the manner in which a prince should behave
   D. it focuses on the value of personal achievement for individual success rather than the civic good

2. The passage can be said to illustrate the transformation of traditional values into Renaissance values, because
   A. it stresses the pursuit of excellence
   B. it extols the virtue of skill in the visual arts rather than the martial arts
   C. it stresses the changing social status of the artist
   D. it values grace

3. The passage illustrates the values of Renaissance humanism, because
   A. it instructs the individual to pay attention to personal appearance
   B. it argues that reason should be the measure of all things
   C. it looks to the ancients for guidance in matters of taste and accomplishment
   D. it encourages all men to aspire to be Courtiers

Short Answer

4. Briefly explain and illustrate the difference between the "civic ideal" in Renaissance humanism and the latter "princely ideal" that supplanted it.

Answers and Explanations

1. **D** is correct because the "princely ideal" of the late Renaissance focused on the value of achievements, such as grace and nonchalance (*sprezzatura*) in promoting individual success, rather than the civic good. A is incorrect because it is too general; all Renaissance ideals promoted individual achievement. B is incorrect because Machiavelli is the author of *The Prince,* not Castiglione. C is incorrect because *The Courtier* offers advice to all would-be gentlemen, not just princes.

2. **B** is correct because, during the Renaissance, skill in the visual arts was more highly valued than skill in the martial arts. A and D are incorrect because individual achievement and grace were valued in both traditional and Renaissance culture. C is incorrect because the passage makes no reference to the social status of artists.

3. **C** is correct because Renaissance humanism looked backward to the accomplishments of ancient Greece and Rome for guidance and inspiration. A is incorrect because attention to personal appearance was not unique to Renaissance humanism. B is incorrect because neither Renaissance humanism nor the passage argued that reason should be the measure of all things. D is incorrect because neither Renaissance humanism nor the passage encouraged all men to be Courtiers.

4. Suggested answer:

   Thesis: The "civic ideal" in Renaissance humanism valued individual achievement in scholarship and the arts for its own sake, as a fulfillment of God's gift and as a part of good citizenship. The "princely ideal" which supplanted it was less idealistic, valuing individual achievement in scholarship and the arts as a tool for individual success.

   Paragraph Outline:

   I. Pico della Mirandola's *Oration on the Dignity of Man* (1486) as an example of the belief in the dignity and potential of man that characterized Renaissance humanism.

   II. Castiglione's *The Book of the Courtier* (1513–1518) and Machiavelli's *The Prince* (1513) as examples of individual achievement and refinement for the purpose of attaining and holding social status and political power.

Rapid Review

The revival of commerce, interest in the classical world, and belief in the potential of human achievement that occurred on the Italian peninsula between 1350 and 1550 is known as the Renaissance. Within the independent, urban city-states of Renaissance Italian society, the successful merchant class sought a well-rounded life of achievement and civic virtue, which led them to give their patronage to scholars and artists. Accordingly, both scholarship and artistic achievement reached new heights, and new philosophies like humanism and Neoplatonism were fashioned. In 1494, mounting jealousy and mistrust between the Italian city-states caused the leaders of Milan to invite intervention by the powerful French monarchy, thereby breaking a delicate balance of power and causing the Italian peninsula to become a battleground in a war for supremacy between European monarchies. The destruction of the independence of the Italian city-states caused the spread and transformation of Renaissance ideals and values. A northern European humanism, less secular than its Italian counterpart, developed and served as the foundation of the Reformation.

CHAPTER 10

The Rise of Natural Philosophy and the Scientific Revolution

IN THIS CHAPTER

Summary: By the mid-sixteenth century, the spirit of Renaissance humanism fused with other traditions to create a Platonic–Pythagorean point of view that sought to identify the fundamental mathematical laws of nature. This chapter focuses on the contributions of Copernicus, Kepler, Galileo, and Descartes to that effort and the ways their views challenged traditional beliefs and authorities.

Key Terms:

- ✪ **Celestial realm** The realm, in the Aristotelian view of the cosmos, above the orbit of the moon.
- ✪ **Elements** The basic components of matter in Aristotelian physics; there were five: earth, water, air, fire, and aether.
- ✪ **Qualities** A term, in Aristotelian physics, for the tendencies of matter; that is, Earth sinks, Air floats, etc.
- ✪ **Geocentric** Earth-centered; the Aristotelian model of the cosmos.
- ✪ **Scholasticism** A term for the pre-Renaissance system of knowledge characterized by the belief that everything worth knowing was written down in ancient texts.
- ✪ **Hermeticism** A tradition of knowledge that taught that the world was infused with a single spirit that could be explored through mathematics, as well as through magic.

- ✪ **Neoplatonism** In the Renaissance and the Early Modern period, a philosophy based on that of Plato, which contended that reality was located in a changeless world of forms and that, accordingly, spurred the study of mathematics.
- ✪ **Platonic–Pythagorean tradition** A tradition of philosophy that developed in the sixteenth and seventeenth centuries, which embraced the works of Plato and Pythagoras and which had as its goal the identification of the fundamental mathematical laws of nature.
- ✪ **Heliocentric** Sun-centered; the model of the cosmos proposed by Nicolas Copernicus in 1534.
- ✪ **Copernicanism** The theory, following Nicolas Copernicus, that the sun is at the center of the cosmos and that the Earth is the third planet from the sun.
- ✪ **Kepler's laws** Three laws of planetary motion developed by Johannes Kepler between 1609 and 1619.
- ✪ ***The Starry Messenger*** Galileo's treatise of 1610, in which he published his celestial observations made with a telescope.
- ✪ ***Dialogue on the Two Chief Systems of the World*** Galileo's treatise of 1632, in which he dismantled the arguments in favor of the traditional, Aristotelian view of the cosmos and presented the Copernican system as the only alternative for reasonable people.
- ✪ ***Discourse on Method*** René Descartes's treatise of 1637, in which he established a method of philosophical inquiry based on radical skepticism.

Introduction

Natural philosophy is a term that refers to the attempt of intellectuals to understand the natural world. The Scientific Revolution is the term given to the rise of a particular kind of natural philosophy that stressed empirical observation and reason. While it is hard to know where to cite the beginning of such a development, many historians point to a key publication by Nicolas Copernicus in 1543 and to Galileo Galilei's challenge to the old Aristotelian view of the cosmos and the authority of the Catholic Church in 1610.

The Traditional View of the Cosmos

The traditional view of the cosmos in European civilization was one that it inherited from the ancient Greek philosopher Aristotle. The Aristotelian cosmos was based on observation and common sense. Because the Earth appeared, to all of one's senses, to stand still, Aristotle believed the earth was the unmoving center point of the cosmos. The moon, the planets, and the stars were understood to move in concentric circular orbits around the earth because that is what they appeared to do. The stars were conceived of as "fixed" into a single sphere because they do not move relative to each other.

The Aristotelian cosmos was divided into two realms:

- The terrestrial realm, which contained the Earth and all matter inside the orbit of the moon
- The celestial realm, or the realm of the heavens, which existed beyond the orbit of the moon

In the Aristotelian cosmos, there were five basic elements, each of which was defined by its qualities:

1. Earth, which was heavy and tended to sink toward the center of the cosmos
2. Water, which was slightly lighter and accumulated on top of the solid Earth
3. Air, which was lighter still
4. Fire, which was the lightest of all and tended to try to rise above all the others
5. Aether, which was perfect matter that existed only in the celestial realm and which moved in uniform circular motion

The qualities of the five types of matter served as the basis of Aristotelian physics. The motion of terrestrial matter was understood to be the result of its composition. For example, if you threw a rock, its motion described a parabola because the force of the throw gave its motion a horizontal component, while its heaviness gave it a vertical component toward the earth. If you filled an air tight bag with air and submerged it in water, it would float to the top because the air was lighter than earth or water. The planets and stars of the celestial realm moved at a uniform rate in perfect circles around the earth because they were composed purely of aether.

To the medieval church scholars who rediscovered and translated the writings of Aristotle, this Earth-centered, or "geocentric," model of the cosmos not only made logical sense, it confirmed the Christian theological doctrine that the perfect kingdom of God awaited in the heavens for those humans who could transcend the corruption of the world.

Alternative Traditions of Knowledge Before the Scientific Revolution

Although the dominant tradition of knowledge in European civilization prior to the Scientific Revolution was scholasticism, which derived its knowledge from ancient texts like those of Aristotle, there were other traditions upon which the Scientific Revolution drew.

Natural Magic, Alchemy, and Hermeticism

One was the tradition of natural magic and alchemy that understood the natural world to be alive with latent power, just waiting to be tapped by those who could learn its secrets. One strain of magical thought drew inspiration from a corpus of texts erroneously attributed to a supposed ancient Egyptian priest, Hermes Trismegistus. Hermeticism taught that the world was infused with a single spirit that could be explored through mathematics as well as through magic.

Neoplatonism

The most powerful and potent of the alternative traditions was developed by Renaissance humanists who rediscovered and revered the work of the ancient Greek philosopher Plato. Plato's writings distinguished between a changeless and eternal realm of being or form and the temporary and perishable world we experience. To the Neoplatonists, mathematics was the language with which one could discover and describe the world of forms. Like the Hermetic tradition, Neoplatonism taught that mathematics described the essential nature and soul of the cosmos, a soul that was God itself.

The Platonic–Pythagorean Tradition

By the advent of the seventeenth century, these alternative traditions had fused into an approach to gaining knowledge of the natural world that has come to be known as the Platonic–Pythagorean tradition (after Plato and the ancient mathematically oriented school of Pythagoras), which had as its goal the identification of the fundamental mathematical laws of nature.

Development of New Institutions

Because the curricula of traditional universities were devoted to the teaching of Aristotle and other authorities in the scholastic tradition, new institutions were required for the alternative traditions to flourish. New institutions that emerged to fill that role included the following:

- Royal courts, where kings, dukes, and other ruling nobles were determined to show off both their wealth and their virtue by patronizing not only great artists and musicians but also natural philosophers
- Royal societies and academies, like the Royal Society of London and the Royal Academy of Sciences in Paris, both established in the 1660s, where organized groups of natural philosophers sought and received the patronage of the Crown by emphasizing both the prestige and the practical applications of their discoveries
- Smaller academies under the patronage of individual nobles, like the *Accademia dei Lincei*, which formed in 1657 under the patronage of the Marquess of Monticelli in Italy
- New universities, particularly in Italy, which were funded by the civic-minded merchants in the Renaissance tradition and which were outside the control of the Church

The Rise of Copernicanism

The central challenge to the traditional view of the cosmos was made in the context of the Church's own effort to reform the calendar and, therefore, the science of astronomy. The annual changes in the position of the sun, the moon, and the planets with respect to the constellations of stars are the means by which human beings construct calendars that keep track of time and predict seasonal climate patterns. In keeping with the philosophy of scholasticism, European Church scholars constructed calendars based on ancient astronomical tables that dated back to the ancient Greek astronomer Claudius Ptolemy. Though amazingly accurate, the multiplication over thousands of years of small errors in the Ptolemaic astronomical tables led to a situation in the early sixteenth century in which the calendars were dramatically out of sync with the actual seasons.

In 1515, a church council appointed to consider calendar reform summoned the Polish churchman and astronomer Nicolas Copernicus to remedy the situation. Educated in a Neoplatonic academy and a proponent of the Platonic–Pythagorean tradition, Copernicus proposed to reconcile the calendar and the actual movements of the heavens by introducing a new sun-centered, or "heliocentric," astronomical model of the cosmos.

Copernicus's proposal alarmed Church authorities for several reasons:

- It questioned the authority of the Aristotelian tradition on which scholasticism relied.
- It contradicted the physical principles that served as the foundation of physics.
- It destroyed the theological coherence of the cosmos.
- It required the Church to admit it had been in error.

Shortly before Copernicus's death in 1543, the Church allowed his theory to be published in a work titled *Revolutionibus Orbium Caelestum* (*On the Revolutions of the Heavenly Spheres*), provided that it be accompanied by a preface stating that the theory was only being presented as a useful hypothetical model, not as a true account of the physical nature of the cosmos. Because Copernicus's great work was written in Latin (which was the language of educated scholars) and because it was a highly technical work, its publication created no great stir. But slowly, over the course of the next 70 years, Copernicanism (as the theory came to be known) spread in circles of men educated both within the Church and in the newer academies and societies.

Kepler's Laws

By the seventeenth century, a loose network of Copernicans championed the new world view as part of a new empirical and mathematical approach to the study of the natural world. One was a German mathematician working in the Hermetic and Neoplatonic traditions, Johannes Kepler, who devoted his life to finding the mathematical harmonies of the cosmos. Between 1609 and 1619, he developed three laws of planetary motion that would come to be known as Kepler's laws:

1. The first law broke with the tradition of conceiving of the planets as moving in uniform circles, suggesting that the planetary orbits took the form of an ellipse, with the sun as one of their foci.
2. The second law abandoned the notion that planetary motion was uniform and asserted that a planet's velocity varied according to its distances from the sun, sweeping out equal areas in equal times.
3. The third law gave a mathematical description for the physical relationship between the planets and the sun, asserting that the squares of the orbital periods of the planets are in the same ratio as the cubes of their average distance from the sun.

Galileo and the Value of Empirical Knowledge

Although Kepler worked in obscurity, Galileo Galilei was an ambitious self-promoter. Dubbing himself a "mathematical philosopher," Galileo championed an approach to knowing the natural world that emphasized the need to apply reason to observational and mathematical data. Also, following the English philosopher Francis Bacon, Galileo combined his approach with an appeal to the practical and pragmatic value of such knowledge.

Having dismantled and analyzed a spyglass he bought from Dutch merchants, Galileo drew up schematics for a larger, more powerful version. The result was the world's first telescope, and Galileo immediately turned his new invention on the heavens. In 1610, Galileo published his findings in a pamphlet titled *Sidereus Nuncius* (*The Starry Messenger*). There, he announced several discoveries, which, although they did not explicitly promote the Copernican theory, did implicitly call into question the veracity of the Aristotelian model. These discoveries included the following:

- The existence of countless stars previously unseen, suggesting that there was much about the cosmos that was not known
- The rugged, crater-filled surface of the moon, suggesting that it was not created of perfect celestial matter
- Four moons orbiting the planet Jupiter, suggesting that it would not be so strange for Earth to have a moon as well

Unfortunately, Galileo mistakenly believed that both a combination of his growing fame and his value to his powerful patron (the Grand Duke of Tuscany, Cosimo de Medici) would protect him from the wrath of the Catholic Church. Because of this mistaken belief, Galileo began to promote more boldly both the Copernican theory and his method of knowing nature through the application of reason to empirical observations. In 1615, he was summoned to Rome, where he narrowly escaped being branded a heretic only because he had a powerful friend, Cardinal Maffeo Barberini, who interceded on Galileo's behalf and managed to convince the Church to brand the Copernican theory "erroneous" rather than "heretical." Galileo was set free with a stern warning. In 1623, Barberini became Pope Urban VIII. The following year, Galileo returned to Rome for a series of discussions with the Pope. He left having been given permission to teach Copernicanism as a theory, but not as a true account of the cosmos.

Over the next decade and a half, Galileo continued to promote his particular brand of natural philosophy. In 1632, chafing against the constrictions put upon him, Galileo effectively took his case to the public by abandoning the Latin prose of the scholarly elite for the vernacular Italian of the masses and publishing a thinly veiled attack on what he considered to be the absurdity of the Church's defense of the Aristotelian model. The book *Dialogue on the Two Chief Systems of the World* dismantled the arguments in favor of the traditional, Aristotelian view of the cosmos and presented the Copernican system as the only alternative for reasonable people. Early the following year, Galileo was summoned before the Inquisition and forced to recant. He was sentenced to spend the rest of his life under house arrest and forbidden to ever publish again. The long-term effect of Galileo's condemnation was to shift the locus of the Scientific Revolution to the Protestant countries of Europe.

Cartesian Skepticism and Deductive Reasoning

Although many of those who took the lead in the Scientific Revolution in the second half of the seventeenth century were born in Protestant countries, René Descartes had been a citizen of Catholic France. But upon hearing of Galileo's condemnation, Descartes relocated to the Netherlands, where he published (in 1637) a challenge to both the authority of scholasticism and to the validity of the Galilean approach. In *Discourse on Method*, Descartes began by sweeping away all previous claims to knowledge by skeptically asserting that "received knowledge"—that is, information that you do not learn for yourself—amounted to nothing more than "opinion." But rather than proceed from observation, Descartes extended his skepticism to the senses, which, he asserted, could easily be fooled; instead, he sought the "clear and distinct idea"—that is, one that could not reasonably be doubted.

The first idea that Descartes could not doubt was that he was thinking, and that if he was thinking, then he must really exist. From that famous formulation—"I think, therefore I am"—Descartes proceeded to deduce a variety of truths, including the existence of God and a cosmos made up of only two things: matter and motion. Putting the sun in the center (as Copernicus had done), Descartes described a solar system in which the planets were simply large chunks of matter that were caught in swirling vortices of smaller matter. This Cartesian approach of deducing the details of nature from a set of clearly defined general propositions appealed to those who sought an intelligible explanation of the cosmos, rather than the mathematical calculations of the Platonic–Pythagorean tradition.

Review Questions

Multiple Choice

Questions 1–3 refer to the following passage:

First. I say that it seems to me that . . . Galileo did prudently to content [himself] with speaking hypothetically, and not absolutely, as I have always believed that Copernicus spoke. . . . But to want to affirm that the sun really is fixed in the center of the heavens and only revolves around itself (i.e., turns upon its axis) without traveling from east to west, and that the earth is situated in the third sphere and revolves with great speed around the sun, is a very dangerous thing, not only by irritating all the philosophers and scholastic theologians, but also by injuring our holy faith and rendering the Holy Scriptures false.

Second. I say that, as you know, the Council [of Trent] prohibits expounding the Scriptures contrary to the common agreement of the holy Fathers. And if [you] would read not only the Fathers but also the commentaries of modern writers on Genesis, Psalms, Ecclesiastes and Josue, you would find that all agree in explaining literally (*ad litteram*) that the sun is in the heavens and moves swiftly around the earth, and that the earth is far from the heavens and stands immobile in the center of the universe. Now consider whether in all prudence the Church could encourage giving to Scripture a sense contrary to the holy Fathers and all the Latin and Greek commentators. Nor may it be answered that this is not a matter of faith, for if it is not a matter of faith from the point of view of the subject matter, it is on the part of the ones who have spoken.

Cardinal Robert Bellarmine, *Letter on Galileo's Theories*, 1615

1. From the passage, it may be inferred that Bellarmine was
   A. willing to have Copernicus's book published
   B. willing to admit that the Earth revolves around the sun
   C. willing to allow the Copernican theory to be taught as a hypothesis
   D. willing to admit that scripture could be false

2. From the passage, one may infer that Galileo worked
   A. in the alchemical tradition
   B. in the Hermetic tradition
   C. in the Platonic–Pythagorean tradition
   D. in the Copernican tradition

3. From the passage, one may infer that Bellarmine believed
   A. that the Council of Trent supported the Copernican theory
   B. that the Copernican theory posed a threat to the authority of the Catholic Church
   C. that the Catholic Church always read scripture literally
   D. that, in the Catholic Church, the structure of the cosmos was not considered a matter of faith

Short Answer

4. Briefly explain ONE similarity and TWO differences between the approach of Galileo and the approach of Descartes to gaining reliable knowledge of the natural world.

Answers and Explanations

1. **C** is correct because, in the passage, Bellarmine says that ". . . Galileo did prudently to content [himself] with speaking hypothetically." A is false because the letter does not speak of Copernicus's book, which was published in 1543. B is incorrect because Bellarmine does not admit that the Earth revolves around the sun; rather, he says that such an assertion "is a very dangerous thing." D is incorrect because Bellarmine says that the holy faith would be injured by "rendering the Holy Scriptures false."

2. **D** is correct because the assertion that the sun "is fixed in the center of the heavens and only revolves around itself (i.e., turns upon its axis) without traveling from east to west, and that the earth is situated in the third sphere and revolves with great speed around the sun" is in the Copernican tradition. A is incorrect because nothing in the passage refers to the alchemical tradition, which understood the natural world to be alive with latent power. B is incorrect because nothing in the passage refers to the Hermetic tradition, which taught that the world was infused with a single spirit. C is incorrect because, although it is true that Galileo worked in the Platonic–Pythagorean tradition (which had as its goal the identification of the fundamental mathematical laws of nature), there is nothing in the passage that allows you to infer that.

3. **B** is correct because the passage indicates that the Copernican theory contradicted the writings of Church scholars and that the Church could not risk sanctioning such a contradiction. A is incorrect because the passage clearly states that the Council of Trent "prohibit[ed] expounding the Scriptures contrary to the common agreement of the holy Fathers." C is incorrect because the passage indicates that a council of scholars had met to *decide* whether, in the case of the structure of the cosmos, scripture was to be taken as offering a literal explanation. D is incorrect because the passage clearly indicates that Bellarmine believed that the structure of the cosmos was a matter of faith.

4. Suggested answer:

   Thesis: Galileo's and Descartes's approaches were similar in that they both began with skepticism. Their approaches were different in two ways: (1) Galileo relied on empirical observation, whereas Descartes considered the senses unreliable. (2) Galileo tended to employ an inductive method, gathering facts and then generalizing from them, while Descartes preferred to deduce general principles and then explain the facts based on those principles.

   Paragraph outline:

   I. Galileo's rejection of the Aristotelian model of the cosmos and the scholastic approach. Descartes's skeptical assertion that "received knowledge"—that is, information that you do not learn for yourself—amounted to nothing more than "opinion."

   II. Galileo's observations of the moon and his inductive argument that those observations refute the claims of Aristotle. Descartes's rejection of observation on the grounds that our senses can be fooled and his deduction of his own existence by the fact that he cannot doubt that he is thinking about the question of his existence.

Rapid Review

By the mid-sixteenth century, the spirit of Renaissance humanism fused with other reviving traditions, such as Hermeticism and Neoplatonism, to create a Platonic–Pythagorean tradition that sought to identify the fundamental mathematical laws of nature. Nicolas Copernicus was the first to challenge the traditional scholastic view of the cosmos by suggesting that the sun—not the Earth—was at the center of the system. But it was in the seventeenth century that Copernicus's successors, taking advantage of new spaces for natural philosophy, promoted new ways of knowing about nature:

- Galileo promoted both the Copernican system and an observationally based inductive method in increasingly bold ways until he was silenced by the Inquisition in 1633.
- René Descartes developed and promoted an alternative method that began with radical skepticism and went on to deduce knowledge about nature by seeking clear and distinct thought.

CHAPTER 11

The Reformation and the Fracturing of Christianity

IN THIS CHAPTER

Summary: In the sixteenth century, the preoccupation of the Roman Church with worldly matters and its failure to meet the needs of an increasingly literate population led to challenges to its doctrine and authority. This chapter describes the rise of Protestant churches in northern Europe and the Catholic Church's response in the Counter-Reformation.

Key Terms:

✪ **Papal States** A kingdom in central Italy, ruled directly by the pope until Italian unification (1866–1870).

✪ **Indulgences** Certificates of absolution sold by the church forgiving people of their sins, sometimes even before they committed them, in return for a monetary contribution. The selling of indulgences was one of the practices that Martin Luther objected to.

✪ **Millenarianism** The belief that one is living in the last days of the world and that the judgment day is at hand (originally tied to the belief that the end would come in the year AD 1000).

✪ **Salvation by Faith Alone** One of the central tenets of Martin Luther's theology: the belief that salvation is a gift from God given to all who possess true faith.

✪ **Scripture Alone (*Sola Scriptura*)** One of the central tenets of Martin Luther's theology: the belief that scripture is the only guide to knowledge of God. (In contrast, the Catholic Church holds that there are two guides to knowledge of God: scripture and Church tradition.)

✪ **Priesthood of All Believers** One of the central tenets of Martin Luther's theology: the belief that all who have true faith are "priests," that is, they are competent to read and understand scripture.

✪ ***The Ninety-Five Theses*** The 95 propositions or challenges to official Church theology posted by Martin Luther on the door of Wittenberg castle church in the autumn of 1517.

✪ **Peace of Augsburg** The treaty, signed in 1555, that established the principle of "whoever rules, his religion" and signaled to Rome that the German princes would not go to war with each other over religion.

✪ **Peasantry** The class of rural, agricultural laborers in traditional European society.

✪ **Huguenots** The sixteenth- and seventeenth-century term for Protestants living in France.

✪ **Edict of Nantes** A royal edict that established the principle of religious toleration in France, proclaimed in 1598 and revoked in 1685.

✪ **Anglican Church** The state church of England, established by Henry VIII in the early sixteenth century when he decided to break from the Church in Rome.

✪ **Dissenters** The collective name for Protestant groups who refused to join the Anglican Church in England.

✪ **Predestination** The Calvinist belief that asserts that God has predetermined which people will be saved and which will be damned.

✪ **The elect** The name given in Calvinist theology to the group of people who have been predestined by God for salvation.

✪ **Anabaptists** A sect of radical Protestant reformers in Europe in the sixteenth century who considered true Protestant faith to require social reform.

✪ **Council of Trent** The reform council of the Catholic Church that began its deliberations in 1545. Despite its reformist aims, it continued to insist that the Catholic Church was the final arbiter in all matters of faith.

✪ **Inquisition** An institution within the Catholic Church, created in 1479 to enforce the conversion of Muslims and Jews in Spain. It was revived and expanded during the Reformation to combat all perceived threats to orthodoxy and the Church's authority.

Introduction

The Reformation in sixteenth-century Europe began as an effort to reform the Christian Church, which many believed had become too concerned with worldly matters. Soon, however, the Church found itself facing a serious challenge from a brilliant German theologian, Martin Luther, and his followers. What began as a protest evolved into a revolution with social and political overtones. By the end of the century, a Europe that had been united by a single Church was deeply divided, as the Catholic and Protestant faiths vied for the minds and hearts of the people.

The Need for a Religious Reformation

By the onset of the sixteenth century, the Christian Church of Europe was facing a serious set of interconnected problems. Concern was growing that the Church had become too worldly and corrupt in its practices. The Church, and particularly the papacy in Rome, was widely seen to be more concerned with building and retaining worldly power and wealth than in guiding souls to salvation. The pope was not only the head of a powerful Church hierarchy, but he was the ruler of the Papal States, a kingdom that encompassed much of the central portion of the Italian peninsula. He collected taxes, kept an army, and used his religious power to influence politics in every kingdom in Europe.

The selling of indulgences (which allowed people to be absolved of their sins, sometimes even before they committed them, by making a monetary contribution to the Church) is just one example of the way in which the church seemed more concerned with amassing power and wealth than with guiding the faithful to salvation. To many common people who yearned for a powerful, personal, and emotional connection with God, the Church not only failed to provide it but worked actively to discourage it in the following ways:

- By protecting the power of the priesthood
- By saying the mass in Latin, a language understood by only the educated elite
- By refusing to allow the printing of the Bible in the vernacular

The Lutheran Revolt

Martin Luther was an unlikely candidate to lead a revolt against the Church. The son of a mine manager in eastern Germany, Luther received a humanistic education, studying law before being drawn to the Church and being ordained as a priest in 1507. Continuing his education, Luther received a doctorate of theology from the University of Wittenberg and was appointed to the faculty there in 1512.

The revolutionary ideas that would come to define Lutheran theology were a product of Luther's personal search. Luther believed that he was living in the last days of the world and that God's final judgment would soon be upon the world. This view, now referred to as millenarianism and widespread in sixteenth-century Europe, led Luther to become obsessed with the question of how any human being could be good enough to deserve salvation. He found his answer through the rigorous study of scripture, and he formulated three interconnected theological assertions:

- Salvation by Faith Alone, which declared that salvation came only to those who had true faith
- Scripture Alone, which stated that scripture was the only source of true knowledge of God's will
- The Priesthood of All Believers, which argued that all true believers received God's grace and were, therefore, priests in God's eyes

Each of Luther's assertions put him in direct opposition to the Church's orthodox theology:

- Salvation by Faith Alone contradicted the Church's assertion that salvation was gained by both having faith and performing works of piety and charity.
- Scripture Alone contradicted the Church's assertion that there were two sources of true knowledge of God: scripture and the traditions of the Church.
- The Priesthood of All Believers contradicted the Church's assertion that only ordained priests could read and correctly interpret scripture.

Creation and Spread of the Protestant Movement

In the autumn of 1517, Luther launched his protest by tacking 95 theses, or propositions, that ran contrary to the theology and practice of the Church to the door of the Wittenberg castle church. His students quickly translated them from Latin into the German vernacular and distributed printed versions throughout the German-speaking kingdoms and provinces. With the aid of the printing press, Luther attracted many followers, but the survival of a Protestant movement was due to the political climate. Had the papacy moved quickly to excommunicate Luther and his followers, the movement might not have survived. However, Luther found a powerful protector in Frederick of Saxony, the prince of Luther's district. Frederick was one of seven electors, the princes who elected the Holy Roman Emperor to whom the princes of the German districts owed their allegiance. Frederick's protection caused the pope to delay Luther's excommunication until 1520. By that time, it was too late: Luther and his followers had established throughout Germany congregations for the kind of Christian worship that, after 1529, would be known as Protestant.

Luther promoted his theology to both the nobility and common people. To the nobility, he wrote an "Address to the Christian Nobility of the German Nation" (1520), which appealed to the German princes' desire for both greater unity and power and to their desire to be out from under the thumb of an Italian pope. To the common people, he addressed "The Freedom of the Christian Man" (1520), in which he encouraged common men to obey their Christian conscience and respect those in authority who seemed to possess true Christian principles. Through this strategy, Luther offered the noble princes of Germany an opportunity to break with the Roman Church and papacy without losing the obedience of the common people. It was an opportunity that was too good to pass up. By 1555, the German princes made it clear that they would no longer bow to Rome; they signed the Peace of Augsburg, which established the principle of "whoever rules, his religion" and signaled to Rome that the German princes would not go to war with each other over religion.

Once it gained a foothold in northern Germany, Protestantism tended to flourish in those areas where the local rulers were either unwilling or not strong enough to enforce orthodoxy and loyalty to Rome. Accordingly, the Protestant movement spread with success to the Netherlands, Scandinavia, Scotland, and England, but it encountered more difficulty and little or no success in southern and eastern Europe. The site of the most bloodshed was France, where Protestantism was declared both heretical and illegal in 1534. Initially French Protestants, known as Huguenots, were tolerated, but a civil war pitting Catholics against Protestants erupted in 1562. Peaceful coexistence was briefly restored by the Edict of Nantes in 1598, which established the principle of religious toleration in France, but the edict would be revoked in 1685.

The English Reformation

The English Reformation was unique. England had long traditions of dissent and anti-clericalism that stemmed from a humanist tradition. In that context, Protestantism in England grew slowly, appealing especially to the middle classes, and by 1524, illegal English-language Bibles were circulating. But as the English monarch Henry VIII tried to consolidate his power and his legacy, he took the existence of a Protestant movement as an opportunity to break from Rome and create a national church, the Church of England or the Anglican Church.

Henry needed a divorce from his wife, Catherine of Aragon, because she could not provide him with a male heir to the throne. He also needed money and land with which to buy the loyalty of existing nobles and to establish loyalty in new ones who would owe their position to him. In 1534, he officially broke with the Church in Rome and had himself declared the head of the new Church of England. In 1536, he dissolved the English monasteries and seized church lands and properties, awarding them to those loyal to him. It soon became apparent, however, that the Church that Henry had created was Protestant only in the sense that it broke from Rome. In terms of the characteristics opposed by most Protestant reformers—its episcopal or hierarchical nature, the existence of priests, and the retention of the sacraments and symbols of the traditional Roman church—the Church of England was hardly Protestant at all.

For the rest of the century, the unfinished Reformation left England plagued by religious turmoil. During the reign of Edward VI, the son of Henry and Jane Seymour, England was officially Anglican, but communities who wished to organize themselves along more Protestant lines grew to sufficient numbers to be known collectively as Dissenters. Upon the accession of Mary I (the daughter of Henry and his first wife, Catherine of Aragon), England was returned to Catholicism and Protestants were persecuted. Under the subsequent reign of Elizabeth I (the daughter of Henry and Anne Boleyn), England was again Anglican. While Catholics were initially persecuted under Elizabeth, there emerged during her long reign a kind of equilibrium in which a modicum of religious toleration was given to all.

Calvin and Calvinism

Once the break from the Roman Church was accomplished, Protestant leaders faced the task of creating new religious communities and systematizing a theology. The most influential of the second-generation Protestant theologians was John Calvin. Converting to Protestantism around 1534, Calvin was forced to leave his native France and flee to Switzerland, whose towns were governed by strong town councils that had historically competed with the Church bishops for local power. Calvin settled in Geneva where, in 1536, the adult male population had voted to become Protestant. For the next 40 years, Calvin worked in Geneva, articulating the theology and structure for Protestant religious communities that would come to be known as Calvinism.

Calvinism accepted both Martin Luther's contentions that salvation is gained by faith alone and that scripture is the sole source of authoritative knowledge of God's will. But on the subject of salvation, Calvin went further, developing the doctrine of Predestination, which asserted that God has predetermined which people will be saved and which will be damned. Those that are predestined to salvation are known as "the elect," and, although their earthly behavior could not affect the status of their salvation, Calvin taught that the elect would be known both by their righteous behavior and by their prosperity, as God would bless all their earthly enterprises.

In Calvinist communities, the structure and discipline of the congregation were integrated into those of the town. In place of the hierarchical structure of the Roman church, Calvinist churches were organized by function:

- Pastors preached the gospel.
- Doctors studied scripture and wrote commentaries.
- Deacons saw to the social welfare of the community.
- Elders governed the church and the community in moral matters and enforced discipline.

Geneva soon became the inspirational center of the Protestant movement.

Social Dimensions and the Radical Reformation

The Protestantism of Martin Luther and John Calvin appealed to the industrious and prosperous commercial and merchant classes. At these higher rungs of the social hierarchy, people could read and react to criticism of both the doctrine and practice of the orthodox Roman Church. The strict discipline of the Calvinist communities mirrored the self-discipline their own professions demanded, and the promise that God would bless the worldly endeavors of the elect provided a self-satisfying justification for the wealth and prosperity that many were enjoying. Further down the social ladder, amongst the artisan and peasant classes, a more radical reformation was being shaped.

The religious beliefs of the poorer and less educated classes were always less uniform than those of the elite. Their knowledge of Christian theology tended to be superficial and wedded to older folklore that deified the forces of nature. What they cared about was that the suffering they endured in this life would be rewarded in the next. Accordingly, leaders of Protestant movements among the artisan and peasant classes interpreted the doctrines of justification by faith alone and predestination to mean that God would never abandon the poor and simple people who suffered and that they could have direct knowledge of their salvation through an inner light that came to them directly from God. In some circles, this was combined with millenarian notions that the judgment day was near, to create a belief that the poor had a special mission to purge the world of evil and prepare it for the second coming of Christ.

The first and largest group of such radical reformers was known as the Anabaptists. In 1534, proclaiming that judgment day was at hand, a group of them captured the German city of Münster, seized the property of non-believers, and burned all books except the Bible. To Protestant and Catholic elites alike, the Anabaptists represented a threat to the social order that could not be tolerated. Their rebellion was subsequently put down by an army led by the Lutheran Prince Philip of Hesse, and the Anabaptist movement was violently repressed and driven underground.

The Catholic Response

Although it was slow to believe that Protestantism could pose a threat to its power, the Roman Church—which was increasingly referred to as "catholic" (meaning one, true, and universal)—began to construct a response by the middle of the sixteenth century. Although sometimes referred to as the Counter-Reformation, the Catholic response actually had two dimensions: one aimed at reforming the Catholic Church and another aimed at exterminating the Protestant movement.

At the center of both dimensions was the Society of Jesus. Founded in 1534 by Ignatius Loyola, the Jesuits (as they came to be known) were a tightly organized order who saw themselves as soldiers in a war against Satan. Strategically, the Jesuits focused on education, building schools and universities throughout Europe. The Jesuits also served as missionaries, and they were often among the first Europeans to visit the new worlds that the Age of Exploration was opening up, thereby establishing a beachhead for Catholicism. Internally, they preached a new piety and pushed the Church to curb its worldly practices and to serve as a model for a selfless, holy life that could lead to salvation.

The Catholic reform movement reached its peak with the Council of Trent, which began its deliberations in 1545. Over many years, the Council passed reforms abolishing the worst of the abuses that had led to Protestant discontent. However, the Council of Trent also symbolized a defeat for Protestants who hoped for reconciliation, as the Council refused to compromise on any of the key theological issues and continued to insist that the Catholic Church was the final arbiter in all matters of faith.

At the heart of the Catholic Church's efforts to defeat Protestantism was the office known as the Inquisition. An old institution within the Church that investigated charges of heresy, its duties were revived and expanded to combat all perceived threats to orthodoxy and the Church's authority. Those who ran afoul of the Inquisition ran the risk of imprisonment, torture, and execution. The Church's other main weapon in its aggressive response to the Reformation was censorship. Books that were considered unorthodox or at odds with the Church's teachings were placed on the *Index of Banned Books*.

Review Questions

Multiple Choice

Questions 1–3 refer to the following passage:

The covenant of life not being equally preached to all, and among those to whom it is preached not always finding the same reception, this diversity discovers the wonderful depth of the Divine judgment. Nor is it to be doubted that this variety also follows, subject to the decision of God's eternal election. If it be evidently the result of the Divine will, that salvation is freely offered to some, and others are prevented from attaining it—this immediately gives rise to important and difficult questions, which are incapable of any other explication, than by the establishment of pious minds in what ought to be received concerning election and predestination. . . that . . . some should be predestined to salvation, and others to destruction. . . . His eternal election, which illustrates the grace of God by this comparison, that He adopts not all promiscuously to the hope of salvation, but gives to some what He refuses to others. . . .

We affirm that this counsel, as far as concerns the elect, is founded on his gratuitous mercy, totally irrespective of human merit; but that to those whom he devotes to condemnation, the gate of life is closed by a just and irreprehensible, but incomprehensible, judgment. In the elect, we consider calling as an evidence of election, and justification as another token of its manifestation, till they arrive in glory, which constitutes its completion. As God seals his elect by vocation and justification, so by excluding the reprobate from the knowledge of his name and the sanctification of his Spirit, he affords an indication of the judgment that awaits them.

John Calvin, *Institutes of the Christian Religion*, 1536

1. From the passage, one may infer that Calvin asserted that
   A. God does not offer salvation to everyone
   B. man is incapable of understanding salvation
   C. one can "elect" to be saved or refuse to be saved
   D. only Protestants are saved

2. From the passage, one may infer that Calvin asserted that the fact that some souls are predestined to eternal condemnation is
   A. due to sins committed by those souls on Earth
   B. due to sins committed in a previous life
   C. not open to human understanding
   D. open to interpretation

3. From the passage, one may infer that Calvin asserted that
   A. finding a "calling" or vocation earns one salvation
   B. finding a "calling" or vocation is evidence that one is predestined to salvation
   C. finding a "calling" or vocation can save the previously damned
   D. finding a "calling" or vocation offers consolation to the damned

Short Answer

4. Briefly explain TWO ways in which Protestant theology differed from Catholic theology and ONE way in which Lutheran theology differed from Calvinist theology.

Answers and Explanations

1. **A** is correct because the passage clearly states that, where salvation is concerned, God "gives to some what He refuses to others." B is incorrect because the passage does offer an explanation of salvation and how it comes to some. C is incorrect because, in the passage, the word "election" refers to God's choosing to elect (or predestine) some souls for salvation. D is incorrect because the passage does not say that all Protestants are saved or that non-Protestants are damned.

2. **C** is correct because the passage asserts that the condemnation of some souls is due to God's "just" but "incomprehensible" judgment. A is incorrect because the passage states that salvation or condemnation is "totally irrespective of human merit." B is incorrect because the passage makes no mention of previous lives. D is incorrect because the passage states that God's judgment is incomprehensible, not open to interpretation.

3. **B** is correct because the passage states that Calvin and his followers "consider calling as an evidence of election." A is incorrect because the passage does not say that finding a calling earns one salvation. C is incorrect because the passage indicates that nothing can save those to whom salvation has been denied. D is incorrect because the passage says nothing about consolation for the damned.

4. Suggested answer:

   Thesis: Protestant theology differed from Catholic theology in its assertion of the doctrine of Scripture Alone and in its denial that good works could earn one's soul salvation. Calvinist theology differed from Lutheran theology in its insistence on the doctrine of Predestination.

   Paragraph Outline:

   I. The Protestant doctrine (articulated by Luther) of *Sola Scriptura* (Scripture Alone), which stated that only scripture provides reliable knowledge of God's will, contradicted the Catholic Church's assertion that both scripture and the traditions of the Church provide reliable knowledge of God's will.

   II. The Protestant doctrines of Faith Alone (Luther) and Predestination (Calvin) contradict the Catholic Church's assertion that good works can earn one salvation.

   III. Luther's doctrine of Faith Alone asserts that anyone who has true faith (thereby receiving God's grace) can be saved. Calvin's doctrine of Predestination asserts that God has predestined some to salvation and some to damnation; no one not elected by God can achieve salvation by developing true faith.

Rapid Review

KEY IDEA

By the sixteenth century, the Christian Church was faced with mounting criticism of its preoccupation with worldly matters. In Germany in 1517, Martin Luther charged that the Church had abandoned scripture and strayed from its mission. He offered an alternative and simplified theology that asserted that salvation came by having faith alone, and that scripture alone was the source of all knowledge about salvation. In England, the powerful monarch Henry VIII used the existence of a Protestant movement to break with Rome in

1524, confiscating church lands and creating the Church of England, which retained the hierarchy and trappings of the Catholic Church. By mid-century, the Protestant movement had diversified and fragmented, as second-generation Protestant theologians faced the task of articulating the specific beliefs and structures of the new Church they were building.

The Catholic response to the Protestant movement, the Counter-Reformation, was two-pronged. The Church carried out many internal reforms that addressed the grievances of the faithful; it also put into motion the Inquisition, which was aimed at stamping out Protestantism.

CHAPTER 12

The Great Voyages of Exploration and Early Colonization

IN THIS CHAPTER

Summary: In the fifteenth century, a more secular and ambitious culture emerged as European nations began to explore and exploit new areas of the globe, including Africa, the Americas, and the East. This chapter describes the growth of global trade, the establishment of European colonies in new regions of the world, and the severe stress on the traditional economic and social organization of Europe caused by the new sources of wealth and power.

Key Terms:

- ✪ **Spice trade** The importation of spices from Asia into Europe, revived during the Renaissance. The need to find shorter, more efficient routes gave impetus to the great voyages of exploration of the fifteenth and sixteenth centuries.
- ✪ *Haciendas* The large estates that produced food and leather goods for the mining areas and urban centers of the Spanish Empire in the New World.
- ✪ **Triangle of Trade** The system of interconnected trade routes that quadrupled foreign trade in both Britain and France in the eighteenth century.
- ✪ **The Middle Passage** The leg of the Triangle of Trade in which African slaves were transported in brutal conditions across the Atlantic Ocean on European trade ships.
- ✪ **Plantations** The large estates in the West Indies, which produced sugar for export to Europe.

Introduction

Around the middle of the fifteenth century, European civilization began to recover from a series of calamities that had destroyed much of the culture that characterized the High Middle Ages. What emerged was a more secular, ambitious culture that began to explore and exploit new areas of the globe, including Africa, the Americas, and the East. The influx of trade, wealth, and new cultural influences put severe stress on the traditional economic and social organization of Europe.

Exploration and Expansion

The marriage of Isabella of Castile and Ferdinand of Aragon in 1469 united two previously unruly Spanish kingdoms. With the resources of the joint kingdoms at their disposal, Isabella and Ferdinand increased Spain's power by promoting overseas exploration. They sponsored the voyages of the Genoese explorer Christopher Columbus, who, sailing west in 1492 in search of a shorter route to the spice markets of the Far East, reached the Caribbean, thereby "discovering" a "New World" for Europeans and setting in motion a chain of events that would lead to the establishment of a Spanish Empire in Mexico and Peru.

Spain was not alone in the fifteenth century in sponsoring seafaring exploration. The Portuguese prince Henry the Navigator sponsored Portuguese exploration of the African coast. By the end of the fifteenth century, Portuguese trading ships were bringing in gold from Guinea. Soon, European powers came to understand that there was also gold to be had in the selling of spices imported from India that were used both to preserve and flavor food. The search for gold and competition for the spice trade combined to inspire an era of daring exploration and discovery:

- In 1487, Bartholomew Dias rounded the Cape of Good Hope at the southern tip of Africa, thereby opening Portuguese trade routes in the East.
- In 1498, Vasco da Gama extended Portuguese trade by reaching the coast of India and returning with a cargo that earned his investors a 60 percent profit.
- The Portuguese formed trading colonies in Goa and Calcutta on India's Malabar Coast.
- Amerigo Vespucci, an Italian sailing for Spain in 1499 and for Portugal in 1501, helped to show that the lands discovered by Columbus were not in the Far East, but rather a new continent, which the German cartographer Martin Waldseemüller dubbed "America" in his honor.
- In 1519, a Spanish expedition led by the Portuguese sailor Ferdinand Magellan sailed west in search of a new route to the Spice Islands of the East. Rounding the tip of South America in 1520, the expedition sailed into the Pacific Ocean and arrived at the Spice Islands in 1521. In 1522, the expedition completed the first circumnavigation of the globe, returning to Spain without Magellan, who had been killed in the Philippines.

The Spanish Empire in the New World

Spain led the way in exploiting the economic opportunities of the New World. The process of exploitation got under way in 1519, when Hernán Cortés landed on the coast of what is now Mexico with 600 troops. Soon thereafter, Cortés marched on the Aztec capital of Tenochtitlán and imprisoned their leader, Montezuma. By 1521, the Aztecs were defeated, and the Aztec Empire was proclaimed New Spain.

In 1531, Francisco Pizarro landed on the western coast of South America with 200 well-armed men and proceeded into the highlands of what is now Peru to engage the Inca civilization. By 1533, the Incas were subdued. Internal divisions within the conquering force initially made it difficult, but by the late 1560s, effective control by the Spanish Crown was established.

The major economic components of the Spanish Empire in the New World included the following:

- Mining, primarily silver from Peru and northern Mexico that was exported to Spain
- Agriculture, through large landed estates called *haciendas*, which produced food and leather goods for the mining areas and urban centers of the New World, and plantations in the West Indies, which produced sugar for export

In both the mining and the agriculture sectors, ownership was in the hands of Spanish-born or -descended overlords, while labor was coerced from the native population.

The establishment of an exploitative foreign empire in the New World had several lasting results on the civilizations of the New World, particularly in Central and South America:

- The establishment of Roman Catholicism in the New World
- The establishment of economic dependence between the New World and Europe
- The establishment of a European-style hierarchical social structure in the cultures of the New World

It also had lasting effects on Spain and, eventually, the rest of Europe:

- A steady rise in prices, eventually producing inflation, due to the increase in available wealth and coinage
- An eventual rise of a wealthy merchant class that sat uneasily in the traditional feudal social structure of Europe
- Raised expectations for quality of life throughout the social structure of Europe

England, France, and the Triangle of Trade

By 1600, England and France were endeavoring to form their own colonies in the New World. They founded settler colonies in North America through the formation of joint stock companies (which allowed private investment combined with investment by the Crown). These colonies soon thrived, initially with considerable help from, and later at the expense of, the indigenous populations.

In the eighteenth century, England and, to a lesser extent, France surpassed Spain, Portugal, and Holland as the dominant economic powers in Europe and in the New World. They did so by controlling the majority of the increasingly lucrative Triangle of Trade that connected Europe to Africa and the Americas. The phrase "Triangle of Trade" refers to a system of interconnected trade routes that quadrupled foreign trade in both Britain and France in the eighteenth century. Here are three characteristics of the Triangle of Trade:

- Manufactured goods (primarily guns and gin) were exported from Europe to Africa.
- Slaves were exported to serve as labor in European colonies in North America, South America, and the Caribbean.
- Raw materials (especially furs, timber, tobacco, rice, cotton, indigo dye, coffee, rum, and sugar) were exported from the colonies to Europe in exchange for slaves and manufactured goods.

Prior to the eighteenth century, the primary destination of Africans taken into slavery by their rivals had been either the Mediterranean basin or Asia. The eighteenth-century expansion of the European colonies greatly increased the demand for African slaves and reoriented the slave trade to the West. The majority of slaves were destined for the West Indies and Brazil, with about 10 percent going to colonies in North America. The transportation of African slaves across the Atlantic Ocean on European trade ships was known as the Middle Passage. As many as 700 slaves per ship were transported, chained below deck in horrific conditions. It is estimated that somewhere between 50,000 and 100,000 Africans were transported each year during the height of the eighteenth-century slave trade.

Review Questions

Multiple Choice

Questions 1–3 refer to the following passage:

The great city of Tenochtitlan is built on the salt lake. . . . [C]onsidering that these people were barbarous, so cut off from the knowledge of God and other civilized peoples, it is admirable to see to what they attained in every respect. . . .

It happened . . . that a Spaniard saw an Indian . . . eating a piece of flesh taken from the body of an Indian who had been killed. . . . I had the culprit burned, explaining that the cause was his having killed the Indian and eaten him which was prohibited by Your Majesty, and by me in Your Royal name. I further made the chief understand that all the people . . . must abstain from this custom . . . I came . . . to teach them that they were to adore but one God . . . that they must turn from their idols, and the rites they had practiced until then, for these were lies and deceptions which the devil . . . had invented. . . . I, likewise, had come to teach them that Your Majesty, by the will of Divine Providence, rules the universe, and that they also must submit themselves to the imperial yoke, and do all that we who are Your Majesty's ministers here might order them.

Hernán Cortés, *Letters to Charles V, King of Spain*, 1521

1. From the passage, one may infer that Cortés saw the people of Tenochtitlán

   A. as more technologically advanced than the Spanish

   B. as disadvantaged by the absence of Christianity in their culture

   C. as ready to convert to Christianity

   D. as morally superior to Europeans

2. From the passage, one may infer that Cortés

   A. believed that God had chosen him to conquer the people of Tenochtitlán

   B. doubted the morality of his mission in the New World

   C. believed that the Spanish had complete authority over the people of Tenochtitlán

   D. intended to set himself up as the God of the people of Tenochtitlán

3. From the passage, one may infer that

   A. Cortés intended to impose the laws of Christianity and Spain on the people of Tenochtitlán

   B. Cortés intended to exterminate the people of Tenochtitlán

   C. Cortés's main mission was to educate the people of Tenochtitlán

   D. the people of Tenochtitlán were devil worshipers

Short Answer

4. Briefly explain TWO ways in which Spanish colonization changed life in the New World.

Answers and Explanations

1. **B** is correct because the passage indicates that Cortés was impressed by the technical accomplishments of the people of Tenochtitlán, *despite* their "barbarous" state, "so cut off from the knowledge of God." A is incorrect because nothing in the passage indicates that Cortés saw the people of Tenochtitlán as *more* advanced than the Spanish. C is incorrect because nothing in the passage indicates that Cortés saw the people of Tenochtitlán as "ready to convert" to Christianity. D is incorrect because the passage indicates that Cortés saw the people of Tenochtitlán as morally *inferior* to Europeans.

2. **C** is correct because both Cortés's willingness to outlaw the eating of flesh and to order the natives to turn away from idols indicate that Cortés believed that he had complete authority over the people of Tenochtitlán. A is incorrect because there is nothing in the passage that indicates that Cortés believed that he had been personally chosen by God. B is incorrect because nothing in the passage indicates that Cortés doubted the moral correctness of his mission. D is incorrect because nothing in the passage indicates that Cortés intended to set himself up as the God of the people of Tenochtitlán.

3. **A** is correct because the banning of cannibalism and the "turning away" from idols referred to in the passage allow one to infer that Cortés intended to impose the laws of Christianity and Spain on the people of Tenochtitlán. B is incorrect because nothing in the passage indicates that Cortés intended to exterminate the people of Tenochtitlán. C is incorrect; despite the reference to "teaching" the people of Tenochtitlán, the passage makes it clear that Cortés's primary mission was to rule the people of Tenochtitlán. D is incorrect because the passage allows one to infer nothing in regard to the worship practices of the people of Tenochtitlán; rather, the passage gives inferences of the ways in which Cortés interpreted those practices.

4. Suggested answer:

   Thesis: Spanish colonization changed life in the New World by creating a new agricultural system and by shifting ownership of both the agricultural and mining sectors away from local populations.

   Paragraph Outline:

   I. Spanish colonization created a new agricultural system in which large estates called *haciendas* produced food and leather goods for the mining areas and urban centers of the New World, and plantations in the West Indies produced sugar for export.

   II. In both the mining and agriculture sectors, ownership was in the hands of Spanish-born or Spanish-descended overlords, while labor was coerced from the native population.

Rapid Review

In the fifteenth century, Isabella and Ferdinand used the resources of the newly united kingdom of Spain to promote overseas exploration. Other European kingdoms followed suit. This led to an unprecedented era of exploration and discovery in the sixteenth and seventeenth centuries and to the building of a Spanish empire in the New World. In the eighteenth century, Britain and France came to dominate the lucrative Triangle of Trade that imported valuable raw materials from North America and the Caribbean to Europe in exchange for slaves acquired from Africa.

CHAPTER 13

Economic Change and Political Consolidation

IN THIS CHAPTER

Summary: In the first half of the seventeenth century, the traditional, hierarchical social structure of European kingdoms came under new pressures. This chapter describes the economic, social, and political changes as economies underwent a transformation from an agrarian base to a more complex economic system that included expanding trade and the growth of a middle class of merchants and professionals.

KEY IDEA

Key Terms:

- ✪ **Peasantry** The class of rural, agricultural laborers in traditional European society.
- ✪ **Nobility** The class of privileged landowners in traditional European society.
- ✪ **Monarchs** The hereditary rulers of traditional European society.
- ✪ **Divine Right of Kings** The theory that contended that monarchs received their right to rule directly from God.
- ✪ **Absolutism** A theory of government that contends that a rightful ruler holds absolute power over his or her subjects.
- ✪ **English Civil War** (1642–1646) The war in which forces loyal to King Charles I fought to defend the power of the monarchy, the official Church of England, and the privileges and prerogatives of the nobility, while forces supporting Parliament fought to uphold the rights of Parliament, to bring an end to the notion of an official state church, and for the ideals of individual liberty and the rule of law.

- **The Commonwealth** (1649–1660) The period during which England was ruled without a monarch, following the victory of the Parliamentary forces in the English Civil War and the subsequent execution of Charles I.
- **Constitutional monarchy** A theory of government that contends that a rightful ruler's power is limited by an agreement with his or her subjects.
- *Intendent* An administrative bureaucrat in absolutist France of the seventeenth century, usually chosen from the middle class, who owed his position and, therefore, his loyalty directly to the state.

Introduction

In the first half of the seventeenth century, the traditional hierarchical structure of European society came under new pressures. This structure was one in which a large class of poor agricultural laborers (the peasantry) supported a small and wealthy class of elites (the nobility). As the monarchs of Europe fought wars to expand their kingdoms and created larger state bureaucracies to manage them, the pressure to raise greater sums of money through taxes stretched the economies and social structures of European societies to the breaking point. Meanwhile, a continuous increase in trade and in the diversification of the economy was creating a new class of people: a middle class made up of merchants and professionals, which did not fit comfortably into the traditional hierarchy.

Economic Stress and Change

A series of unusually harsh winters that characterized the "little ice age" of the 1600s led to a series of poor harvests, which, in turn, led to malnutrition and disease. In an effort to cope with increasing poverty, members of the besieged agricultural class opted to have smaller families. This combination of famine, poverty, and disease led to a significant decrease in the population during this period.

These "natural" problems that plagued the peasantry of Europe were exacerbated during this period by increasing demands from the nobility that ruled them. The endless warfare waged by the rival monarchs of Europe during this period further depleted the agricultural population through the conscription of its young men into the army and taking them off to war. War also required money, which the monarchs and their governments attempted to raise by increasing taxes. Because the nobility was largely exempt from taxes, the peasantry bore the brunt of this new economic burden. In many places, the peasantry resisted violently in a series of tax revolts, but temporary concessions won by them were quickly reversed.

More successful resistance to the monarchs' desire for increased power and wealth came from provincial nobles, town officials, and church leaders. The outcomes of these power struggles varied from kingdom to kingdom.

Britain: The Rise of Parliament

In Britain, these tensions came to a head in the form of a struggle between the monarchs of the Stuart dynasty and the English Parliament. Already an old and important institution by 1600, the English Parliament was an assembly of elites who advised the king. But it differed from its counterparts in the other European kingdoms in several important ways:

- Its members were elected by the property-holding people of their county or district.
- Eligibility for election was based on property ownership, so its members included wealthy merchants and professional men, as well as nobles.
- Members voted individually, rather than as an order or class.

As a result, the English Parliament of the seventeenth century was an alliance of nobles and well-to-do members of a thriving merchant and professional class that saw itself as a voice of the "English people," and it soon clashed with the monarch it had invited to succeed the heirless Elizabeth I.

When James Stuart, the reigning king of Scotland (known there as James VI), agreed to take the throne of England as James I (r. 1603–1625), he was determined to rule England in the manner described by the theory of absolutism. Under this theory, monarchs were viewed as having been appointed by God (an appointment known as the "Divine Right of Kings"). As such, they were entitled to rule with absolute authority over their subjects. Despite the tension between Parliament and the monarchy, James I's reign was characterized by a contentious but peaceful coexistence with Parliament.

A religious element was added when James's son and successor, Charles I (r. 1625–1649), married a sister of the Catholic king of France. That, together with his insistence on waging costly wars, led to a confrontation with Parliament. Having provoked the Scots into invading England by threatening their religious independence, Charles I was forced to call on the English Parliament for yet more funds. Parliament responded by making funds contingent on the curbing of monarchical power. This led to a stalemate, which degenerated into the English Civil War (1642–1646). Forces loyal to the king fought to defend the power of the monarchy, the official Church of England, and the privileges and prerogatives of the nobility; forces supporting Parliament fought to uphold the rights of Parliament, to bring an end to the notion of an official state church, and for notions of individual liberty and the rule of law. The victory of the Parliamentary forces led to the trial and execution of Charles I for treason and to the establishment of the Commonwealth period (1649–1660), in which Britain was governed without a king.

France: The Construction of a State

Several key differences allowed for a far different outcome in France. A series of religious and dynastic wars in the sixteenth century produced a kingdom in which the religious issue had been settled firmly in favor of the Catholic majority. The lack of religious turmoil in the seventeenth century allowed the French monarchy to cement an alliance with both the clergy and the merchant class, and to use the great administrative expertise of both to begin to build a powerful centralized government. Both Louis XIII (r. 1610–1643) and Louis XIV (r. 1643–1715) relied on well-connected Catholic cardinals to oversee the consolidation of royal power by transferring local authority from provincial nobility to a bureaucracy that was both efficient and trustworthy.

As chief minister to Louis XIII, Cardinal Richelieu used the royal army to disband the private armies of the great French aristocrats and to strip the autonomy granted to the few remaining Protestant towns. More significantly, he stripped provincial aristocrats and elites of their administrative power by dividing France into some 30 administrative districts and putting each under the control of an *intendent*, an administrative bureaucrat who owed his position, and therefore his loyalty, directly to Richelieu.

Central and Eastern Europe: Compromise

Whereas the contests for power and sovereignty in Britain and France had clear winners and losers, similar contests in the European kingdoms further to the east resulted in a series of compromises between monarchs and rival elites.

In general, European kingdoms in eastern and central Europe, such as Brandenburg-Prussia, the independent German states, Austria, and Poland, were less economically developed than their western counterparts. The economies of Britain and France in the seventeenth century were based on an agricultural system run by a free and mobile peasantry and supplemented by an increasingly prosperous middle class consisting of artisans and merchants in thriving towns. In contrast, the landholding nobility of the kingdoms in central and eastern Europe during this period managed to retain control of vast estates worked by serfs, agricultural laborers who were bound by the land. By doing so, they were able to avoid the erosion of wealth that weakened their counterparts in Britain and France.

Review Questions

Multiple Choice

Questions 1–3 refer to the following passage:

The only way to erect . . . a Common Power, as may be able to defend them from the invasion of [foreigners] and the injuries of one another, and thereby to secure them in such sort, as that by their own industry, and by the fruits of the Earth, they may nourish themselves and live contentedly is, to confer all their power and strength upon one Man, or upon one Assembly of men, that may reduce all their Wills, by plurality of voices, unto one Will . . . and therein to submit their Wills, everyone to his Will, and their judgments, to his judgment. This is more than Consent, or Concord; it is a real Unity of them all, in one and the same Person, made by Covenant of every man with every man, in such manner, as if every man should say to every man, I Authorize and give up my Right of Governing myself to this Man, or to this Assembly of men, on this condition, that thou give up thy Right to him, and Authorize all his Actions in like manner. . . . [And] being thereby bound by Covenant . . . cannot lawfully make a new Covenant, amongst themselves, to be obedient to any other, in anything whatsoever, without his permission.

Thomas Hobbes, *Leviathan,* 1651

1. From the passage, one may infer that Hobbes was an advocate of
   A. absolutism
   B. constitutionalism
   C. socialism
   D. millenarianism
2. From the passage, one may infer that Hobbes was proposing a system of government
   A. based on conditional consent between the governing and the governed
   B. based on a limited concord between the governing and the governed
   C. based on an unbreakable covenant between the governing and the governed
   D. based on the concept of representational democracy
3. From the passage, one may infer that Hobbes
   A. was an advocate of representative democracy
   B. was opposed to the deposing of Charles I and the establishment of the Commonwealth government in England
   C. was opposed to the centralization of power in government
   D. was an advocate of an unwritten constitution

Short Answer

4. Briefly explain ONE similarity and TWO differences between the English and French experience of the consolidation of political power in the seventeenth century.

Answers and Explanations

1. **A** is correct because the phrases "confer all their power and strength," "submit their Wills," and "I Authorize and give up my Right of Governing myself" all indicate an advocacy of absolutism. B is incorrect because the passage makes no mention of limiting the power of the sovereign by a constitution. C is incorrect because the passage makes no reference to the collectivist principles of socialism. D is incorrect because the passage makes no reference to the millennial belief in the imminent end of the world.

2. **C** is correct because the passage explicitly calls for an unbreakable "Covenant of every man with every man, in such manner, as if every man should say to every man, I Authorize and give up my Right of Governing." A is incorrect because the covenant discussed in the passage is not conditional in any way. B is incorrect because the covenant discussed in the passage is not limited in any way. D is incorrect because the passage makes no reference to any kind of democracy.

3. **B** is correct because the passage establishes that Hobbes was an advocate of an unbreakable political covenant, and one may therefore infer that he was opposed to the deposing of the reigning monarchy and the establishment of a commonwealth based on conditional consent. A is incorrect because the passage makes no mention of any kind of democracy. C is incorrect because the passage indicates the advantages of centralized power. D is incorrect because the passage establishes Hobbes's opposition to any kind of constitution because it would limit the power of the sovereign.

4. Suggested answer:

   Thesis: In the seventeenth century, the people of both England and France experienced attempts by their kings to consolidate political power around the monarchy. In the English situation, that effort was complicated by religious differences and was ultimately unsuccessful. In the French case, the power of a dominant Church was used in the service of the monarchy, and the effort was ultimately successful.

   Paragraph Outline:

   I. Efforts by the monarchs of England (James I and Charles I) and the monarchs of France (Louis XIII and XIV) to consolidate power in the seventeenth century

   II. Split between the monarchists' advocacy of the Church of England and the Parliamentarians' advocacy of further Protestant reform in England. Bourbon use of the Church as a bureaucratic mechanism for the consolidation of political power in France.

   III. English Civil War and defeat of the monarchists' efforts to consolidate power in England. Successful consolidation of political power by the Bourbon monarchy in France.

Rapid Review

During the period from 1600 to 1648, the dynamics of the traditional, hierarchical social structure of European kingdoms came under new pressures. As their economies underwent a transformation from a purely agricultural base to a more complex system that included expanding trade and the uneven growth of a middle class of merchants and professionals, European monarchs attempted to solidify their claims to sovereignty.

In both Britain and France, the power struggle between the monarch and the elites was won by the side who managed to form an alliance with the wealthy merchant and professional classes. In the European kingdoms farther east, however, these classes failed to gain in wealth and numbers as their counterparts in Britain and France had done. As a result, the stalemate between royal and aristocratic wealth and power remained more balanced, necessitating compromise.

CHAPTER 14

Economic Change and the Expansion of the State

IN THIS CHAPTER

Summary: In the eighteenth century, the influx of capital generated by colonial trade in Great Britain and France spurred changes in agricultural and manufacturing production that destroyed the last vestiges of feudalism and converted the peasantry and guildsmen into wage laborers. This chapter describes these economic changes, the resulting social and political changes in Great Britain and France, and the efforts of other European powers to catch up.

Key Terms:

- ✪ **The Commonwealth** The period (1649–1660) during which England was ruled without a monarch, following the victory of the Parliamentary forces in the English Civil War and the subsequent execution of Charles I.
- ✪ **The Restoration** The period of English history (1660–1688) following the Commonwealth and preceding the Glorious Revolution. It encompassed the reigns of Charles II (1660–1685) and James II (1685–1688).
- ✪ **The Glorious Revolution** The quick, nearly bloodless uprising (1688) that co-ordinated Parliament-led uprisings in England with the invasion of a Protestant fleet and army from the Netherlands and led to the expulsion of James II and the establishment of a constitutional monarchy in England under William and Mary.
- ✪ **Constitutional monarchy** A theory of government that contends that a rightful ruler's power is limited by an agreement with his or her subjects.

- ✪ *Second Treatise of Civil Government* A philosophical treatise (1690) by the Englishman John Locke, which became the primary argument for the establishment of natural limits to governmental authority.
- ✪ **Versailles** The great palace of the French monarchs, located 11 miles outside of Paris, which was the center of court life and political power in France from 1682 until the French Revolution in 1789.
- ✪ **Tsars** The hereditary monarchs of Russia.
- ✪ **Law Code of 1649** Legislation in Russia that converted the legal status of groups as varied as peasants and slaves into that of a single class of serfs.
- ✪ **Manorial system** The traditional economic system of Europe, developed in the medieval period, in which landowning elites (lords of the manor) held vast estates divided into small plots of arable land farmed by peasants for local consumption.
- ✪ **Cash crops** Crops grown for sale and export in the market-oriented approach that replaced the manorial system during the Agricultural Revolution of the eighteenth century.
- ✪ **Enclosure** The building of hedges, fences, and walls to deny the peasantry access to traditional farming plots and common lands, which had been converted to fields for cash crops during the Agricultural Revolution of the eighteenth century.
- ✪ **Putting-out system (also "cottage industry")** A system in which rural peasants engaged in small-scale textile manufacturing. It was developed in the eighteenth century to allow merchants, faced with an ever-expanding demand for textiles, to get around the guild system.
- ✪ **Guilds** Exclusive organizations that monopolized the skilled trades in Europe from the medieval period until broken by the development of cottage industry in the eighteenth century.
- ✪ **Flying shuttle** A machine invented in 1733 by John Kay that doubled the speed at which cloth could be woven on a loom, creating a need to find a way to produce greater amounts of thread faster.
- ✪ **Spinning jenny** A machine invented in the 1760s by James Hargreaves that greatly increased the amount of thread a single spinner could produce from cotton, creating a need to speed up the harvesting of cotton.
- ✪ **Cotton gin** A machine invented in 1793 by an American, Eli Whitney, that efficiently removed seed from raw cotton, thereby increasing the speed with which it could be processed and sent to the spinners.
- ✪ **Diplomatic Revolution** The mid-eighteenth-century shift in European alliances, whereby the expansionist aims of Frederick II of Prussia caused old enemies to become allies. Prussia, fearful of being isolated by its enemies, forged an alliance in 1756 with its former enemy Great Britain; Austria and France, previously antagonistic toward one another, responded by forging an alliance of their own.
- ✪ **The Seven Years' War (1756–1763)** A conflict that pitted France, Austria, Russia, Saxony, Sweden, and (after 1762) Spain against Prussia, Great Britain, and the German state of Hanover in a contest for control of both the European Continent and the New World in North America.

Introduction

In the second half of the seventeenth century and into the eighteenth century, Great Britain and, to a lesser extent, France, surpassed Spain, Portugal, and Holland as the dominant economic and political powers in Europe. As they did so, the political struggle among the elites reached their respective climaxes.

Great Britain and France rose to prominence by controlling the majority of the increasingly lucrative Triangle of Trade that connected Europe to Africa and the Americas (see Chapter 12). The resulting wealth and prosperity set in motion a series of innovations that radically changed European agricultural and manufacturing production, which in turn produced changes in the social structure of Europe. Competition between Great Britain and France, and the desire of their eastern European rivals to catch up, led to innovations in diplomacy and war—the twin processes by which eighteenth-century European rulers built and expanded their states.

Great Britain: The Triumph of Constitutionalism

The Commonwealth (1649–1660) deteriorated into a fundamentalist Protestant dictatorship under the rule of the Parliamentary army's leading general, Oliver Cromwell. Upon Cromwell's death in 1658, English Parliamentarians worked to establish a Restoration (1660–1688) of the English monarchy, inviting the son of the king they executed to take the throne as Charles II (1660–1685).

The relative peace of the Restoration period broke down when Charles's brother, a Catholic, ascended the throne as James II (1685–1688). James was determined to establish religious freedom for Catholics, to avenge his father, and to restore absolute monarchy to Great Britain. To thwart James's plans, Parliament enlisted the aid of the king's eldest daughter, Mary, the Protestant wife of William of Orange of the Netherlands. The quick, nearly bloodless uprising that coordinated Parliament-led uprisings with the invasion of a Protestant fleet and army from the Netherlands led to the quick expulsion of James II in 1688. This is known as the Glorious Revolution. The reign of William and Mary marks the clear establishment of a constitutional monarchy, a system by which the monarch rules within the limits of the laws passed by a legislative body. The text written by the leading legal spokesman of the Parliamentary faction, John Locke's *Second Treatise of Civil Government* (1690), is still read today as the primary argument for the establishment of natural limits to governmental authority.

France: The Triumph of Absolutism

The policies of Cardinal Richelieu were continued by his successor, Cardinal Jules Mazarin, and perfected by Louis XIV (r. 1643–1715) when he took full control of the government upon Mazarin's death in 1661. To the intimidation tactics practiced by Richelieu and Mazarin, Louis added bribery. Building the great palace at Versailles, 11 miles outside of Paris, Louis presented the nobility of France with a choice: oppose him and face destruction or join him and be part of the most lavish court in Europe. In choosing to spend most of their time at Versailles, French nobles forfeited the advantages that made their English Parliamentary counterparts so powerful: control of both the wealth and loyalty of their local provinces and districts. As a result, Louis XIV became known as "the Sun King," because all French life seemed to revolve around him as the planets revolved around the sun.

Russia: Tsarist Absolutism

The seventeenth-century kingdom farthest to the east proved to be an exception to the rule, as its monarchs, the *tsars*, managed to achieve a high degree of absolutism despite an agricultural economy based on serfdom and the lack of an alliance with a thriving middle class.

Beginning in 1613 and reaching its zenith with the reign of Peter the Great (1689–1725), the Romanov tsars consolidated their power by buying the loyalty of the nobility. In return for their loyalty, the Romanov tsars gave the nobility complete control over the classes of people below them. A prime example is the Law Code of 1649, which converted the legal status of groups as varied as peasants and slaves into that of a single class of serfs. Under the Romanov tsars, the Russian nobility also enjoyed the fruit of new lands and wealth acquired by aggressive expansion of the Russian empire eastward into Asia.

With the nobility firmly tied to the tsar, opposition to the tsar's power manifested itself only periodically in the form of revolts from coalitions of smaller landholders and peasants angered by the progressive loss of their wealth and rights. Such revolts, like the revolts of the Cossacks in the 1660s and early 1670s, were ruthlessly put down by the tsar's increasingly modern military forces. The smaller landholders and peasants were controlled thereafter by the creation of a state bureaucracy modeled on those of western Europe, and by encouraging the primacy and importance of the Russian Orthodox Church, which taught that the traditional social hierarchy was mandated by God.

Breaking the Traditional Cycle of Population and Productivity

The enormous wealth generated by the British and French colonies and the Triangle of Trade created pressure for social change that eventually affected the whole populations of both Great Britain and France. The effects were felt more strongly in Great Britain and led to changes that, taken together, constituted the first phase of the Industrial Revolution, which began in Great Britain and then spread eastward throughout Europe. This Industrial Revolution broke the traditional cycle of population and productivity.

The traditional cycle of population and productivity worked like this:

- Population and productivity rose together, as an increase in the number of people working in an agricultural economy increased the agricultural yield.
- Eventually, the agricultural yield reached the maximum amount that could be produced given the land available and the methods in use.
- For a while, population would continue to rise, but eventually, as the number of people far outstripped the agricultural yield, food became scarce and expensive.
- Scarcity and high prices eventually caused the population to decline.
- When the population was safely below the possible productivity, the cycle began again.

In the eighteenth century, several developments related to new wealth combined to break this cycle:

- Agriculture became market oriented.
- Rural manufacturing spread capital throughout the population.
- Increased demand led to technical innovation.

The new market orientation of agriculture created a shift from farming for local consumption to a reliance on imported food sold at markets. The introduction of rural manufacturing put larger amounts of currency into the system and made the working population less dependent on land and agricultural cycles, thereby breaking the natural check on population growth.

Market-Oriented Agriculture

The rise in population created more mouths to feed. The existence of a vast colonial empire of trade created an increasingly wealthy merchant class of individuals who both bought land from, and affected the behavior of, traditional landholding elites. The result was the destruction of the traditional manorial system in which landowning elites (lords of the manor) held vast estates divided into small plots of arable land farmed by peasants for local consumption and vast grounds, known as commons, where peasants grazed their livestock. That system was slowly replaced by a market-oriented approach in which cash crops were grown for sale and export.

The shift to a cash-crop system created pressure, which led to the reorganization of the social structure of the countryside. The traditional landowning elites abandoned their feudal obligations to the peasantry and adopted the attitude of the merchant class. Cash crops created a demand for larger fields. Landowners responded by instituting a process known as "enclosure," because of the hedges, fences, and walls that were built to deny the peasantry access to the commons, which had been converted to fields for cash crops. Later, the landowners extended enclosure into other arable lands, breaking traditional feudal agreements and gradually transforming much of the peasantry into wage labor. By the middle of the eighteenth century, three-quarters of the arable land in England was enclosed informally or "by agreement" (though the peasantry had not, in fact, been given any choice); after 1750, the process continued more formally as land was enclosed via acts of Parliament.

Rural Manufacturing

The increase in population also created greater demand for the other necessities of life, particularly clothing. In the feudal system, all aspects of textile production had been under the control of guilds (which were organizations of skilled laborers, such as spinners and weavers), which enjoyed the protection of town officials. Membership in a guild was gained only through a lengthy apprenticeship. In that way, the guilds kept competition to a minimum and controlled the supply of textiles, thereby guaranteeing that they could make a decent living. In the eighteenth century, merchants faced with an ever-expanding demand for textiles had to find a way around the guild system; the result was a system of rural manufacturing, known variously as cottage industry or the putting-out system.

In the putting-out system, merchants went into the countryside and engaged the peasantry in small-scale textile production. Each month, a merchant would provide raw material and rent equipment to peasant families. At the end of the month, he would return and pay the family for whatever thread or cloth they had produced. Initially, peasant families supplemented their agricultural income in this way; eventually, some of them gave up farming altogether and pooled their resources to create small textile mills in the countryside. As the system grew, the guilds of the town were unable to compete with the mills, and cottage industry replaced the urban guilds as the center for textile production.

The new system of rural manufacturing went hand in hand with the shift to market-oriented agriculture; the destruction of the manorial system could not have been accomplished if the cash flowing into the economy did not find its way into the hands of the rural population. The creation of cottage industries provided the cash that enabled rural families to buy their food, rather than having to grow it themselves.

However, the social change that accompanied the destruction of both the manorial system and the guilds also brought hardship and insecurity. The enclosure movement meant that thousands of small landholders, tenant farmers, and sharecroppers lost their land and their social status. Forced to work for wages, their lives and those of their families were now at the mercy of the marketplace. The destruction of the guilds produced similar trauma for the artisans whose livelihood had been protected by the guilds and their families. For both the peasantry and the artisans, the economic and social changes of the eighteenth century meant the destruction of their traditional place and status in society: they were now faced with both new opportunity and great insecurity.

Technical Innovations in Agriculture and Manufacturing

It is important to remember that technical innovations are always responses to new challenges. The people of earlier centuries did not fail to innovate because they were less intelligent; they simply had no need for the innovations. The ever-growing population and demand for food and goods in the eighteenth century created a series of related demands that eventually led to technical innovations in both agriculture and manufacturing. Single innovations often created a need for further innovation in a different part of the process.

The key technical innovation in the agricultural sector in the eighteenth century was the replacement of the old three-field system (in which roughly one-third of the land was left fallow to allow the soil to replenish itself with the necessary nutrients to produce crops) with new crops, such as clover, turnips, and potatoes, which replenished the soil while also producing foodstuffs that could be used to feed livestock in winter. More and healthier livestock contributed to the creation of products as varied as dairy and leather.

In the manufacturing sector, a number of interconnected technical innovations greatly increased the pace and output of the textile industry:

- In 1733, John Kay invented the flying shuttle, which doubled the speed at which cloth could be woven on a loom, creating a need to find a way to produce greater amounts of thread faster.
- In the 1760s, James Hargreaves invented the spinning jenny, which greatly increased the amount of thread a single spinner could produce from cotton, creating a need to speed up the harvesting of cotton.
- In 1793, the American Eli Whitney invented the cotton gin, which efficiently removed seed from raw cotton, thereby increasing the speed with which it could be processed and sent to the spinners.

These technical innovations greatly increased the pace and productivity of the textile industry. The need to supervise these larger, faster machines also contributed to the development of textile mills, which replaced the scattered putting-out system by the end of the eighteenth century.

Eastern Ambition

The prosperity and power of Great Britain and France caused their eastern European rivals to try to strengthen and modernize their kingdoms.

Prussia

In Prussia, Frederick William I built a strong centralized government in which the military, under the command of the nobles, played a dominant role. In 1740, his successor Frederick II (the Great) used that military to extend Prussia into lands controlled by the Hapsburgs. Challenging the right of Maria Theresa to ascend the throne of Austria (which was a right guaranteed her by a document known as the Pragmatic Sanction), Frederick II marched troops into Silesia. In what came to be known as the War of the Austrian Succession (1740–1748), Maria Theresa was able to rally Austrian and Hungarian troops to fight Prussia and its allies, the French, Spanish, Saxons, and Bavarians, resulting in a standoff.

Russia

In Russia, the progress toward modernization and centralization made under Peter the Great had largely been undone in the first half of the eighteenth century. However, under the leadership of Catherine the Great, Russia defeated the Ottoman Turks in 1774, thereby extending Russia's borders as far as the Black Sea and the Balkan Peninsula. In 1775, Russia joined with Prussia and Austria to conquer Poland and divide its territories among the three of them.

War and Diplomacy

In eighteenth-century Europe, state-building was still primarily conducted through war and diplomacy. The competition between Great Britain and France in the Triangle of Trade meant that they would contend militarily for control of colonies in North America and the Caribbean, but the desire to weaken one another also led them to become entangled in land wars in Europe.

The expansionist aims of Frederick II of Prussia led to a shift in diplomatic alliances that is now referred to as the Diplomatic Revolution:

- Prussia, fearful of being isolated by its enemies, forged an alliance in 1756 with its former enemy, Great Britain.
- Austria and France, previously antagonistic toward one another, were so alarmed by the alliance of Prussia and Great Britain that they forged an alliance of their own.

Colonial and continental rivalries combined to bring all of the great European powers into conflict during the Seven Years' War (1756–1763). Land and sea battles were fought in North America (where the conflict is sometimes referred to as the French and Indian War), Europe, and India. The European hostilities were concluded in 1763 by a peace agreement that essentially reestablished prewar boundaries. The North American conflict, and particularly the fall of Quebec in 1759, shifted the balance of power in North America to the British. The British had similar success in India.

As the eighteenth century progressed, the nature of European armies and wars changed in ways that would have profound implications for the ruling regimes:

- The size of the standing armies increased.
- The officer corps became full-time servants of the state.
- Troops consisted of conscripts, volunteers, mercenaries, and criminals who were pressed into service.
- Discipline and training became harsher and more extensive.

At the same time, weapons and tactics changed to accommodate the new armies:

- Muskets became more efficient and more accurate.
- Cannons became more mobile.
- Wars were now decided not by a decisive battle, but by a superior organization of resources.
- Naval battles were now often more crucial than land battles.

Review Questions

Multiple Choice

Questions 1–3 refer to the following passage:

> The political dominance of large landowners determined the course of enclosure. . . . [I]t was their power in Parliament and as local Justices of the Peace that enabled them to redistribute the land in their own favor.
>
> A typical round of enclosure began when several, or even a single, prominent landholder initiated it . . . by petition to Parliament. . . . [T]he commissioners were invariably of the same class and outlook as the major landholders who had petitioned in the first place, [so] it was not surprising that the great landholders awarded themselves the best land and the most of it, thereby making England a classic land of great, well-kept estates with a small marginal peasantry and a large class of rural wage laborers.
>
> Joseph R. Stromberg, "English Enclosures and Soviet Collectivization: Two Instances of an Anti-Peasant Mode of Development," 1995

1. From the passage, one may infer that Stromberg sees the seventeenth-century English Parliament and justices of the peace as
   A. protectors of the rights of agricultural laborers
   B. political innovations
   C. a check on agricultural innovation
   D. instruments of the landowning class
2. From the passage, one may infer that Stromberg interprets the petitioning process by which enclosure was carried out to have
   A. favored the interests of urban industry
   B. favored the interests of the landowning class
   C. been fair and balanced
   D. promoted cottage industry
3. From the passage, one may infer that Stromberg understands the enclosure movement to have made England into a society characterized by
   A. great economic inequity
   B. great economic opportunity
   C. industrialization
   D. urbanization

Short Answer

4. Briefly explain the rise of technical innovation in eighteenth-century agriculture. Illustrate your explanation with THREE examples.

Answers and Explanations

1. **D** is correct as the passage asserts that Parliament and local justices of the peace "enabled [large landowners] to redistribute the land in their own favor." A is incorrect as the passage indicates that Parliament and local justices of the peace looked out for the interests of the landowning classes, not of the agricultural laborers. B is incorrect because nothing in the passage refers to political innovation. C is incorrect because the passage indicates that Parliament and local justices of the peace helped to bring about enclosure, which was an agricultural innovation.

2. **B** is correct because the passage indicates that the commissioners who oversaw the petitioning process were of the landowning class and "awarded themselves the best land and the most of it." A is incorrect because the passage makes no reference to urban industry. C is incorrect because the passage clearly indicates that the process favored the landowning class. D is incorrect because the passage makes no reference to cottage industry.

3. **A** is correct because the last sentence of the passage indicates that enclosure created an England in which the landowning classes had great, landed estates, while the peasantry was "marginal," and the rest of the population were reduced to being "wage laborers." B is incorrect because the passage makes no reference to enclosure furthering economic opportunity. C and D are incorrect because the passage makes no reference to industrialization or urbanization.

4. Suggested answer:

   Thesis: The rise of technical innovation in eighteenth-century agriculture was a response to the rising demand for food and goods created by an increasing population. The process of innovation was spurred on by its reciprocal nature, as innovation in one sector of the process created a demand for innovation in other sectors.

   Paragraph Outline:

   I. For example, the increasing population created an increased demand for textile production. That demand created a need for faster ways to process larger amounts of wool and cotton goods. As a response, the flying shuttle was developed in 1733 to increase the speed at which cloth could be woven; the spinning jenny was developed in the 1760s to increase the amount of thread that could be spun by a single spinner; and the cotton gin was developed in 1793 to increase the speed with which seeds could be removed from cotton.

   II. The process of innovation in one aspect of textile production created a demand for innovation in other aspects. By doubling the speed at which cloth could be woven, the flying shuttle created a demand for greater amounts of thread. That demand was met by the spinning jenny, which increased the amount of thread that could be produced by a single spinner, but that in turn created a demand for faster, more efficient harvesting of cotton. That demand was met by the cotton gin.

Rapid Review

In the eighteenth century, Great Britain and France continued down their respective paths toward constitutionalism and absolutism. Concurrently, they came to dominate the lucrative Triangle of Trade, which allowed valuable raw materials from North America and the Caribbean to be imported to Europe in exchange for slaves acquired from Africa.

The influx of capital generated by the colonial trade served as a spur for unchecked population growth made possible by an agricultural revolution and the creation of a system of rural manufacturing. The changes in agricultural and manufacturing production destroyed the last vestiges of an economic system (manorialism) and a social system (feudalism) that dated back to the medieval period. In that process, both the traditional European peasantry and the guildsmen were converted to wage labor.

The intensifying rivalry between Great Britain and France, and the growing ambition of their eastern European counterparts, led to a series of mid-century wars, including the War of the Austrian Succession and the Seven Years' War. Rivalries also led to a series of innovations in diplomacy and warfare.

CHAPTER 15

The Enlightenment

IN THIS CHAPTER

Summary: In the eighteenth century, many of the educated elite in France and England, inspired by Newton's discovery of the laws of physics, tried to discover through reason the "natural laws" for social and political order. This chapter looks at the beliefs of the most influential thinkers of the Enlightenment and how the more egalitarian and democratic thought of this period contributed to an atmosphere of political and social revolution that flourished in Europe at the end of the century.

Key Terms:

- ✪ *Second Treatise of Government* Philosophical treatise (1690) by the Englishman John Locke, which became the primary argument for the establishment of natural limits to governmental authority.
- ✪ **Civil society** The society formed when free individuals come together and surrender some of their individual power in return for greater protection.
- ✪ *Spirit of the Laws* The Baron de Montesquieu's treatise of 1748, in which he expanded on John Locke's theory of limited government and outlined a system in which government was divided into branches in order to check and balance its power.

- ⊙ *Essay Concerning Human Understanding* John Locke's treatise of 1689–1690, which argued that humans are born *tabula rasa* (as "blank slates"), contradicting the traditional Christian notion that humans were born corrupt and sinful and implying that what humans become is purely a result of what they experience.

- ⊙ *Wealth of Nations* Adam Smith's treatise of 1776, which argued that there are laws of human labor, production, and trade, which stem from the unerring tendency of all humans to seek their own self-interest.

- ⊙ **Invisible hand** A phrase, penned by Adam Smith in *Wealth of Nations* (1776), to denote the way in which natural economic laws guide the economy.

- ⊙ *The Vindication of the Rights of Women* Mary Wollstonecraft's treatise of 1792, in which she argued that reason was the basis of moral behavior in *all* human beings, not just in men.

- ⊙ **Salons** Places where both men and women gathered, in eighteenth-century France, to educate themselves about and discuss the new ideas of the Enlightenment in privacy and safety.

- ⊙ *Philosophe* Public intellectuals of the French Enlightenment who believed that society should be reformed on the basis of natural law and reason.

- ⊙ **Masonic lodges** Secret meeting places established and run by Freemasons, whose origins dated back to the medieval guilds of the stonemasons. By the eighteenth century, the lodges were fraternities of aristocratic and middle-class men (and occasionally women) who gathered to discuss alternatives to traditional beliefs.

- ⊙ **Deism** The belief that the complexity, order, and natural laws exhibited by the universe were reasonable proof that it had been created by a God who was no longer active.

- ⊙ **Enlightened despotism** The hope shared by many *philosophes* that the powerful monarchs of European civilization, once educated in the ideals of the Enlightenment, would use their power to reform and rationalize society.

- ⊙ *Candide* Voltaire's sprawling satire of European culture, penned in 1759, which has become the classic example of Enlightenment period satire.

- ⊙ *Encyclopedia* Produced by the tireless efforts of its co-editors, Denis Diderot and Jean le Rond d'Alembert (1751–1772), the entries of the *Encyclopedia* championed a scientific approach to knowledge and labeled anything not based on reason as superstition.

- ⊙ *System of Nature* The Baron d'Holbach's treatise of 1770, which was the first work of Enlightenment philosophy to be openly atheist and materialist.

- ⊙ *The Social Contract* Jean-Jacques Rousseau's treatise of 1762, in which he wrote, "Man is born free; and everywhere he is in chains." He argued that a virtuous citizen should be willing to subordinate his own self-interest to the general good of the community and that the government must be continually responsible to the general will of the people.

- ⊙ **Almanacs** Popular eighteenth-century texts that incorporated much of the new scientific and rational knowledge of the Enlightenment.

- ⊙ **Philosophical texts** The underground book trade's code name for banned books, which included some versions of philosophical treatises, and bawdy, popularized versions of the *philosophes'* critique of the Church and the ruling classes.

Introduction

 KEY IDEA "The Enlightenment" refers to an eighteenth-century cultural movement whose proponents argued that society and its laws should be based on human reason, rather than on custom or tradition. Its roots can be traced to the late seventeenth century, when thinkers and writers began praising the method of inquiry and the accomplishments of Isaac Newton. Following Newton, political writers like John Locke began suggesting that there were natural laws that govern human behavior that could be discovered through reason. In the eighteenth century, intellectuals known as *philosophes* developed a program for reforming society along the lines of reason, which they initially hoped to implement by educating the powerful rulers, or "enlightened despots," of Europe. Later in the century, when enlightened despotism seemed to have failed, Enlightenment ideals began to be applied in more revolutionary contexts.

The Triumph of Newtonian Science

Isaac Newton was an Englishmen who was educated at Cambridge University at a time when its faculty was committed to the advancement of Neoplatonism and to the rejection of Cartesianism. As a fellow of Trinity College, Cambridge, Newton lived a solitary life and was driven by the notion that God had left clues to His true nature in the laws that governed the natural world. Newton was intensely focused on solving the mystery of planetary motion. Using a mathematical system of his own creation, which he called "fluxions" (and which we now refer to as calculus), and following Kepler's suggestion that the paths of planetary orbits were elliptical, Newton was able to calculate the orbits of the planets precisely by assuming that each particle of matter, no matter how large or small, was drawn to every other piece of matter by a force that he called universal gravitation.

Newton published his results in 1687 in his great work, the *Principia Mathematica* (*The Mathematical Principles of Natural Knowledge*), in which he stated, "Every particle of matter in the universe attracts every other particle with a force varying inversely as the square of the distance between them and directly proportional to the product of their masses." The *Principia* not only provided the correct calculations for planetary motion, it set out "definitions" and "laws of motion," which demonstrated how mathematical philosophy was henceforth to be done.

For the rest of the seventeenth century, the methods of Newton and Descartes served as competing models, with Newtonianism reigning in Great Britain and Cartesianism dominating in continental Europe. But by the dawn of the eighteenth century, Newtonianism had won out and served as a model not just for natural philosophy, but for an approach to the understanding of human society—an approach that would come to be known as the Enlightenment.

New Ideas About Natural Law, Human Nature, and Society

Isaac Newton had shown that, through the rigorous application of empirical observation and reason, humans could discern the laws that God had created to govern the natural world. His eighteenth-century successors, the *philosophes*, argued that the same process could lead to knowledge of the natural laws that govern human behavior. Accordingly, the Enlightenment view of society rested upon certain assumptions about the "natural state" of human beings.

Thomas Hobbes

One assumption about human nature that was foundational to Enlightenment thought was the belief that human beings could discern and would naturally follow their own self-interest. Thomas Hobbes, the author of *Leviathan* (1651), asserted that self-interest motivated nearly all human behavior. Specifically, Hobbes argued that human beings were naturally driven to quarrel by competition, diffidence, and glory. Hobbes therefore concluded that "without a common power to keep them in awe," the natural state of man was one of war.

John Locke

More typical of Enlightenment thought about human nature were the ideas of John Locke. In his *Essay Concerning Human Understanding* (1689–1690), Locke argued that humans are born *tabula rasa* (as "blank slates"). This contradicted the traditional Christian notion that humans were born corrupt and sinful, and it implied that what humans become is purely a result of what they experience. Accordingly, Locke argued that educational and social systems that taught and rewarded rational behavior would produce law-abiding and peaceful citizens.

Locke shared Hobbes's belief in self-interest, and its importance in Locke's thought can be seen in his influential theory of private property, which appeared in his *Second Treatise of Government* (1690). Locke argued that God created the world and its abundance so that humans might make it productive. To ensure that productivity, God established a natural right to property. Private property is created, Locke argued, when an individual mixes a common resource with his individual labor. For example, when an individual does the work of cutting down a tree and crafting the wood into a chair, he has mixed a common resource with his individual labor to create something that did not exist before. That creation is his private property and, therefore, his incentive to be productive.

Adam Smith

A typical eighteenth-century example of self-interest as natural law can be seen in the work of Adam Smith, who applied Enlightenment ideals to the realm of economics. In *Wealth of Nations* (1776), Smith argued that there were laws of human labor, production, and trade that stemmed from the unerring tendency of all humans to seek their own self-interest. The economic laws that Smith identified, such as the law of supply and demand, are all by-products of human self-interest. Smith asserted that the sum total of these natural economic laws functioned like an "invisible hand" that guided the economy. Efforts by governments to alter the natural laws of an economy, such as putting a tax or tariff on foreign products, would ultimately fail, Smith argued. Accordingly, Smith and his followers advocated a hands-off, or *laissez-faire*, economic policy.

Mary Wollstonecraft

In 1792, the English *philosophe* Mary Wollstonecraft published *The Vindication of the Rights of Women*, in which she argued that reason was the basis of moral behavior in all human beings (not just men). From that basis, she went on to assert that the subjugation of women in European society was based on irrational belief and the blind following of tradition, and she challenged all men of reason to acknowledge the equality and human rights of all men and women.

New Political Ideas

Enlightenment ideals about natural law, human nature, and society led Enlightenment thinkers to ponder the question of the origin and proper role of government. Both Locke and Hobbes wrote in the context of the English Civil War that pitted Royalists against

Parliamentarians. The Royalists supported the traditional power and privilege of the aristocracy and the king. In contrast, the Parliamentarians were seeking to limit the power and privilege of the aristocracy and the king.

Thomas Hobbes

Hobbes was a Royalist. From his point of view, the Parliamentarians had brought chaos to England by naively ignoring the fact that the natural state of humanity was war. Peace, Hobbes argued in *Leviathan*, required a government capable of simultaneously striking the fear of death in its subjects and guaranteeing that lawful subjects would attain a good quality of life. In order to accomplish these tasks, the government required absolute power, which it acquired by entering into an unbreakable contract, or sacred covenant, with the people.

John Locke and Cesare Beccaria

Locke, a Parliamentarian, agreed that men were often ruled by their passions. But in the *Second Treatise*, he argued that in civil society, men settled disputes dispassionately and effectively by creating a system of impartial judges and communal enforcement. In such a system, the power of government came from the consent of the people, and its use was limited to protecting the people's natural rights, particularly their right to property. Any government that did not use its power to protect the rights of its people was no longer legitimate and both could and should be deposed.

In the eighteenth century, it was Locke's vision of government and law that came to dominate the Enlightenment. The Italian philosopher Cesare Beccaria carried Locke's line of thinking about the proper function of government further, arguing in *Crime and Punishment* (1764) that the purpose of punishment should be to rehabilitate and reintegrate the individual into society. Accordingly, the severity of the punishment should reflect the severity of the crime.

Baron de Montesquieu

The Baron de Montesquieu was a French aristocrat and judge who expanded on Locke's theory of limited government by investigating the effects of climate and custom on human behavior. In *Spirit of the Laws* (1748), he stressed the importance of the rule of law and outlined a system in which government was divided into branches in order to check and balance its power.

Thomas Jefferson

Thomas Jefferson established the notion that the only legitimate role of a government was to guarantee its citizens the "inalienable rights to life, liberty, and the pursuit of happiness," which became the philosophical justification for the American Declaration of Independence from the rule of George III and Great Britain in 1776.

The *Philosophes* and Enlightened Despotism

The term *philosophe*, originally just the French term for *philosopher*, came to identify a new breed of philosopher, one dedicated to educating the broader public. Many were popularizers of the ideas of others, looking to spread an ideal of a society governed by reason. To reach the broadest possible audience, they wrote in many different genres: histories, novels, plays, pamphlets, and satires, as well as traditional philosophical treatises.

The phrase "enlightened despotism" referred to the hope shared by many *philosophes* that the powerful monarchs of European civilization, once educated in the ideals of the Enlightenment, would use their power to reform and rationalize society. To one degree or another, many eighteenth-century European monarchs instituted reforms, but within limits:

- Frederick II (the Great) of Prussia abolished serfdom, instituted a policy of religious toleration, and attracted French Protestants and dissidents, such as Voltaire, to his kingdom, but Prussia remained a militaristic state under an absolutist regime, and Voltaire eventually became disenchanted.
- Joseph II of Austria legislated religious toleration for Lutherans and Calvinists, abolished serfdom, and passed laws that liberalized the rules governing the press, but when pamphlets about the French Revolution appeared, he reimposed censorship.
- Catherine II (the Great) of Russia read the works of the *philosophes*, befriended Voltaire and Diderot, and called for a legislative commission to study reform, but she dismissed the commission before most of its findings had even been reported and had no intention of departing from absolutism.

In the final analysis, enlightened despotism was the use of certain Enlightenment ideals to help monarchs modernize and reform certain government and social institutions for the purpose of centralizing and strengthening their grasp on power. In the end, the interests of a ruling monarch ran counter to the more democratic and egalitarian ideals of the Enlightenment.

Salons and Lodges

The development and spread of an intellectual movement required places for people to congregate and share ideas. While *philosophes* could be found in most major European cities, the culture of salons flourished in Paris, making it the center of the Enlightenment. Originally, the term *salon* had referred to the room in aristocratic homes where the family and its guests gathered for leisure activities. During the Enlightenment, however, aristocratic and, eventually, upper middle-class women transformed such rooms (and the term) by turning them into a place where both men and women gathered to educate themselves about and discuss the new ideas of the age in privacy and safety. In the more prestigious houses, the leading *philosophes* were often invited to give informal lectures and to lead discussions.

It was through the salons that women made their most direct contribution to the Enlightenment. As hostesses, they controlled the guest list and enforced the rules of polite conversation. They were, therefore, in control of what ideas were discussed in front of which influential men, and were somewhat able to affect the reception that those ideas were given. Additionally, they controlled an extensive international correspondence network, as they decided which letters from *philosophes* in other cities were to be read, discussed, and replied to.

Another eighteenth-century home of Enlightenment thought was the Masonic lodge. The lodges were established and run by Freemasons, whose origins dated back to the Medieval guilds of the stonemasons. By the eighteenth century, the lodges had become fraternities of aristocratic and middle-class men (and occasionally women) who gathered to discuss alternatives to traditional beliefs. Following the customs of the old guilds, the Masonic fraternities were run along democratic principles, the likes of which were new to continental Europe. Linked together by membership in the Grand Lodge, the lodges formed a network of communication for new ideas and ideals that rivaled that of the salons. Some of the most influential men of the eighteenth century were Masons, including the Duke of Montagu in England, Voltaire and Mozart in France, and Benjamin Franklin in America. In Berlin, Frederick the Great cultivated the Masonic lodges as centers of learning.

Skepticism, Religion, and Social Criticism

Skepticism, or the habit of doubting what one has not learned for oneself, was also a key element of the Scientific Revolution that was developed more widely during the Enlightenment. A particular target of Enlightenment skeptics was religion. In his *Historical and Critical Dictionary* (1697), the French religious skeptic Pierre Bayle included entries for numerous religious beliefs, illustrating why they did not, in his opinion, stand the test of reason. More generally, Bayle argued that all dogmas, including those based on scripture, should be considered false if they contradicted conclusions based on clear and natural reasoning.

The most prevalent form of religious belief among the *philosophes* was deism. The deists believed that the complexity, order, and natural laws exhibited by the universe were reasonable proof that it had been created by a God. But reason also told them that once God had created the universe and the natural laws that govern it, there would no longer be any further role for Him in the universe. A typical deist tract was John Toland's *Christianity Not Mysterious* (1696). There, Toland argued that the aspects of Christianity that were not compatible with reason should be discarded and that Christians should worship an intelligible God.

Some *philosophes* went further with their skepticism. The Scottish philosopher David Hume rejected Christianity, arguing that Christianity required a belief in miracles and that the notion of miracles was contradicted by human reason. Hume also attacked the deist position, arguing that the order humans perceived in the universe was probably the product of human minds and social conventions, concluding that all religion was based on "hope and fear." In the final analysis, Hume contended that reason must be the ultimate test and that belief should be in proportion to evidence.

The most famous skeptic of the Enlightenment wrote under the pen name of Voltaire. He raised satire to an art form and used it to criticize those institutions that promoted intolerance and bigotry. For his criticism of the French monarchy, aristocracy, and the Church, he was briefly imprisoned in the Bastille. While in exile in England, he became an admirer of Newton and Locke. In *Letters Concerning the English Nation* (1733), he compared the constitutional monarchy, rationalism, and toleration that he found in England with the absolutism, superstition, and bigotry of his native France. Later, he produced a sprawling satire of European culture in *Candide* (1759). For a time he lived and worked with the most accomplished female *philosophe*, Madame du Châtelet, who made the only French translation of *Newton's Principia*.

The Arts in the Enlightenment

The eighteenth century saw the creation of new opportunities for artists, as the rise of a wealthy middle class broke the aristocratic monopoly on artistic patronage. The tastes of middle-class or bourgeois patrons were simpler than those of their aristocratic counterparts; the art produced for them was, consequently, less grand and less stylized. The middle class particularly patronized the visual arts and demanded genre paintings that depicted more realistic scenes and themes from everyday life. The paintings and engravings of William Hogarth, such as the series titled *Marriage à la Mode* (c. 1744), are examples of this genre.

The Radical Enlightenment

As the monarchs and ruling regimes of Europe showed the limits of enlightened despotism, the elements of Enlightenment thought came together in increasingly radical ways. The multi-volume *Encyclopedia* (1751–1772) was produced by the tireless efforts of its co-editors, Denis Diderot and Jean le Rond d'Alembert. Their stated goal was to overturn the barriers of superstition and bigotry and to contribute to the progress of human knowledge. The entries of the *Encyclopedia* championed a scientific approach to knowledge and labeled anything not based on reason as superstition. Its pages were strewn with Enlightenment thought and the rhetoric of natural rights that was egalitarian and democratic. King Louis XV of France declared that the *Encyclopedia* was causing "irreparable damage to morality and religion," and twice banned its publication.

Another more radical position was that of the German-born French *philosophe*, the Baron d'Holbach, whose philosophy was openly atheist and materialist. In *System of Nature* (1770), d'Holbach offered the eighteenth-century reader a view of the world as a complex system of purely material substances, acting and developing according to purely mechanical laws of cause and effect, rather than having been imposed by a rational God.

Perhaps the most influential radical voice emerged at mid-century, articulating a view of human nature that differed from Locke's *tabula rasa* and that suggested different political implications. In *Emil* (1762), Jean-Jacques Rousseau argued that humans were born essentially good and virtuous but were easily corrupted by society. Accordingly, Rousseau argued that the early years of a child's education should be spent developing the senses, sensibilities, and sentiments.

Politically, Rousseau agreed with his predecessors that individuals come together to form a civil society and give power to their government by their consent. But where Locke and Montesquieu were content with a constitutional monarchy, Rousseau's model was the ancient Greek city-state in which citizens participated directly in the political life of the state. He expressed his discontent with the political state of affairs in *The Social Contract* (1762): "Man is born free; and everywhere he is in chains." Accordingly, Rousseau believed that the virtuous citizens should be willing to subordinate their own self-interest to the general good of the community, and he argued that a lawful government must be continually responsible to the general will of the people. Toward the end of the century, as the ruling regimes of continental Europe mobilized to protect their power and privilege, it would be Rousseau's version of the Enlightenment that resonated with an increasingly discontented population.

The Other Enlightenment

The Enlightenment of the *philosophes*, with their salons and lodges, was primarily a cultural movement experienced by aristocrats and upper middle-class people. But further down the social hierarchy, a version of the Enlightenment reached an increasingly literate population in the following ways:

- Excerpted versions of the *Encyclopedia*
- Popular almanacs, which incorporated much of the new scientific and rational knowledge
- "Philosophical texts," the underground book trade's code name for banned books, which included some versions of philosophical treatises, and bawdy, popularized versions of the *philosophes'* critique of the Church and the ruling classes

In these texts the most radical of Enlightenment ideals—particularly those of Rousseau and d'Holbach—together with satirical lampooning of the clergy and the ruling class, reached a broad audience and helped to undermine respect for and the legitimacy of the ruling regimes.

Review Questions

Multiple Choice

Questions 1–3 refer to the following passage:

The political liberty of the subject is a tranquility of mind, arising from the opinion each person has of his safety. In order to have this liberty, it is requisite the government be so constituted as one man need not be afraid of another.

When the legislative and executive powers are united in the same person, or in the same body of magistrates, there can be no liberty; because apprehensions may arise, lest the same monarch or senate should enact tyrannical laws, to execute them in a tyrannical manner.

Again, there is no liberty, if the power of judging be not separated from the legislative and executive powers. Were it joined with the legislative, the life and liberty of the subject would be exposed to arbitrary control, for the judge would then be the legislator. Were it joined to the executive power, the judge might behave with all the violence of an oppressor. . . .

The executive power ought to be in the hands of a monarch; because this branch of government, which has always need of expedition, is better administered by one than by many: Whereas, whatever depends on the legislative power, is oftentimes better regulated by many than by a single person.

The Baron Montesquieu, *The Spirit of the Laws*, 1748

1. From the passage, one may infer that Montesquieu was an advocate of what political ideology born during the Enlightenment?
   A. Classical conservatism
   B. Classical liberalism
   C. Absolutism
   D. Deism

2. The author of the passage is arguing that tyranny is best avoided by
   A. direct representation of the people in government
   B. virtual representation of the people in government
   C. the consolidation of power within the government
   D. a division of power within the government

3. From the passage, one may infer that the author believed that the power to implement the law is best assigned to
   A. a king or queen
   B. an assembly
   C. a judiciary
   D. the people

Short Answer

4. Briefly explain the concept of enlightened despotism and illustrate, with TWO examples, why it ultimately failed.

Answers and Explanations

1. **B** is correct because the passage's emphasis on individual liberty identifies its author as an advocate of classical liberalism. A is incorrect because nothing in the passage advocates the conservative reverence for tradition and traditional institutions. C is incorrect because the emphasis on individual liberty and on the limited nature of political power is in opposition to absolutism. D is incorrect because nothing in the passage allows you to infer anything about the religious beliefs of the author.

2. **D** is correct because the passage proposes to protect liberty by dividing power between the legislative, executive, and judicial branches of government. A and B are incorrect because the passage makes no reference to representation. C is incorrect because the passage argues that power should be split between branches of the government, not consolidated into one branch as absolutism would recommend.

3. **A** is correct because the passage states that the executive power (the power to implement a law) "ought to be in the hands of the monarch." B is incorrect because the passage states that the executive power (the power to implement a law) "ought to be in the hands of the monarch," and because it states that such power "is better administered by one than by many." C is incorrect because the passage states that the executive power (the power to implement a law) "ought to be in the hands of the monarch." D is incorrect because the passage states that the executive power (the power to implement a law) "ought to be in the hands of the monarch," and because it makes no mention of "the people."

4. Suggested answer:

   Thesis: Enlightened despotism was the hope, shared by many *philosophes*, that the powerful monarchs of European civilization, if educated in the ideals of the Enlightenment, would use their power to reform and rationalize society. It ultimately failed because Enlightenment reform was fundamentally opposed to the political interests of a reigning monarch.

   Paragraph Outline:

   I. Voltaire initially put his hopes in Frederick II (the Great) of Prussia. Educated in Enlightenment ideals, Frederick instituted several Enlightenment reforms in his early career (by abolishing serfdom, instituting a policy of religious toleration, and attracting French Protestants and dissidents) but ultimately refused to curb the power and influence of the Prussian military elite because it went against his desires for both a strong military and unconditional power.

   II. Joseph II of Austria granted religious toleration for Lutherans and Calvinists, abolished serfdom, and passed laws that liberalized the rules governing the press. But when pamphlets appeared praising the reforms demanded by the French Revolution, he reimposed censorship.

Rapid Review

Near the end of the seventeenth century, the English physicist Isaac Newton showed, through empirical observation and reason, that one could discern the laws that God had created to govern the cosmos. In the eighteenth century, writers known as *philosophes* developed and popularized a vision of society based on Newton's emphasis on reason. They wrote philosophical treatises, histories, novels, plays, pamphlets, and satires critical of traditional social and political conventions and institutions, like absolute monarchy and the Church. Initially, they hoped to reform society by educating the powerful monarchs of European kingdoms. When that strategy (known as enlightened despotism) faltered, the movement found new venues, such as salons and Masonic lodges, and the more egalitarian and democratic aspects of Enlightenment thought came to dominate, contributing to an atmosphere of political and social revolution that flourished in modern Europe at the end of the eighteenth century.

CHAPTER 16

The French Revolution and Empire

IN THIS CHAPTER

Summary: In France in 1789, bourgeois representatives of the Third Estate, influenced by the Enlightenment, launched a revolution aimed at curbing the power and privilege of the nobility and clergy and establishing a constitutional monarchy. This chapter reviews the various phases of the French Revolution as it moved further to the left toward the Reign of Terror and then back to the right (Thermidor). It also describes the rise of Napoleon Bonaparte and the creation of a Europe-wide French Empire.

Key Terms:

- ✪ **Bourgeoisie** A term for the merchant and commercial classes of eighteenth- and nineteenth-century France. In Marxist social critique, the class that owns the means of production and exploits wage laborers.
- ✪ **Ancien Régime (also Old Regime)** The traditional social and political hierarchy of eighteenth-century France.
- ✪ **Estates General** The representative body of eighteenth-century France. Members representing each of the three Estates met to hear the problems of the realm and pleas for new taxes. In return, they were allowed to present a list of their own concerns and proposals, called *cahiers*, to the Crown.
- ✪ **National Assembly** The name taken by the representatives of the Third Estate on June 17, 1789, declaring themselves to be the legislative body of France. This event is often seen as the beginning of the French Revolution's moderate phase.

- ✪ **"Declaration of the Rights of Man and of the Citizen"** A declaration adopted by the National Assembly of France on August 27, 1789, espousing individual rights and liberties for all citizens.
- ✪ *Sans-culottes* The working people (bakers, shopkeepers, artisans, and manual laborers) who asserted their will in the radical phase of the French Revolution (1791–1794). They were characterized by their long working pants, hence, *sans-culottes* (literally "without short pants").
- ✪ **Girondins** A faction within the National Convention of France, during the French Revolution, whose membership tended to come from the wealthiest of the bourgeoisie. They opposed the execution of Louis XVI.
- ✪ **Jacobins** A faction within the National Convention of France, during the French Revolution, whose members came from the lower strata of the bourgeoisie. They were adamant proponents of the execution of Louis XVI.
- ✪ **Committee of Public Safety** A twelve-man committee created in the summer of 1793 and invested with nearly absolute power in order that it might secure the fragile French Republic from its enemies.
- ✪ **Reign of Terror** The period of the French Revolution during which Robespierre, the leader of the Committee of Public Safety, created tribunals in the major cities of France to try individuals suspected of being enemies of the Revolution. During the Reign of Terror, between September 1793 and July 1794, between 200,000 and 400,000 people were sentenced to prison; between 25,000 and 50,000 of them are believed to have died either in prison or at the guillotine.
- ✪ **Directory** A five-man board created to handle the executive functions of the government during Thermidor, the third and final phase of the French Revolution (1794–1799).
- ✪ **Napoleonic Code (also known as the Civil Code of 1804)** A system of uniform law and administrative policy that Napoleon created for the empire he was building in Europe.
- ✪ **Continental System** A system established by Napoleon in order to weaken Britain by forbidding the continental European states and kingdoms under French control from trading with Great Britain.
- ✪ **Concert of Europe** The alliance created in November 1815 that required important diplomatic decisions to be made by all four great powers—Austria, Russia, Prussia, and Great Britain—"in concert" with one another.

Introduction

Between 1789 and 1799, the Kingdom of France underwent a political revolution that unfolded in three phases:

- A moderate phase (1789–1791), in which the politically active portions of the bourgeoisie, or merchant class, attempted to curb the power and privilege of the monarchy, the aristocracy, and the clergy and create a limited constitutional monarchy similar to that which existed in Great Britain
- A radical phase (1791–1794), in which the politicized urban working class of Paris seized control and attempted to create a democratic republic and a more materially and socially egalitarian society

- An end phase known as Thermidor (1794–1799), in which the moderate bourgeois faction reasserted itself and concentrated simply on restoring order

By 1799, the Thermidorian government, known as the Directory, was totally dependent on the military for its ability to govern. In November of that year, a military general, Napoleon Bonaparte staged a coup d'état and embarked on an ambitious campaign to create a French Empire that would span most of Europe. Upon his defeat in 1815 by a coalition of European powers, the French monarchy was restored, and the Kingdom of France was returned to its traditional boundaries.

The *Ancien Régime* in Crisis

The phrase *Ancien Régime*, or Old Regime, refers to the traditional social and political hierarchy of eighteenth-century France. It was composed of three "Estates":

- The First Estate, made up of the clergy, included all ordained members of the Catholic Church in France.
- The Second Estate, made up of the nobility, included all titled aristocrats.
- The Third Estate, made up of the citizenry, included everyone who was not either clergy or nobility and whose membership accounted for 96 percent of the population of France.

Together, the clergy and the nobility wielded enormous power and enjoyed tremendous privilege, while the various groups that made up the Third Estate bore the tax burden.

The Catholic Church in France functioned as a branch of the government bureaucracy. It registered births, marriages, and deaths; collected certain kinds of agricultural taxes; and oversaw both education and poverty relief. The Church owned approximately 10 percent of all the land in France but paid no taxes to the government; instead, it made an annual gift to the Crown in an amount of its own choosing. The clergy who populated the hierarchical structure of the Catholic Church in France ranged from poor, simple parish priests to the powerful cardinals, who were connected to the pope in Rome, and who often served as chief advisors in the government of the French king.

The nobility were the traditional landowning elite of France, though by this period they often supplemented their fortunes through banking and commerce. They owned somewhere between 25 and 33 percent of the land in France but were exempt from most taxes, despite the fact that they still collected various types of manorial dues from peasant farmers. Members of the nobility held most of the high offices in the French government, army, and Church.

The citizenry can roughly be divided into three social groups:

- The bourgeoisie, including merchants, manufacturers, bankers, lawyers, and master craftsmen
- The peasantry, including all agricultural laborers, ranging from very prosperous land owners to poor sharecroppers and migrant workers
- Urban laborers, including journeymen craftsmen, mill and other small-scale manufacturing workers, and all wage laborers who populated the cities and towns of France

By 1787, the government of King Louis XVI was in financial crisis. When he took the throne in 1774, Louis XVI had inherited a huge and ever-increasing national debt, most of it incurred by borrowing money to finance wars and maintain an army. With interest on the debt mounting and bankers refusing to lend the government more money, Louis and his ministers attempted to reform the tax system of France and to pry some of the vast wealth out of the hands of the nobility. When the nobility resisted, he was forced to do something that had not been done since 1614; he called into session the Estates General. The Estates General was the closest thing to a legislative assembly that existed in eighteenth-century France. Members representing each of the three Estates met to hear the problems of the realm and to hear pleas for new taxes. In return, they were allowed to present a list of their own concerns and proposals, called *cahiers*, to the Crown. When the representatives arrived at Versailles, the palace of Louis XVI, in April 1789, the representatives of the Third Estate presented a series of proposals that were revolutionary in nature.

The Moderate Phase of the French Revolution (1789–1791)

The representatives of the Third Estate, in reality all members of the bourgeoisie, demanded that the number of representatives for the Third Estate be doubled in order to equal the number of representatives in the other two Estates combined and that representatives of all three Estates meet together and vote by head rather than by Estate. These demands were designed to give the Third Estate a chance to pass resolutions by persuading a single member of the nobility or clergy to side with them. The demands of the Third Estate posed a dilemma for Louis XVI: granting their demands would give the Third Estate unprecedented power, and that power would come at the expense of the nobility and the clergy, but could perhaps be used to achieve the tax reforms that Louis and his ministers needed to address France's financial crisis.

Demand for a New Constitution

While Louis considered his options, the representatives of the Third Estate grew bolder. Arguing that they were the voice of the nation, on June 17, 1789, they declared themselves to be the National Assembly of France. When they were locked out of their meeting hall three days later, they pushed their way into Louis's indoor tennis court and vowed that they would not disband until a new constitution had been written for France. This proclamation became known as the Tennis Court Oath. On June 27, Louis decided in favor of the Third Estate, decreeing that all members should join the National Assembly.

Fear Causes Parisians to Storm the Bastille

While the bourgeois leaders of the new National Assembly worked on writing a constitution for France, the uncertainty of the situation created an atmosphere of fear and mistrust. Nervous nobles began to demand that Louis break up the new Assembly, which in turn demanded an explanation for the arrival of new regiments of mercenary troops in Versailles. By July 1789, much of the urban population of Paris, which now looked to the Assembly as its champion, believed that the nobility and, perhaps, the king intended to remove the Assembly by force. Their fears focused on the infamous Bastille, a prison fortress in Paris, which they wrongly believed housed the guns and ammunition that would be needed for the job.

On July 14, an angry crowd marched on the Bastille. The nervous governor of the Bastille ordered the crowd to disperse; when they refused, he had his guard fire into the crowd. The crowd responded by storming the Bastille. By the time it was over, 98 people had been killed and 73 wounded. The governor and his guard were killed, and their heads were paraded on pikes through the city. In the aftermath, Louis's advisors urged him to flee Versailles and raise an army to crush the Assembly and restore order to Paris. Louis decided to try to soothe the city instead, and he promised to withdraw the mercenary troops.

Rural Unrest Emboldens the Assembly

While order was restored in Paris, it was disintegrating in the countryside, where peasants, aware that the nobility had been weakened and fearful that they would soon reassert their power with a vengeance, seized the opportunity to act. They raided granaries to ensure that they would be able to have affordable bread and attacked the *chateau* of the local nobility in order to burn debt records. In the context of that rural unrest, sometimes known as the Great Fear, the Assembly passed the August Decrees, in which most of the traditional privileges of the nobility and the clergy were renounced and abolished. In an attempt to assure all citizens of France of their intention to bring about a new, more just society, on August 27, 1789, the Assembly adopted "The Declaration of the Rights of Man and of the Citizen," a document that espoused individual rights and liberties for all citizens.

By the end of the summer of 1789, severe economic stress, in the form of high bread prices and unemployment, again prompted the people of Paris to take action. Prompted by rumors that the nobility in Louis's court were plotting a coup, and spurred on by an active tabloid press, the people of Paris rioted on October 5, 1789. This event came to be known as the October Riot. The next day, a contingent of Parisian women organized an eleven-mile march from Paris to the king's palace at Versailles. Along the way, they were joined by the Paris Guards, a citizen militia, and together they forced their way into the palace and insisted that Louis accompany them back to Paris. He did, and within two weeks the National Assembly itself had relocated from Versailles to Paris. The March to Versailles, as it came to be known, demonstrated two important things:

- First, the crowds of Paris did not yet look upon Louis XVI as their enemy; they had marched to Versailles to retrieve him because they believed that if he were with them in Paris, rather than isolated in Versailles where he was surrounded by his aristocratic advisors, he would side with them and support the Assembly's efforts.
- Second, the crowd of Paris, and their willingness to do violence, had become a powerful political force.

The relocation of both the king and the National Assembly to Paris, within easy reach of the Parisian crowd, set the stage for the radical phase of the evolution.

The Radical Phase of the French Revolution (1791–1794)

The end of the October Riot marked the beginning of a two-year period of relative calm. A gradual improvement in the economy eased the tension in Paris, and the Assembly's most determined aristocratic enemies either fled to the countryside or emigrated. The Assembly used this period of relative calm to complete the constitution and to draft and pass the Civil Constitution of the Clergy, a piece of legislation that turned clergymen into employees of the government and turned Church property into property of the state. The Assembly soon sold off the confiscated property to pay off part of the national debt, but the attack on the clergy and the Church turned many faithful Catholics against the Assembly.

When Louis XVI signed the new constitution into law on September 15, 1791, the goals of the bourgeois leaders of the Assembly had been fulfilled: the power of the nobility and the Church had been diminished, and France was now a constitutional monarchy. Four developments conspired to send the Revolution into a more radical phase (each of which is reviewed in the sections that follow this list):

- The king's attempt to secretly flee Paris in June 1791
- The outbreak of war with Austria and Prussia in April 1792

- The division of the National Assembly into political factions
- The rise of a politicized laboring faction, known as the *sans-culottes* because of the long work pants they wore

The King's Attempt to Secretly Flee Paris

The king's attempt to flee Paris and head north to rally supporters, an event that came to be known as the Flight to Varennes, was disastrous. He and the royal family were apprehended and forcibly returned to Paris. He was officially forgiven by the Assembly, but he had forever lost the trust of the people of Paris.

The Outbreak of War with Austria and Prussia

The war with Austria and Prussia came about partly because French aristocratic émigrés had been urging the Austrian and Prussian monarchies to come to the aid of the embattled Louis XVI. But both Louis and the Assembly wanted the war, Louis because he believed that the country would have to turn to him to lead it in a time of war, and the Assembly because they believed it would unite the people of France in a common cause. However, when the combined forces of the Austrian and Prussian armies invaded France, the French army collapsed, and the country went into a panic.

The Division of the National Assembly into Political Factions

The development of political factions within the Assembly revealed the differing opinions about the goals and aims of the Revolution that had always lurked under the surface of its united front against the nobility and the clergy. In October 1791, an attempt to defuse factional rivalries by dissolving the National Assembly and electing a new Legislative Assembly failed to solve the problem.

The Rise of a Politicized Laboring Faction: the *Sans-Culottes*

From the beginning, the Parisian crowd and its willingness to do violence had been a factor in the Revolution. But it had been a force with essentially traditional and conservative aims, insisting that the king pay attention to, and take proper care of, his people. By 1792, the crowd was different; the working people (bakers, shopkeepers, artisans, and manual laborers, characterized by their long working pants) were now seen attending meetings of political clubs and discussing the reforms that were still needed, reforms that would bring about true equality.

Once the men and women of the *sans-culottes* began to assert themselves, political power belonged to whomever they supported. This fact became evident on August 10, 1792, when a crowd stormed first the royal palace and then the hall of the Assembly. Unable to resist the crowd, the leaders of the Assembly voted to depose and imprison the king and to immediately convene a new National Convention to deal with the crises facing the country.

The Vote to End the French Monarchy

The membership of the National Convention was elected by universal manhood suffrage, where each adult male was entitled to a single vote. Accordingly, the members of the National Convention were more radical than their predecessors. In September 1792, the Convention voted to abolish the monarchy and to proclaim France a republic. It also managed to reorganize the French army and push the invading Austrian and Prussian forces back across the border. When the Convention proclaimed the war an extension of the Revolution and vowed to carry it anywhere people yearned for liberty and freedom, the monarchies of Europe responded by forming a coalition to crush the Revolution.

In January 1793, the Convention put Louis XVI on trial for treason. The debate that followed his conviction revealed a split between two powerful factions within the Convention. The Girondins, whose membership tended to come from the wealthiest of the bourgeoisie, were mostly opposed to executing him; the Jacobins, whose members came from the lower strata of the bourgeoisie, were adamant that he must die. The vote was close, but the Jacobins prevailed, and Louis XVI was sent to the guillotine on January 21, 1793.

A New Constitution and Robespierre's Reign of Terror

The execution of the king, combined with a decision to increase the number of men conscripted into the army, caused large anti-Convention uprisings throughout France. In Paris, the Jacobins used the revolt as an opportunity to purge the Girondins from the Convention. In June 1793, a Jacobin-led mob occupied the Convention hall and refused to leave until the Girondins resigned. Those Girondins who refused to resign were arrested. The purged Convention then passed the Law of the Maximum to cap the price of bread and other essentials and drafted a new constitution that guaranteed universal manhood suffrage, universal education, and subsistence wages. In order to secure the egalitarian, democratic republic espoused by the new constitution, the Convention created a twelve-man Committee of Public Safety and invested it with almost total power in order that it might secure the fragile republic from its enemies. Within the Committee, a young lawyer from the provinces, Maximilien Robespierre, gained control through his ability to persuade both his fellow Jacobins and the *san-culottes* crowd to follow him.

Under Robespierre's leadership, the Committee instituted what has come to be known as the Reign of Terror. Arguing that, in times of revolution, terror was the necessary companion to virtue, Robespierre created tribunals in the major cities of France to try individuals suspected of being enemies of the Revolution. During the period of the Terror, between September 1793 and July 1794, between 200,000 and 400,000 people were sentenced to prison; between 25,000 and 50,000 of them are believed to have died either in prison or at the guillotine.

Among the victims of the Terror were those who rivaled Robespierre for power. In April 1794, when Robespierre had the popular and influential Jacobin leader, Georges-Jacques Danton, arrested and executed for daring to suggest that it was time to reassess the Terror, he lost the support of both the Jacobins and the crowd. In July 1794, Robespierre was arrested, tried, and executed by the same Terror machine that he had created. The execution of Robespierre marked the end of the radical phase of the Revolution, as an exhausted Paris, devoid of its radical leaders, succumbed to a reassertion of power by the propertied bourgeoisie.

The Final Phase of the French Revolution: Thermidor and the Rise of Napoleon (1794–1799)

For several months following the execution of Robespierre, the revolutionary Terror was replaced by a terror of reaction, as armed bands of men, hired by the wealthier bourgeois elites, roamed the cities hunting down and killing remaining Jacobins. In the Convention, the ascendant moderates wrote a new constitution that limited the right to vote for members of legislative bodies to wealthy property owners and removed price controls. The executive functions of the government were placed in the hands of a five-man board known as the Directory. Increasingly, the Directory relied on the military to keep order and to protect it from both the *sans-culottes*, who stormed the Convention in May 1795, and from the Royalists, who attempted a coup five months later.

When the war against the European coalition began to go badly, conservative factions within the Convention conspired with the ambitious and popular army general, Napoleon Bonaparte, to overthrow the Directory. On November 9, 1799, the conspirators staged a successful coup, and Napoleon acquired the powers necessary to govern as "first consul." By 1804, Napoleon had rid himself of his co-conspirators and had France proclaimed an "empire" and himself "emperor." He governed France with a mixture of reform and traditionalism and oversaw the military expansion of the French Empire until his defeat at the hands of coalition forces at the Battle of Waterloo in 1815.

Post-Revolutionary France and the Napoleonic Code

By the time Napoleon had himself declared emperor in 1804, he was well on his way to completing the process, begun by the Revolution, of creating a strong central government and administrative uniformity in France.

To solidify his position, Napoleon took the following measures:

- Suppressing Royalists and Republicans through the use of spies and surprise arrests
- Censoring and controlling the press
- Regulating what was taught in schools
- Reconciling France with the Roman Church by signing the Concordat of 1801, which stipulated that French clergy would be chosen and paid by the state but consecrated by the pope

To provide a system of uniform law and administrative policy, Napoleon created the Civil Code of 1804, more widely known as the Napoleonic Code. It incorporated many principles that had been espoused during the Revolution, some revolutionary and some reactionary. In accordance with revolutionary principles, the Code:

- Safeguarded all forms of property
- Upheld equality before the law
- Established the right to choose a profession
- Guaranteed promotion on merit for employees of the state

In accordance with reactionary principles, the Code:

- Upheld the ban on working men's associations
- Upheld the patriarchal nature of French society by granting men extensive rights over their wives and children

As Napoleon conquered Europe, he spread the Code across the continent. The overall effect of the Code on Europe was to erode the remnants of the old feudal system by further weakening the traditional power of the nobility and clergy.

Napoleon's Empire

Between 1805 and 1810, Napoleon's forces won a series of battles that allowed France to dominate all of continental Europe, except the Balkan Peninsula. These key victories included the following:

- The Battle of Austerlitz (December 1805), defeating Russo-Austrian forces
- The Battle of Jena (October 1806), defeating Prussian forces
- The Battle of Friedland (June 1807), defeating Russian forces

The resulting French Empire consisted of some states that were annexed directly into the French Empire, including the following:

- Belgium
- Germany to the Rhine
- The German coastal region to the western Baltic
- West-central Italy, including Rome, Genoa, and Trieste

Also included in the Empire were five satellite kingdoms ruled by Napoleon's relatives:

- Holland, ruled by his brother Louis
- Westphalia, ruled by his brother Jérôme
- Spain, ruled by his brother Joseph
- The Kingdom of Italy, ruled by his stepson Eugène
- The Kingdom of Naples, ruled by his brother-in-law Joachim Murat

The remaining portions of the Empire consisted of a series of subservient states and confederations, which included the following:

- The Confederation of the Rhine, eventually consisting of 18 German states that had been part of the now-defunct Holy Roman Empire
- The 19 cantons of the Swiss Confederation
- The Duchy of Warsaw, carved out of Prussia's Polish lands

Those European states that remained independent from France were reluctant allies that simply had no choice but to bow to Napoleon's power. Such states included the following:

- Austria, where Francis II ruled a kingdom diminished by the disintegration of the Holy Roman Empire
- Prussia, now much smaller for losing its Polish lands and other areas to the Confederation of the Rhine
- Russia, which, following the defeat at Friedland, signed the Treaty of Tilsit on July 7, 1807, recognizing France's claims in Europe
- Sweden
- Denmark

The one European nation that still threatened Napoleon was Great Britain, whose superior naval power, as exemplified by its victory over the combined French and Spanish fleets at the Battle of Trafalgar on October 21, 1805, made it unconquerable. In order to weaken Great Britain, Napoleon established what came to be known as the Continental System, whereby the Continental European states and kingdoms under French control were forbidden to trade with Great Britain.

The Decline and Fall of Napoleon and His Empire

The decline and fall of Napoleon and his empire were due to a combination of flawed policies and growing resistance to his rule. The trade restrictions of the Continental System failed to weaken Great Britain and succeeded instead in being a constant source of resentment amongst the conquered states of Europe. The British responded with a counterblockade that damaged the French economy and engaged in a lively smuggling enterprise with the rest of Europe. The combination of the restrictions of the Continental System and general resentment of French rule led to the growth of a new national spirit in many parts of continental Europe.

Spain

In Spain, popular resistance to the rule of Napoleon's brother Joseph was immediate. There were demonstrations and riots in Madrid. The brutal repression with which Napoleon's troops met these demonstrations only stiffened opposition, the spirit of which was captured forever in Francisco de Goya's painting titled *The Third of May, 1808*, which depicts a French firing squad executing helpless Spanish protestors. Opposition to French domination grew into what has been called the first example of guerrilla warfare, as loosely organized pockets of opposition carried out raids throughout Spain in a sporadic and unpredictable way, which the French could do little to prevent.

Germany

In Germany a new sense of nationalism grew in response to French domination. The sense of independence that was once a source of pride in the independent principalities and duchies was now perceived as a fatal weakness that had made Germany vulnerable to the French. In response, opposition forces in Germany began to work together, and many looked to Prussia for leadership. For its own part, Prussia quietly modernized its civil institutions and its army and waited for an opportunity to rise up against its French overlords.

Russia

In Russia, the competing ambitions of Tsar Alexander I and Napoleon led to renewed hostilities. In June 1812, Napoleon invaded Russia with a *Grande Armée* ("Great Army") of over 600,000 troops. The Russian army retreated, stripping towns of supplies and burning croplands as they went. In September, the Russian army turned on the tired and hungry French troops at Borodino, some 70 miles east of Moscow, and fought one of the bloodiest battles of the nineteenth century. The Russians withdrew, opening the way to Moscow, but the French army lost over 40,000 men. On September 14, Napoleon led his army into Moscow to find that the Russians had deserted it and set it aflame. Napoleon reluctantly retreated, but it was too late. In November and December, the Russian winter and advancing Russian troops eventually finished off the Grande Armée, undersupplied and too far from home. Nearly 500,000 French troops were lost in all; Napoleon abandoned them and dashed back to Paris.

Exile to Elba

News of the defeat of the Grande Armée in Russia galvanized resistance to Napoleon's rule throughout Europe. Napoleon raised a new army, but it lacked the supplies and veterans lost in Russia. In October 1813, a coalition of forces from Austria, Russia, Prussia, and Sweden defeated Napoleon's forces at Leipzig. In November, a combined force of British and Spanish troops crossed the Pyrenees into France and took Paris. The victorious coalition exiled Napoleon to the island of Elba, off the coast of Italy.

The Battle of Waterloo

In 1815, Napoleon staged one last comeback, returning to France and raising one last army. He was defeated at the Battle of Waterloo in Belgium by coalition forces led by the Duke of Wellington. Napoleon was finished. He was captured and imprisoned on the island of St. Helena in the South Atlantic, where he died six years later.

Restoration

In November 1814, representatives from the four major powers that had combined to defeat Napoleon—Great Britain, Russia, Prussia, and Austria—met in Vienna for a peace conference. Those representatives—Lord Castlereagh, Tsar Alexander I, Baron Hardenberg, and Prince Klemens von Metternich—were all conservative members of the aristocracy. Accordingly, the goal of the conference was to reestablish the foundations of aristocratic dominance that had been challenged by the French Revolution. They were guided by the twin principles of legitimacy and stability. The concept of legitimacy dictated that all European territories should be returned to the control of the aristocratic house that had governed before Napoleon had redrawn the map. But the concept of stability meant a restoration of a balance of power in Europe. Accordingly, the important elements of the resulting settlement consisted of both tradition and innovation. The important components of the settlement included the following:

- The restoration of the monarchy in Spain under Ferdinand VII
- The restoration of the monarchy in France under Louis XVIII
- The reconstitution of France inside borders that were nearly those of 1789
- The ceding of parts of Saxony, Westphalia, and the Rhine to Prussia
- The unification of the Austrian Netherlands (Belgium) and the Dutch Republic to form a single kingdom of the Netherlands under the House of Orange
- The placing of the kingdoms of Lombardy and Venetia in Italy, and of the states in the German Confederation, under the control of Austria

In an attempt to secure the balance of power created by the Vienna Settlement, the leaders of Austria, Russia, Prussia, and Great Britain entered into a military alliance designed to make aggression by individual states or kingdoms impossible. The alliance, created in November 1815, came to be known as the Concert of Europe, for the way in which it required important diplomatic decisions to be made by all four great powers "in concert" with one another. In 1818, France, having paid its war indemnities, joined the alliance.

Review Questions

Multiple Choice

Questions 1–3 refer to the following passage:

But, to found and consolidate democracy, to achieve the peaceable reign of the constitutional laws, we must end the war of liberty against tyranny and pass safely across the storms of the revolution: such is the aim of the revolutionary system that you have enacted. Your conduct, then, ought also to be regulated by the stormy circumstances in which the republic is placed; and the plan of your administration must result from the spirit of the revolutionary government combined with the general principles of democracy.

Now, what is the fundamental principle of the democratic or popular government—that is, the essential spring which makes it move? It is virtue; I am speaking of the public virtue which . . . is nothing other than the love of country and of its laws. . . .

If the spring of popular government in time of peace is virtue, the springs of popular government in revolution are at once virtue and terror: virtue, without which terror is fatal; terror, without which virtue is powerless. Terror is nothing other than justice, prompt, severe, inflexible; it is therefore an emanation of virtue; it is not so much a special principle as it is a consequence of the general principle of democracy applied to our country's most urgent needs.

It has been said that terror is the principle of despotic government. Does your government therefore resemble despotism? Yes, as the sword that gleams in the hands of the heroes of liberty resembles that with which the henchmen of tyranny are armed.

Maximilien Robespierre, "Speech of February 5, 1794"

1. From the passage, one may infer that, for Robespierre, the goal of the Revolution was
   A. to create a tyranny of the virtuous
   B. to create a constitutional monarchy
   C. to create a democratic republic governed by the rule of law
   D. to create an absolute monarchy

2. From the passage, one may infer that Robespierre argued that the use of terror was
   A. immoral and indicative of tyranny
   B. a necessary means to a just end
   C. fatal to the Revolution
   D. an indication of powerlessness

3. From the passage, one may infer that Robespierre's response to the charge that his revolutionary government had become despotic was
   A. that the resemblance to despotism was superficial
   B. that despotism was necessary to establish a virtuous monarchy
   C. that, as a hero, he was entitled to despotic rule
   D. despotism was inevitable

Short Answer

4. Briefly give TWO illustrations of the existence of a "radical phase" of the French Revolution and explain ONE cause of the shift to that phase.

Answers and Explanations

1. **C** is correct because the passage argues that a war of liberty is being fought in order to bring about a democracy and "the peaceable reign of the constitutional laws." A is incorrect because the passage argues that tyranny is a tool, not a goal of the Revolution. B and D are incorrect because the passage makes no reference to a monarchy as a goal of the Revolution.

2. **B** is correct because the passage states that virtue without terror is powerless against tyrannical enemies. A is incorrect because the passage argues that terror is a tool and that the morality of its usage depends upon the goal of the user. C is incorrect because the passage argues that terror is necessary for the success of the Revolution, not fatal to it. D is incorrect because the passage states that it is virtue that is powerless in times of revolution, unless it is paired with terror.

3. **A** is correct because the passage states that his government resembles despotism only as "the sword that gleams in the hands of the heroes of liberty resembles that with which the henchmen of tyranny are armed"; that is, only superficially. B is incorrect because the passage states that the redemptive goal of the Revolution is the institution of a virtuous *republic*, not monarchy. C is incorrect because the passage disputes the notion that his government has become despotic. D is incorrect because the passage argues that the Revolution can be successful in its battle against despotism if it is willing to use terror.

4. Suggested answer:

   Thesis: The existence of a radical phase of the French Revolution can be detected in the passage of the Civil Constitution of the Clergy in July 1790 and in the vote to abolish the monarchy in September 1792. One explanation for the advent of this phase was the rise of the *sans-culottes*.

   Paragraph Outline:

   I. The passage of the Civil Constitution of the Clergy in July 1790 is evidence of a radical phase because its subordination of the clergy to the new French state was not a goal of the original, moderate leaders of the Revolution, who wanted only to curb the privileges of the clergy.

   II. The vote to abolish the monarchy in September 1792 is evidence of a radical phase because the abolition of the French monarchy was not a goal of the original, moderate leaders of the Revolution, who wanted only to curb the absolutist tendencies of the king and his government.

   III. One explanation for the shift to a radical phase is the rise of the *sans-culottes*, the working people (bakers, shopkeepers, artisans, and manual laborers) of Paris. They helped to cause the radical phase because they had the willingness and the numerical strength to violently impose the more radical agenda of Convention members like Robespierre.

Rapid Review

When Louis XVI was forced by financial difficulties to call the seldom-used Estates General into session in 1789, the bourgeois representatives of the Third Estate launched a revolution aimed at curbing the power and privilege of the nobility and the clergy, and they attempted to turn France into a constitutional monarchy. Supported by the Paris crowd, the leaders of the newly formed National Assembly nearly succeeded, but foreign intervention, persistent resistance from the nobility, the indecisiveness of Louis XVI, and the development of factions within the Assembly allowed new, more radical leaders to win over the *sans-culottes* who now made up the Parisian crowd and set the Revolution on a more radical course. Besieged by a coalition of European powers and beset with factional strife, the radicals resorted to a Reign of Terror, which eventually consumed them.

By 1794, the propertied bourgeoisie reasserted itself and concentrated on restoring order and repealing the gains made by the radicals. In 1799, their executive organ, known as the Directory, was overthrown by a military general, Napoleon Bonaparte. He gradually assumed dictatorial powers and attempted to create a Europe-wide French Empire. Upon his defeat in 1815 by coalition forces, the French monarchy was restored, and the Kingdom of France was restored to its pre-Revolutionary boundaries.

CHAPTER 17

The Industrial Revolution

IN THIS CHAPTER

Summary: Between 1820 and 1900, the increasing demand for goods was met by the creation of the factory system, which standardized and increased industrial production. This chapter reviews the Industrial Revolution in Great Britain, its uneven spread across Europe, and the social effects of industrialization, including urbanization, standardization of work, and changes to the class system. The chapter also describes new modes of scientific explanation, such as the kinetic theory of gases and Darwin's theory of evolution by natural selection.

Key Terms:

KEY IDEA

- ✪ **Industrial Revolution** The phase of the industrialization process, lasting roughly from 1820 to 1900, characterized by the advent of large-scale iron and steel production, the application of the steam engine, and the development of a railway system.
- ✪ **Factory system** A system of production created in order to better supervise labor. In the factory system, workers came to a central location and worked with machines under the supervision of managers.
- ✪ **Division of labor** A technique whereby formerly complex tasks that required knowledge and skill were broken down into a series of simple tasks, aided by machines.

- ✪ **Bessemer process** A process, invented in the 1850s by English engineer Henry Bessemer, that allowed steel to be produced more cheaply and in larger quantities.
- ✪ **Steam engine** A power source that burns coal to produce steam pressure. First used in the early eighteenth century to pump water out of coal mines, it came to be used to drive machinery as diverse as the bellows of iron forges, looms for textile manufacture, and mills for grain, and, in the nineteenth century, as a source of locomotive power.
- ✪ **Internal combustion engine** Developed in 1886 by two German engineers, Gottlieb Daimler and Karl Benz, an engine that burns petroleum as fuel. When mounted on a carriage, it was used to create the automobile.
- ✪ **The Railway Boom** The rapid development of a railway system, beginning in Great Britain in the 1830s. The development of railway systems further spurred the development of heavy industry, as railroads facilitated the speedy transportation of iron and steel while simultaneously consuming large quantities of both.
- ✪ **Class consciousness** A sense of belonging to a "working class" that developed among European workers during the Industrial Revolution of the nineteenth century. It was a result of their working together in factories and living together in isolated slums.

Introduction

During the eighteenth century, the development of a more diverse economy propelled by a system of rural manufacturing (sometimes referred to as proto-industrialization or even the "First Industrial Revolution") radically increased the demand for manufactured goods. In response, nineteenth-century entrepreneurs and inventors created a new, more mechanized system of production, known as the factory system. This new system of production, coupled with the introduction of new sources of power, led to what is termed the Industrial Revolution (or sometimes the "Second Industrial Revolution"). This process of heavy, concentrated industrialization, lasting roughly from 1820 to 1900, was characterized by the advent of large-scale iron and steel production, the application of the steam engine, and a the development of a railway system. The Industrial Revolution of the nineteenth century transformed almost every aspect of European life.

The Factory System and the Division of Labor

The factory system was created in order to better supervise labor. In the old, rural manufacturing system (or cottage industry) that characterized European proto-industrialization, peasants were left on their own to work at the spinning wheel or the loom. Both the quality and the efficiency of their work depended on factors that were beyond the entrepreneur's control. In contrast, under the factory system, workers came to a central location and worked with machines under the supervision of managers.

The factory system employed a technique that has come to be known as the division of labor, whereby formerly complex tasks that required knowledge and skill were broken down into a series of simple tasks, aided by machines. The division of labor had several simultaneous effects:

- It replaced skilled craftsman with unskilled labor, thereby increasing the supply of labor and decreasing the wages that needed to be paid.
- It increased the volume that manufacturers could produce, thereby allowing them to sell products for less and still increase profits.
- It initially drew more women and children into the workforce.
- As machines did more and more of the work, the number of workers needed decreased, creating unemployment and competition for jobs.

Iron and Steel

The iron and steel industry helped to drive the Industrial Revolution of the nineteenth century. The new machines of the textile industry created increased demand for the iron from which they were partly constructed. New, larger armies demanded more iron for guns, cannon, and ammunition. The growing population required even more iron for nails and tools.

Traditionally, the fuel for the iron-smelting process was charcoal, which came from wood. By the eighteenth century, dwindling forests limited the charcoal supply, and steel was smelted in blast furnaces, using coal as the fuel. In the 1850s, Henry Bessemer, an English engineer, discovered a way to manufacture steel more cheaply and in larger quantities. The use of the Bessemer process (as it came to be called), together with the use of the steam engine to power smelting furnaces, increased the supply of iron and steel to the point at which it could meet ever-growing demand. In 1860, Great Britain, France, Germany, and Belgium produced approximately 125,000 tons of steel. By 1913, they produced nearly 32 million tons.

New Sources of Power

Coal

Coal mines provided the most important fuel of the Industrial Revolution. Initially, coal was used to heat homes and to fuel the blast furnaces of the expanding iron and steel industry. Later, demand increased even further as steam engines devoured mass quantities of coal for fuel. Wherever there were natural deposits of coal, huge mining industries grew up around them; agricultural production in these areas was largely abandoned, and the peasants were drawn by the thousands to subterranean work in the mines.

Steam

The perfection of the steam engine increased both the scale and the pace of heavy industry by replacing human muscle and hydropower. The steam engine was first used in the early eighteenth century to pump water out of coal mines. It was perfected and made more efficient by Thomas Newcomen and James Watt. The improved version was used to drive machinery as diverse as the bellows of iron forges, looms for textile manufacture, and mills for processing grain. The shift to steam power allowed entrepreneurs to relocate their mills away from water sources. During the 1820s, entrepreneurs began to exploit the potential of the steam engine as a source of locomotive power; its first use in this way was to power ships. In the 1830s, it was adapted to power railway locomotives.

Electricity

Toward the end of the nineteenth century, the Second Industrial Revolution received another boost from the widespread application of electrical power. More versatile and more easily transported than steam engines, electrical generators were used to power a wide variety of small- and large-scale factories and mills. By 1881, the first large-scale public power plant was constructed in Great Britain, and over the next two decades, plants were built and lines were run to illuminate houses across Europe.

Petroleum and the Internal Combustion Engine

In 1886, two German engineers, Gottlieb Daimler and Karl Benz, perfected the internal combustion engine, which burned petroleum as fuel, and mounted it on a carriage to create the first automobile. The early German automobiles were luxury items, but in 1908, the American Henry Ford produced the "Model T," an automobile for the common man, which he began to mass-produce, creating yet another large factory-based industry. The internal combustion engine, along with its cousin the diesel engine, made transportation and travel cheaper and, therefore, more widely available.

The Railway Boom

In the 1820s, the British inventor George Stephenson developed a railway line with trains pulled by steam-powered locomotives. The Stockton and Darlington Line opened in 1825, and by 1830, another major line traveled between Liverpool and Manchester. The speed and reliability of the new locomotives made them a huge success, which led to what would come to be known as the Railway Boom of the 1830s and 1840s, as competitors quickly developed their own systems. The development of railway systems further spurred the development of heavy industry, as railroads facilitated the speedy transportation of iron and steel while simultaneously consuming large quantities of both.

The Reciprocal Nature of Heavy Industry

The four major components of the Second Industrial Revolution—the iron and steel industry, the coal industry, steam power, and the railways—had a reciprocal effect on one another:

- The iron and steel industry required improvements in the steam engine to run its blast furnaces, greater amounts of coal to fuel the engines, and railways to transport both the coal and the smelted iron and steel.
- The coal industry required more and improved steam engines to pump water out of the mines and to power digging machinery; it also required railways to transport the coal.
- The steam power industry required iron and steel to forge the engines, coal to run them, and railways to transport them.
- The railways required huge amounts of steel and iron for the construction of the engines, cars, and tracks; steam engines to drive the locomotives; and coal to fuel the engines.

Working together, these four industries created an ever-increasing cycle of supply and demand that drove the Second Industrial Revolution of the nineteenth century.

The Spread of Industrialization

The process of industrialization varied greatly across Europe. The Industrial Revolution started in Great Britain and spread eastward across continental Europe.

Great Britain Industrializes First

Great Britain had several natural advantages that help to explain why it was the first to industrialize and why it held the lead for more than a century:

- It had a well-developed commercial economy that created a merchant class with capital to invest.
- Great Britain's extensive river system was ideal for transporting goods throughout the country.
- The country was rich in coal and iron deposits, two key components of the Industrial Revolution.
- Unlike much of Europe, Great Britain had no internal tariffs to inhibit trade.
- It had a uniform and stable monetary system and a national banking system.

Industrialization Spread Eastward Across Europe

As the Industrial Revolution spread to the continent, it moved eastward in a way that can be described by three generalizations:

- The farther east, the later the process began; for example, France industrialized later than Great Britain, Germany later than France, and Russia last.
- The farther east, the faster the process occurred (because innovations could be copied or purchased, rather than invented and developed); for example, France industrialized at a faster pace than Great Britain, Germany faster still, and Russia fastest of all.
- The farther east, the more the government was involved (because governments feared the political and military effects of falling behind their rivals, they invested heavily in industrialization); for example, there was no government involvement in the industrialization of Great Britain, some in France, more in Germany, and in Russia industrialization was almost totally government driven.

Uneven Development

By 1850, large-scale industrialization had spread to northeastern France, Belgium, the northern German states, and northwestern Italy. The southern, central, and eastern areas of Europe—such as Italy, Poland, and Russia—lagged behind due to insufficient natural resources and the lack of a commercialized agricultural system that would allow for a mobile workforce. These areas retained their rural character.

Russia lagged behind until two successive tsars—Alexander III (1881–1894) and Nicholas II (1894–1917)—determined that Russia should become an industrial power. In 1892, Alexander III appointed Serge Witte finance minister. Under Witte's leadership, Russia became an iron- and steel-producing nation. By the end of the nineteenth century, factories had arisen in Moscow and St. Petersburg. By 1904, the construction of a trans-Siberian railroad, which linked the European portion of Russia with the far east of Russia, was nearly completed.

Social Effects of Industrialization

The Second Industrial Revolution transformed European society in significant ways:

- Urbanization increased rapidly, as the population moved into hastily built housing in cities to be nearer to the factories.
- Families were separated, as the place of work shifted from the home to factories.
- Work lost its seasonal nature, as workers were required to follow a routine schedule.
- The pace of work, driven by machines, increased dramatically.
- The overall health of the workforce declined because of the harsh and unhealthy conditions of the factories.
- The availability of work became unpredictable, as it rose and fell with the demand for goods.
- Gradually, women who had first been drawn into cities to work in the factories lost their manufacturing jobs as machines decreased the demand for labor; cut off from their families, many had no other option than prostitution.
- Artisans and craftsmen lost their livelihoods, unable to compete with the lower cost of mass-produced goods.
- The traditional impediment to marriage, which was the need for land, disappeared and people began to marry younger.
- A much greater portion of the population could afford factory-made goods.
- There was further change in the class structure, as industrialization created both a class of newly wealthy industrialists and a precariously situated lower-middle class of managers and clerks.
- Close working and living conditions produced a sense of class consciousness among the working class.

Science in an Industrial Age

Advances in gas theory and a spirit of scientific realism dominated the physical sciences in the nineteenth century. Physicists in this period concentrated on providing a scientific understanding of the processes that drove the engines of the Industrial Revolution. In the middle of the nineteenth century, the German physicist Rudolf Clausius and the Scottish physicist James Maxwell developed a kinetic theory of gases. Their theory envisioned gas pressure and temperature as resulting from a certain volume of molecules in motion. Such an approach allowed them to analyze, and therefore to measure and predict, pressure and temperature statistically. Later in the century, physicists such as Robert Mayer, Hermann von Helmoltz, and William Thompson pursued this kind of statistical analysis to articulate the laws of thermodynamics.

The success of "matter-in-motion" models in physics created a wider philosophical movement that argued that all natural phenomena could and should be understood as a result of matter in motion. The movement, known as materialism, was first articulated by a trinity of German natural philosophers: Karl Vogt, Jakob Moleschott, and Ludwig Büchner. By the end of the nineteenth century, materialism had become the foundational assumption of the scientific view of the world.

The natural sciences of the nineteenth century were dominated by Charles Darwin's theory of evolution by natural selection. As a young man, Darwin had sailed around the globe as a naturalist for the *H. M. S. Beagle*. During the *Beagle*'s five-year voyage, commencing December 27, 1831, and ending on October 2, 1836, Darwin collected specimens for shipment home to England and made observations on the flora and fauna of the many continents he explored. Twenty-three years later, he published a book titled *On the Origin of Species by Means of Natural Selection, or the Preservation of Favoured Races in the Struggle for Life.* In *Origin of Species,* Darwin offered an answer to the two questions at the heart of nineteenth-century natural science: why was there so much diversity among living organisms, and why did organisms seem to "fit" into the environments in which they lived? Darwin's answer, unlike earlier answers that referred to God's will and a process of creation, was materialist. He argued that both the wide range of diversity and the environmental "fit" of living organisms to their environment were due to a process he termed "natural selection." The fact that many more organisms were born than could survive led, Darwin explained, to a constant "struggle for existence" between individual living organisms. Only those individuals who survived the struggle passed their physical characteristics onto their offspring. Over millions of years, that simple process had caused populations of organisms to evolve in ways that produced both the amazing diversity and the environmental "fit."

Origin of Species went through six editions, and Darwin's theory became the central organizing principle of the science of biology, which developed in the late nineteenth and early twentieth centuries. In 1871, Darwin published *The Descent of Man*, which explained Darwin's views on how human beings had come into existence through the process of natural selection.

Review Questions

Multiple Choice

Questions 1–3 refer to the following two passages:

> The blessings which physio-mechanical science has bestowed on society, and the means it has still in store for ameliorating the lot of mankind, have been too little dwelt upon. . . . [I]n the factory, every member of the loom is so adjusted, that the driving force leaves the attendant nearly nothing at all to do, certainly no muscular fatigue to sustain, while it procures for him good, unfailing wages, besides a healthy workshop gratis: whereas the non-factory weaver, having everything to execute by muscular exertion, finds the labor irksome, makes in consequence innumerable short pauses, separately of little account, but great when added together; earns therefore proportionally low wages, while he loses his health by poor diet and the dampness of his hovel. . . .
>
> The constant aim and effect of scientific improvement in manufactures are philanthropic, as they tend to relieve the workmen either from niceties of adjustment which exhaust his mind and fatigue his eyes, or from painful repetition of efforts which distort or wear out his frame.
>
> Andrew Ure, *The Philosophy of the Manufacturers*, 1835

> Any man who has stood at twelve o'clock at the single narrow door-way, which serves as the place of exit for the hands employed in the great cotton-mills, must acknowledge, that an uglier set of men and women, of boys and girls, taking them in the mass, it would be impossible to congregate in a smaller compass. Their complexion is sallow and pallid—with a peculiar flatness of feature, caused by the want of a proper quantity of adipose [fatty] substance to cushion out the cheeks. Their stature low—the average height of four hundred men, measured at different times, and different places, being five feet six inches. Their limbs slender, and playing badly and ungracefully. A very general bowing of the legs. Great numbers of girls and women walking lamely or awkwardly, with raised chests and spinal flexures. Nearly all have flat feet, accompanied with a down-tread, differing very widely from the elasticity of action in the foot and ankle, attendant upon perfect formation. . . . A spiritless and dejected air, a

sprawling and wide action of the legs, and an appearance, taken as a whole, giving the world but "little assurance of a man."

P. Gaskell, *The Manufacturing Population of England*, 1833

1. From the two passages, one can infer that, in Great Britain in the 1830s,
   A. there was general consensus about the benefits of industrialization for British laborers
   B. there was scientific evidence for the detrimental effects of industrialization on British laborers
   C. there was a wide difference of opinion about the benefits of industrialization for British laborers
   D. there was a general consensus about the detriments of industrialization for British laborers

2. From the passage, one can infer that Ure and Gaskell strongly disagreed about
   A. the degree to which British labor has become industrialized
   B. the physical effects of industrial production on the industrial worker
   C. the effect of industrialization on the wages of industrial workers
   D. the economic benefits of industrialization for Great Britain

3. From the passages, one can infer that, in Great Britain in the 1830s,
   A. it was being widely argued that industrial production was physically detrimental to industrial workers
   B. efforts to reform working conditions in factories were under way
   C. it was being widely argued that women and children should not be working in factories
   D. it was being widely argued that industrial production was economically beneficial to industrial workers

Short Answer

4. Briefly explain the reciprocal nature of industrial production in this period and give TWO examples that illustrate the point.

Answers and Explanations

1. **C** is correct because the two passages could be used as evidence for the existence of a wide difference of opinion about the benefits of industrialization for British laborers. A and D are incorrect because the differing opinions expressed in the two passages argue against there being any consensus of opinion on the benefits of industrialization for British laborers. B is incorrect because neither passage offers scientific evidence.

2. **B** is correct because Ure states that industrial work leaves the worker "nearly nothing at all to do" and causes "no muscular fatigue," while Gaskell details the numerous detrimental physical effects of industrialized work. A is incorrect because the two passages offer no evidence of disagreement over the degree to which British labor had become industrialized. C is incorrect because only Ure addresses the effects of industrialization on wages. D is incorrect because neither passage addresses the effects of industrialization on the economy of Great Britain.

3. **A** is correct because the fact that Gaskell explicitly makes the argument, while Ure (a defender of industrial production) feels it necessary to refute the charge, allows one to infer that it was an argument that was fairly widely made. B is incorrect because neither passage refers to the existence of a reform movement. C is incorrect because Ure makes no mention of women and children, and Gaskell's implication is not sufficient to infer

that such a view was widely held. D is incorrect because Gaskell makes no mention of it and Ure's assertion is insufficient to infer that it was widely held.

4. Suggested answer:

Thesis: The four major components of the Industrial Revolution—the iron and steel industry, the coal industry, steam power, and the railways—had a reciprocal effect on one another because each developed in response to a demand created by the others, and each stimulated further demand for the others.

Paragraph Outline:

I. The iron and steel industry required improvements in the steam engine to run its blast furnaces, greater amounts of coal to fuel the engines, and railways to transport both the coal and the smelted iron and steel.

II. The coal industry required more and improved steam engines to pump water out of the mines and to power digging machinery; it also required railways to transport the coal.

Rapid Review

Between 1820 and 1900, the demand for goods on the part of a steadily increasing population was met by entrepreneurs who created the factory system. The new system standardized and increased industrial production. As the century went on, the development of four interrelated heavy industries—iron and steel, coal mining, steam power, and railroads—combined to drive Europe's economy to unprecedented heights, constituting an industrial revolution. The urbanization, standardization of work, and effects of the class system wrought by the Second Industrial Revolution significantly transformed social life in Europe.

The changes wrought by the Industrial Revolution led to the development of materialist modes of scientific explanation, manifested in the physical sciences by the kinetic theory of gases and in the natural sciences by Darwin's theory of evolution by natural selection.

CHAPTER 18

Cultural Responses to Revolution and Industrialization

IN THIS CHAPTER

Summary: In the nineteenth century, intellectuals developed various ideologies in order to make sense of a rapidly changing world. Among the political and cultural ideologies explained in this chapter are conservatism, liberalism, anarchism, utopian socialism, scientific socialism or communism, romanticism, nationalism, and social Darwinism. Further down the social hierarchy, the laboring classes violently resisted innovations which threatened their livelihood.

Key Terms:

- ✪ **Conservatism** A nineteenth-century ideology that held that tradition was the only trustworthy guide to social and political action.
- ✪ **Liberalism** An eighteenth- and nineteenth-century ideology that asserted that the task of government was to promote individual liberty.
- ✪ **Socialism** An ideology that sought to reorder society in ways that would end or minimize competition, foster cooperation, and allow the working classes to share in the wealth being produced by industrialization.
- ✪ **Utopian socialism** A form of socialism that envisioned, and sometimes tried to establish, ideal communities (or utopias) where work and its fruit were shared equitably.
- ✪ **Psychological socialism** A variety of nineteenth-century utopian socialism that saw a conflict between the structure of society and the natural needs and tendencies of human beings. Its leading advocate was Charles Fourier, who argued that the ideal society was one organized on a smaller, more human scale.

- **Technocratic socialism** A variety of nineteenth-century utopian socialism that envisioned a society run by technical experts who managed resources efficiently and in a way that was best for all. The most prominent nineteenth-century advocate of technocratic socialism was the French aristocrat Henri Comte de Saint-Simon.
- **Scientific socialism/communism** An ideology dedicated to the creation of a class-free society through the abolition of private property.
- **Anarchism** A nineteenth-century ideology that saw the modern state and its institutions as the enemy of individual freedom and recommended terrorism as a way to disrupt the machinery of government.
- **Romanticism** A nineteenth-century ideology that urged the cultivation of sentiment and emotion by reconnecting with nature and with the past.
- **Nationalism** A nineteenth-century ideology that asserted that a nation was a natural, organic entity whose people shared a cultural identity and a historical destiny.
- **Social Darwinism** A nineteenth-century ideology that asserted that competition was natural and necessary for the evolutionary progress of a society.

Introduction

The French Revolution had challenged Europeans' beliefs in and assumptions about society; the Industrial Revolution seemed to be transforming society at a dizzying pace. In order to cope with these changes, and to answer the questions posed by them, nineteenth-century Europeans offered a number of significant cultural responses.

Political Ideologies in the Nineteenth Century

One such response was the creation of a number of political ideologies, each claiming to hold the key to creating the best society possible.

Conservatism

In the nineteenth century, conservatism was the ideology that asserted that tradition was the only trustworthy guide to social and political action. Conservatives argued that traditions were time-tested, organic solutions to social and political problems. Accordingly, nineteenth-century conservatives supported monarchy, the hierarchical class system dominated by the aristocracy, and the Church. They opposed innovation and reform, arguing that the French Revolution had demonstrated that reform led directly to revolution and chaos. Supporters of the conservative position originally came from the traditional elites of Europe, the landed aristocracy.

The British writer and statesman Edmund Burke is often considered "the father of conservatism," as his *Reflections on the Revolution in France* (1790) seemed to predict the bloodshed and chaos that characterized the radical phase of the revolution. The French writer Joseph de Maistre's *Essay on the General Principle of Political Constitutions* (1814) is a prime example of nineteenth-century conservatism's opposition to constitutionalism and reform.

Liberalism

Liberalism was the nineteenth-century ideology asserting that the task of government was to promote individual liberty. Liberals viewed many traditions as impediments to that freedom and, therefore, campaigned for reform. Pointing to the accomplishments of the Scientific Revolution, nineteenth-century liberals asserted that there were God-given, natural rights and laws that individuals could discern through the use of reason. Accordingly, they supported innovation and reform (in contrast to conservatives), arguing that many traditions were simply superstitions. They promoted constitutional monarchy over absolutism, and they campaigned for an end to the traditional privileges of the aristocracy and the Church in favor of a meritocracy and middle-class participation in government. Supporters of liberalism originally came from the middle class.

Two British philosophers, John Locke and Adam Smith, are usually thought of as the fathers of liberalism. In *The Second Treatise of Government* (1690), Locke made the argument for the existence of God-given natural rights and asserted that the proper goal of government was to protect and promote individual liberty. In *Wealth of Nations* (1776), Smith made the case for the existence of economic laws that guided human behavior like an "invisible hand." Smith also promoted the notion of *laissez-faire* ("let it be") governance, which stated that governments should not interfere with the natural workings of an economy, a notion that became one of the basic tenets of liberalism in the nineteenth century.

Late-eighteenth- and early-nineteenth-century thinkers extended and cemented Smith's ideas. In *An Essay on the Principle of Population* (1798), Thomas Malthus asserted that free and constant competition would always be the norm in human societies because the human species would always reproduce at a greater rate than the food supply. By mid-century, liberal economic thinkers alleged that there was an "iron law of wages," which argued that competition between workers for jobs would always, in the long run, force wages to sink to subsistence levels. This "law" is sometimes attributed to the English economist David Ricardo, but it was promoted most prominently by the German sociologist Ferdinand LaSalle.

As the nineteenth century progressed, liberalism evolved. The followers of the English philosopher Jeremy Bentham espoused utilitarianism, which argued that all human laws and institutions ought to be judged by their usefulness in promoting "the greatest good for the greatest number" of people. Accordingly, they supported reforms to sweep away traditional institutions that failed the test and to create new institutions that would pass it. Utilitarians tended to be more supportive of government intervention than other liberals. For example, they drafted and supported new legislation to limit the hours that women and children could work in factories and to regulate the sanitary conditions of factories and mines.

Early-nineteenth-century liberals had been leery of democracy, arguing that the masses had to be educated before they could usefully contribute to the political life of the country. But by mid-century, liberals began advocating democracy, reasoning that the best way to identify the greatest good for the greatest number was to maximize the number of people voting. The best example of mid-century utilitarian thought is John Stuart Mill's *On Liberty* (1859), which argued for freedom of thought and democracy, but also warned against the tyranny of the majority. Together, Mill and his companion Harriet Taylor led the liberal campaign for women's rights, Taylor publishing *The Enfranchisement of Women* (anonymously in 1851) and Mill publishing *The Subjection of Women* (1869).

Utopian Socialism

Socialism in the nineteenth century was the ideology that emphasized the collective over the individual and challenged the liberal notion that competition was natural. Socialists sought to reorder society in ways that would end or minimize competition, foster cooperation, and allow the working classes to share in the wealth being produced by industrialization.

The earliest forms of socialism have come to collectively be called utopian socialism for the way in which they envisioned, and sometimes tried to establish, ideal communities (or utopias) where work and its fruit were shared equitably. In the nineteenth century, there were three distinct forms of utopian socialism (described in the following sections).

Technocratic Socialism

This type of utopian socialism envisioned a society run by technical experts who managed resources efficiently and in a way that was best for all. The most prominent nineteenth-century advocate of technocratic socialism was a French aristocrat, Henri Comte de Saint-Simon, who renounced his title during the French Revolution and spent his life championing the progress of technology and his vision of a society organized and run by scientifically trained managers or "technocrats."

Psychological Socialism

This type of utopian socialism saw a conflict between the structure of society and the natural needs and tendencies of human beings. Its leading nineteenth-century advocate was Charles Fourier, who argued that the ideal society was one organized on a smaller, more human scale. He advocated the creation of self-sufficient communities, called "phalansteries," consisting of no more than 1,600 people, in which the inhabitants did work that suited them best.

Industrial Socialism

This type of utopian socialism argued that it was possible to have a productive, profitable industrial enterprise without exploiting workers. Its leading advocate was a Scottish textile manufacturer, Robert Owen. Owen set out to prove his thesis by setting up industrial communities, like the New Lanark cotton mill in Scotland and, later, a larger manufacturing community in New Harmony, Indiana, which paid higher wages and provided food, shelter, and clothing at reasonable prices.

Scientific Socialism and Communism

By the middle of the nineteenth century, the exploitation of European workers had grown more evident, and the dreams of the utopian socialists seemed less plausible. In their place arose a form of socialism based on what its adherents claimed was a scientific analysis of society's workings. The most famous and influential of the self-proclaimed scientific socialists was the German revolutionary Karl Marx. In *The Communist Manifesto* (1848), a slim pamphlet distributed to workers throughout Europe, Marx and his collaborator, Friedrich Engels, argued that "all history is the history of class struggle." In the *Manifesto*, and later in the much larger *Capital* (vol. 1, 1867), Marx argued that a human being's relationship to the means of production gave him a social identity. In the industrial age of the nineteenth century, Marx argued, only two classes existed: the bourgeoisie, who controlled the means of production, and the proletariat, who sold their labor for wages. The key point in Marx's analysis was that the bourgeoisie exploited the proletariat because competition demanded it; if a factory owner chose to treat his workers more generously, then he would have to charge more for his goods, and his competitors would drive him out of business. (That, in short, is what happened to Robert Owen as a result of his experiments.)

Marx's analysis led him to adopt a position that came to be known as communism, which declared that the only way to end social exploitation was to abolish private ownership of the means of production. If no one could claim to own the means of production, then there could be no distinction between owner and worker; all class distinctions would disappear, and the workers would be free to distribute the benefits of production more equally.

Anarchism

Anarchism was the nineteenth-century ideology that saw the state and its governing institutions as the ultimate enemy of individual freedom. Early anarchists drew inspiration from the writings of Pierre Joseph Proudhon who argued that man's freedom had been progressively curtailed by industrialization and larger, more centralized governments. Anarchy had the greatest appeal in those areas where governments were most oppressive; in the nineteenth century, that meant Russia. There, Mikhail Bakunin, the son of a Russian nobleman, organized secret societies whose goal was to destroy the Russian state forever. Throughout Europe, nineteenth-century anarchists engaged in acts of political terrorism, particularly attempts to assassinate high-ranking government officials.

Cultural Ideologies in the Nineteenth Century

Other ideologies developed in the nineteenth century that sought to reach beyond "mere politics." Two of the most influential were Romanticism and nationalism.

Romanticism

Romanticism was a reaction to the Enlightenment and industrialization. The nineteenth-century Romantics rebelled against the Enlightenment's emphasis on reason and urged the cultivation of sentiment and emotion. Fittingly, Romantics tended to avoid political tracts and expressed themselves mostly through art and literature. Their favorite subject was nature.

The roots of Romanticism are often traced back to the works of Jean-Jacques Rousseau, because in *Emil* (1762), he had argued that humans were born essentially good and virtuous but were easily corrupted by society, and that the early years of a child's education should be spent developing the senses, sensibilities, and sentiments. Another source of Romanticism was the German *Sturm und Drang* ("Storm and Stress") movement of the late eighteenth century, exemplified by Johann Wolfgang von Goethe's *The Sorrows of Young Werther* (1774), which glorified the "inner experience" of the sensitive individual.

In response to the rationalism of the Enlightenment (and to some degree, of liberalism), the Romantics offered the solace of nature. Good examples of this vein of nineteenth-century Romanticism are the works of the English poets William Wordsworth and Samuel Taylor Coleridge, who extolled the almost mystical qualities of the lake country of northwest England.

Romantic painters, like John Constable in England and Karl Friedrich Schinkel in Germany, offered inspiring landscapes and images of a romanticized past. Beethoven, Chopin, and Wagner expressed the imaginative, intuitive spirit of Romanticism in music.

Nationalism

In the nineteenth century, nationalism was the ideology that asserted that a nation was a natural, organic entity whose people were bound together by shared language, customs, and history. Nationalists argued that each nation had natural boundaries, shared cultural traits, and a historical destiny to fulfill. Accordingly, nineteenth-century nationalists in existing nation-states like Britain and France argued for strong, expansionist foreign policies. Nationalists in areas like Germany and Italy argued for national unification and the expulsion of foreign rulers.

In the early nineteenth century, nationalism was allied to liberalism. Both shared a spirit of optimism, believing that their goals represented the inevitable, historical progress of humankind. In the non-unified lands of Germany and Italy, occupation by Napoleonic France had helped to foster a spirit of nationalism. Under Napoleon's rule, Germans and Italians came to think of their own disunity as a weakness. The best early examples of this kind of nationalism are the works of German writers Johann Gottlieb Fichte, whose *Addresses to the German Nation* (1808) urged the German people to unite in order to fulfill their historical role in bringing about the ultimate progress of humanity, and Georg Wilhelm Friedrich Hegel, who argued that every nation had a historical role to play in the unfolding of the universe and that Germany's time to take center stage in that drama had arrived.

Like the Romantics, early-nineteenth-century nationalists emphasized the role that environment played in shaping the character of a nation and sentimentalized the past. A good example of Romantic nationalism is the work of Ernst Moritz Arndt, who urged Germans to unify through a shared heritage and through love of all things German. Strains of Romanticism can also be seen in the work of the great Italian nationalist of the early nineteenth century, Giuseppe Mazzini, whose nationalist movement, Young Italy, made appeals to unity based on natural affinities and a shared soul.

Social Darwinism

The socialist notion that competition was unnatural was countered by yet another nineteenth-century ideology that came to be known as social Darwinism. In 1859, the British naturalist Charles Darwin published *The Origin of Species*, which argued that all living things had descended from a few simple forms. In *Origin of Species*, Darwin described a complex process in which biological inheritance, environment, and competition for resources combined over millions of years to produce the amazing diversity in living forms that exists in the world.

The philosopher Herbert Spencer argued that Darwin's theory proved that competition was not only natural, but necessary, for the progress of a society. Spencer coined the phrase "survival of the fittest" (a phrase adopted by Darwin in the sixth and final edition of *Origin of Species*) and argued along liberal lines that government intervention in social issues interfered with natural selection and, therefore, with progress. By the last decades of the nineteenth century, social Darwinism was being used to argue that imperialism, the competition between nations for control of the globe, was a natural and necessary step in the evolution of the human species. Eugenics, the notion that a progressive, scientific nation should plan and manage the biological reproduction of its population as carefully as it planned and managed its economy, also flourished in the last decades of the nineteenth century.

Violent Resistance of the Laboring Classes

When the increased use of machines in industrial and agricultural production threatened the livelihood of skilled laborers, workers responded with violent resistance. In Britain, textile workers resisted the introduction of stocking frames, spinning frames, and power looms by destroying the machines, giving birth to what became known as the Luddite movement. In the countryside, workers resisted the introduction of threshing machines by burning hayricks in what became known as the Swing Riots.

Review Questions

Multiple Choice

Questions 1–3 refer to the following passage:

> WHERE is the German's fatherland?
> The Prussian land? The Swabian land?
> Where Rhine the vine-clad mountain laves?
> Where skims the gull the Baltic waves?
> Ah, no, no, no!
> His fatherland's not bounded so!
> Where is the German's fatherland?
> Bavarian land? or Stygian land?
> Where sturdy peasants plough the plain?
> Where mountain-sons bright metal gain?
> Ah, no, no, no!
> His fatherland's not bounded so! . . .
> Where is the German's fatherland?
> Then name, oh, name the mighty land!
> Wherever is heard the German tongue,
> And German hymns to God are sung!
> This is the land, thy Hermann's land;
> This, German, is thy fatherland.

Ernst Moritz Arndt, *The German Fatherland*, c. 1812

1. From the passage, one may infer that Arndt was a supporter of which nineteenth-century ideology?
   A. Conservatism
   B. Liberalism
   C. Nationalism
   D. Anarchism

2. From the passage, one may infer that the poem was written to
   A. celebrate the unification of Germany
   B. urge German-speaking people to seek unity
   C. indicate the superiority of Prussian culture
   D. celebrate the beauty of Germany

3. From the passage, one may infer that Arndt held that the German kingdoms of Prussia, Swabia, and Bavaria were
   A. German nation-states
   B. part of a German empire
   C. part of the French Empire
   D. part of the true Germany

Short Answer

4. Briefly define Romanticism and illustrate your definition with TWO examples.

Answers and Explanations

1. **C** is correct because the passage indicates that Arndt believed that the true boundaries of a nation were shared language and culture. A is incorrect because the passage does not extol the virtues of tradition as a nineteenth-century conservative would. B is incorrect

because the passage does not extol the virtues of individual liberty as a nineteenth-century liberal would. D is incorrect because the passage does not identify the state as the enemy of liberty as a nineteenth-century anarchist would.

2. **B** is correct because the passage urges German-speaking people to ignore the political divisions and provincialism of their current situation and to understand that a German fatherland exists wherever German is spoken and German customs are observed. A is incorrect because the passage cannot be celebrating a unification that would not come until 1871. C is incorrect because the passage is praising German-ness, not Prussia. D is incorrect because the poem does not speak of beauty.

3. **D** is correct because the passage indicates that all of the customary German and German-speaking kingdoms are really part of the true Germany. A is incorrect because the passage says that one will not find a fatherland in those kingdoms, and because those kingdoms are not nation-states. B is incorrect because nothing in the passage indicates that Arndt thought in terms of a German empire. C is incorrect because nothing in the passage refers to the French Empire.

4. Suggested answer:

Thesis: Romanticism was the nineteenth-century ideology that urged the cultivation of sentiment and emotion by reconnecting with nature and with the past. Two examples of Romanticism in the nineteenth century are Goethe's *The Sorrows of Young Werther* and the works of English lake poets.

Paragraph Outline:

I. Johann Wolfgang von Goethe's *The Sorrows of Young Werther* (1774) illustrates the Romantic cultivation of sentiment by the way in which it glorified the "inner experience" of its young protagonist.

II. The works of the lake poets, such as William Wordsworth and Samuel Taylor Coleridge, illustrate the Romantic call to reconnect with nature by the way in which they extolled the almost mystical qualities of the lake country of northwest England.

Rapid Review

In the nineteenth century, intellectuals articulated numerous ideologies in order to make sense of a rapidly changing world. By the end of the century, a thinking person could choose from a spectrum of ideologies, which included and can be categorized and summarized as follows:

Political Ideologies

- Conservatism: championing tradition
- Liberalism: urging reform
- Anarchism: scheming to bring down the state
- Utopian socialisms: emphasizing the collective over the individual
- Scientific socialism and communism: espousing the abolition of the private ownership of the means of production

Cultural Ideologies

- Romanticism: encouraging the cultivation of sentiment and emotion
- Nationalism: preaching cultural unity
- Social Darwinism: advocating the benefits of unfettered competition

CHAPTER 19

Mass Politics and Nationalism

IN THIS CHAPTER

Summary: In the nineteenth century, increased political participation by the masses supported the growth of nationalism, resulting in the establishment of the nation-state as the dominant unit of European political organization. The unifications of Germany and Italy by the conservative aristocracy, the nationalities problem of Austria-Hungary, the fall of the Second Empire in France, and the growth of democracy in Great Britain are among the topics reviewed in this chapter on the effects of growing political participation and nationalism.

Key Terms:

- ✪ *Carbonari* Secret groups of Italian nationalists active in the early part of the nineteenth century. In 1820, the *Carbonari* had briefly succeeded in organizing an uprising that forced King Ferdinand I of the Kingdom of the Two Sicilies to grant a constitution and a new Parliament.
- ✪ *Risorgimento* The mid-nineteenth-century Italian nationalist movement composed mostly of intellectuals and university students. From 1834 to 1848, the *Risorgimento* attempted a series of popular insurrections and briefly established a Roman Republic in 1848.
- ✪ *Junkers* A powerful class of landed aristocrats in nineteenth-century Prussia who supported Bismarck's plan for the unification of Germany.

- ✪ *Realpolitik* A political theory, made fashionable by Bismarck in the nineteenth century, which asserted that the aim of any political policy should be to increase the power of a nation by whatever means and strategies were necessary and useful.
- ✪ **The nationalities problem** The name given to the conflict between the 10 distinct linguistic and ethnic groups that lived within the borders of Austria-Hungary and their German-speaking rulers.
- ✪ **Russianization** Alexander III's attempt, in the 1880s, to make Russian the standard language and the Russian Orthodox Church the standard religion throughout the Russian Empire.
- ✪ **Chartism** A movement in Britain (1837–1842) in support of the People's Charter, a petition that called for universal manhood suffrage, annual Parliaments, voting by secret ballot, equal electoral districts, the abolition of property qualifications for Members of Parliament, and the payment of Members of Parliament.

Introduction

In the hundred years following the fall of Napoleon's empire, classes of people who were traditionally left out of the politics of Europe's nations and empires demanded participation in a variety of ways. One context in which the advent of mass politics contributed to significant change was in the triumph of the nation-state as the primary unit of political organization.

Nationalism and State-Building

Over the course of the nineteenth century, nationalism triumphed over all other competing ideologies. In areas where people lived under foreign domination, nationalism was used by conservative statesmen to bring about the unification of Italy and Germany. In the Hapsburg Empire, the nationalist aspirations of ethnic minorities worked to undermine Austrian domination. In France and Russia, the force of nationalism was used to end the remaining dreams of liberals and to strengthen the hold of autocratic rulers.

The Triumph of Conservative Nationalism

In the first half of the nineteenth century, liberals and nationalists tended to ally themselves against the forces of conservatism. Both believed that political sovereignty resided in the people, and they shared an optimistic belief that progress toward their goals was inevitable. Campaigns for liberal reform (which attempted to break the conservative aristocracy's grip on political power and to promote individual rights) tended to merge with the struggle for national rights or self-determination. Accordingly, most liberals supported the idea of free and unified nation-states in Germany and Italy, the rebirth of Poland, and Greek independence; most conservatives opposed these ideas.

However, both partial victory and eventual defeat drove a wedge between liberals and nationalists. When liberals won temporary victories over conservative aristocrats between 1830 and 1838, fundamental differences between the agendas of liberal reformers and nationalists began to emerge. The emphasis on individual liberty and limited government did not mesh well with the nationalist emphasis on the collective national tribe or with the desire of nationalists for a strong national government. In short, liberals believed in promoting the rights of *all peoples*; nationalists cared only about their *own* rights.

When, in 1848, the more radical liberal agenda of democratic reform emerged, the conservative tendencies of nationalism came to the fore. Nationalists not only shared the conservatives' belief in the value of historical traditions, they tended to mythologize the past and dream of a return to an era of national glory. Ultimately, however, what drove a wedge between liberals and nationalists was the failure of liberals to hold the power they had temporarily seized. As the conservative reaction in the second half of 1848 smashed liberal movements everywhere in Europe, nationalists dreaming of a strong, unified country free from foreign rule increasingly turned to conservative leaders. Both the unification of Italy and the unification of Germany were primarily engineered by and for the conservative aristocrats.

The Unification of Italy

The Forces Against Unity in Italy

The settlement after the defeat of Napoleon in 1815 had greatly disappointed those hoping for an Italian nation-state. The Italian peninsula consisted of separate states controlled by powerful enemies of Italian nationalism:

- The Hapsburg Dynasty of Austria controlled, either directly or through its vassals, Lombardy and Venetia in the north, and the duchies of Tuscany, Parma, and Modena.
- The pope governed an area known as the Papal States in central Italy.
- A branch of the Bourbon dynasty (which ruled France) controlled the Kingdom of the Two Sicilies in the south.
- An Italian dynasty, the House of Savoy, controlled both the island of Sardinia in the south and Piedmont in the northwest.

In addition to political divisions and foreign interests, the Italian peninsula was also divided by economic and cultural differences:

- The northern areas of the peninsula were well developed economically and more sophisticated culturally than the still largely rural and agricultural areas of the south.
- Culturally, the people of the more developed northern region felt little connection to the poor peasants in the south, who often spoke an entirely different dialect.
- Socially and politically, the middle-class merchants and manufacturers, located mostly in the north, wanted a greater degree of unity for easier trade and tended to support liberal reforms; they were opposed by the staunchly conservative, traditional landed elites.

Italian Nationalism to 1850

Italian nationalism had been forged in opposition to Napoleon's rule. After 1815, dreams of a unified Italy were kept alive in secret societies like the *Carbonari*, secret clubs whose members came mostly from middle-class families and from the army. In 1820, the *Carbonari* had briefly succeeded in organizing an uprising that forced King Ferdinand I of the Kingdom of the Two Sicilies to grant a constitution and a new Parliament. But Austrian troops, with the blessing of the Concert of Europe, crushed the revolt. The Austrians put down a similar revolt by the *Carbonari* in Piedmont from 1831 to 1832.

In the 1840s, Giuseppe Mazzini's Young Italy had carried the banner of Italian nationalism. Both a Romantic and a liberal, Mazzini fought for the establishment of an Italian republic that would serve, as he believed ancient Rome had, as a beacon for the rest of humanity. By mid-century, Mazzini had forged a movement known as the *Risorgimento*, which was composed mostly of intellectuals and university students who shared his idealism. From 1834 to 1848, the *Risorgimento* attempted a series of popular insurrections, briefly establishing a Roman Republic in 1848 until it was crushed (like its liberal counterparts throughout Europe) by the forces of reaction. In defeat, it was evident that the *Risorgimento* had failed to win the support of the masses.

Cavour and Victory over Austria

At mid-century, a new leader of Italian nationalist hopes emerged in the person of Count Camillo Benso di Cavour, the chief minister of King Victor Emmanuel II of the Kingdom of Piedmont-Sardinia. Cavour differed from Mazzini and other previous leaders of the Italian nationalist movement in several significant ways:

- Cavour was a conservative aristocrat with ties to the most powerful Italian ruler on the peninsula, rather than a middle-class intellectual.
- Cavour advocated a constitutional monarchy under King Victor Emmanuel II, rather than a republic.
- Cavour was a cautious and practical statesman, rather than an idealist.

Cavour's strategy was that of an opportunist: he sought to increase the amount of territory under the control of Piedmont whenever possible and to weaken the opponents of Italian unification by playing them against each other. Between 1855 and 1860, Cavour took advantage of several such opportunities and managed to unite all of northern Italy under Piedmont:

- In 1855, Cavour brought Piedmont and its army into the Crimean War on the side of England and France, who were fighting Russia. This resulted in no immediate gains, but the peace conference afforded Cavour an opportunity to denounce the Austrian occupation of Italian lands.
- In 1858, Cavour reached a secret agreement with Napoleon III of France, gaining a promise of French support should Austria attack Piedmont.
- In 1859, Cavour goaded the Austrians into attacking Piedmont by mobilizing forces and refusing an ultimatum to disarm. French and Piedmontese troops defeated the Austrians at the Battles of Magenta and Solferino, driving the Austrians out of Lombardy. Further gains by Piedmont were thwarted by Napoleon III's abrupt signing of the Treaty of Villafranca with the Austrians.
- By 1860, inspired by the Piedmontese victory over Austria, the majority of the northern and north-central duchies shook off their Austrian rulers and voluntarily united with Piedmont.

Garibaldi and Victory in the South

The success of northern Italians in throwing off Austrian domination inspired their southern counterparts. A series of peasant revolts, tinged with anti-Bourbon sentiment, arose in the south. Southern Italian nationalists found a different kind of leader in Giuseppe Garibaldi and, in 1860, launched a series of popular uprisings, which put all of southern Italy under his control. The southern nationalist movement differed from its northern counterpart in several significant ways:

- Garibaldi was a Romantic nationalist who had been an early supporter of Mazzini.
- The southern movement was a genuine revolt of the masses, rather than the political maneuverings of a single kingdom.

- Garibaldi hoped to establish an Italian republic that would respect the rights of individuals and improve the lot of the peasants and workers.

In May 1860, Garibaldi raised an army of 1,000 red-shirted Italian patriots and landed in Sicily to aid a peasant revolt underway there. In a few short months, Garibaldi and his red-shirts provided leadership to a nationalist revolt that took control of most of southern Italy and set its sights on Rome.

The Kingdom of Italy and the Completion of Italian Unification

Cavour publicly condemned Garibaldi's conquests but secretly aided them. When Garibaldi's troops began to threaten Rome, Cavour persuaded Napoleon III, who had sworn to protect the pope, to allow the Piedmontese army to invade the Papal States in order to head off Garibaldi. By September 1860, Piedmont controlled the Papal States and set up a ring around Rome.

When Piedmontese forces, led by King Victor Emmanuel II, met Garibaldi and his forces outside Rome in September 1860, Garibaldi submitted and presented all of southern Italy to Victor Emmanuel; in the end, Garibaldi's dream of a unified Italy was stronger than his commitment to the idea of a republic. In March 1861, the Kingdom of Italy was formally proclaimed. It was a constitutional monarchy under Victor Emmanuel II with a parliament elected by limited suffrage. It consisted of all of the Italian peninsula, except the city of Rome (which was still ruled by the pope and protected by French troops) and the province of Venetia (which was still occupied by Austrian troops). The unification of Italy was completed when Venetia became part of the Kingdom of Italy during the Austro-Prussian War of 1866 and Rome (with the exception of Vatican City) followed during the Franco-Prussian War of 1870.

The Unification of Germany

Forces Against Unity in Germany

Unlike Italy, Germany in the middle of the nineteenth century was free of direct foreign domination. It existed as a loose confederation of independent states. Within that loose confederation, several forces worked against national unity:

- Cultural differences between the rural, conservative, Protestant north and the urban, liberal, Catholic south
- A long history of proud independence on the part of the individual German states
- The powerful influence of Hapsburg Austria, which controlled or influenced a large portion of the German Confederation

Prussian Leadership

With the failure of the liberal Frankfurt Assembly in 1848, leadership in the German nationalist movement passed to Prussia. Prussia was a strong northern kingdom ruled by the Hohenzollern dynasty and supported by a powerful class of landed aristocrats known as *Junkers*. Prussia also had the strongest military in Germany, and in 1845, Prussia led the way in establishing the *Zollverein*, a large free-trade zone. This combination of military and economic power led many Germans to look to Prussia for leadership.

Bismarck and War with Denmark and Austria

In 1861, Prussia's new monarch, William I, wanted to reorganize and further strengthen the military, but the liberal legislature resisted, and a power struggle between the monarch and the legislature ensued. William turned to the conservative *Junker* Otto von Bismarck to be his prime minister. Bismarck forced a showdown, and it quickly became apparent that the support of the Prussian people was with the king, the army, and Bismarck. With the power of the army behind him and the government fully established, Bismarck set out a policy to unify Germany under the Prussian crown, which came to be known as *Realpolitik* and asserted that the aim of Prussian policy would be to increase its power by whatever means and strategies were necessary and useful. Bismarck asserted that the unification of Germany would be accomplished by a combination of "blood and iron."

Bismarck quickly concluded that a war with Austria was inevitable, and he engineered one in an episode that has come to be known as the *Schleswig-Holstein Affair*. He began by enlisting Austria as an ally in a war with Denmark over two duchies, Schleswig and Holstein, which had large German-speaking populations. Once Denmark was forced to cede the two duchies, Bismarck provoked an argument with Austria over control of them. Bismarck's next moves were a perfect illustration of *Realpolitik* in action:

- First, Bismarck obtained Italian support for with a war with Austria by promising Italy the province of Venetia.
- Next, he ensured Russian neutrality by supporting Russia's actions against its rebellious Polish subjects.
- Then, he met secretly with Napoleon III of France and persuaded him that a weakening of Austrian power was in the best interests of France.
- Finally, and only after those preparations were in place, he carried out a series of diplomatic and military maneuvers that provoked Austria into declaring war.

In the resulting Austro-Prussian War of 1866, Prussian troops surprised and overwhelmed a larger Austrian force, winning victory in only seven weeks. The result was the expulsion of Austria from the old German Confederation and the creation of a new North German Confederation, which was completely under the control of Prussia.

War with France

All that remained for Bismarck was to draw the south German states into the new Confederation. But the south (which was predominantly Catholic and liberal) feared being absorbed by the Protestant and authoritarian Prussians. Bismarck concluded that only one thing would compel the south Germans to accept Prussian leadership: a war with a powerful foreign enemy. So he set about engineering one.

The opportunity came when both France and Prussia got involved in a dispute over the vacant throne in Spain. Bismarck, with the support of the Prussian military leadership, edited a communication between Napoleon III and William I (a communication now known as the Ems Telegram) to make it seem as though they had insulted one another, which Bismarck then released to the press. Tempers flared, and France declared war. The south German states rallied to aid Prussia. Combined German forces quickly routed the French troops, capturing Napoleon III and taking Paris in January 1871.

The Second Reich

On January 18, 1871, the unification of Germany was completed. The heads of all the German states gathered in the Hall of Mirrors in the Palace of Versailles outside Paris and proclaimed William I kaiser (emperor) of the German Empire (formally the Second Reich, honoring the old Holy Roman Empire as the First Reich). The new empire took the provinces of Alsace and Lorraine from France and billed the French 5 billion francs as a war indemnity.

Mass Politics and Nationalism in the Hapsburg Empire

In the dual monarchy of Austria-Hungary, mass politics continued to mean competition between nationalities for greater autonomy and relative supremacy within the empire. In an age of nation-building, the Hapsburg Empire, with its Austrian minority dominating an empire consisting of Hungarians (also known as Magyars), Czechs, Serbs, Romanians, and other ethnic groups, was an anachronism. The forces of nationalism, therefore, worked to tear the empire apart. After Austria's defeat by Prussia in 1866, the Austrian Emperor Franz Joseph attempted to deal with what has come to be called "the nationalities problem." By agreeing to the Compromise of 1867, he set up the dual monarchy of Austria-Hungary. Franz Joseph served as the ruler of both Austria and Hungary, each of which had its own parliament. This arrangement essentially set up an alliance between the Austrians and the Hungarians against the other ethnic groups in the empire. The introduction of universal manhood suffrage in 1907 made Austria-Hungary so difficult to govern that the emperor and his advisors began bypassing the parliament and ruling by decree.

Mass Politics and Nationalism in France

Louis-Napoleon Bonaparte had originally been elected president of the Second Republic in 1848. When the National Assembly refused to amend the constitution to allow him to run for a second term, he staged a coup d'état on December 2, 1851. The public overwhelming sided with Louis-Napoleon, who granted them universal manhood suffrage. They responded, in two plebiscites, by voting to establish a Second Empire and to make Louis-Napoleon hereditary emperor.

Like his namesake, Louis-Napoleon attempted to increase his popularity by expanding the Empire, but soon his foreign adventures began to erode his popularity. By 1870, the liberal parliament had begun to reassert itself. The humiliating defeat in the Franco-Prussian War brought down both Louis-Napoleon and the Second Empire, and it also set in motion a battle between monarchists and the people of Paris who, having defended Paris from the Germans while the aristocrats fled, now considered themselves to represent the nation of France. When elections in 1871 resulted in a victory for the monarchists, the people of Paris refused to accept the results and set up their own democratic government, which came to be known as the Paris Commune. The Commune ruled the city of Paris in February and March 1871, before being crushed by the French Army.

Monarchists initially controlled the government of the new Third Republic, but they remained divided between factions. By the end of the 1870s, France was governed by a liberal government elected by universal manhood suffrage. However, in the late 1880s, conservative nationalists supported an attempted coup by General George Boulanger. The attempt—which has come to be known as the Boulanger Affair—failed, but it underscored the fragility of French democracy and the volatility of mass politics in France.

Mass Politics and Nationalism in Russia

At mid-century, Russia's government was the most conservative and autocratic in Europe. The peasants of Russia were still bound to the land by serfdom. The Crimean War (1853–1856), in which Russia essentially battled Great Britain and France for control of parts of the crumbling Ottoman Empire, damaged the reputation of both the tsar and the military. Alexander II, who ascended the throne in 1855, was determined to strengthen

Russia by reforming and modernizing it. He abolished serfdom, made the judiciary more independent, and created local political assemblies.

However, Russia was plagued by its own nationalities problem. Alexander attempted to deal with it by relaxing restrictions on the Polish population within the Russian Empire, but this fanned the flames of nationalism and led to an attempted Polish Revolution in 1863. Alexander responded with increased repression of Poles and other ethnic minorities within the Russian Empire. And after an attempt on his life in 1866, Alexander gave up all notions of liberal reform and proceeded to turn Russia into a police state. In response, mass politics took the form of terrorism. Radical groups like the People's Will carried out systematic acts of violent opposition, including the assassination of Alexander II with a bomb in 1881. His successor, Alexander III, responded by waging war on liberalism and democracy. Initiating a program of "Russianization," he attempted to standardize language and religion throughout the Russian Empire.

Mass Politics and Nationalism in Great Britain

Mass participation in politics in Great Britain in the nineteenth century (in the form of mass demonstrations and riots) provided the pressure that enabled liberals to force through the Great Reform Bill of 1832, enfranchising most of the adult, male middle class.

In the decades that followed, the liberals seemed satisfied with limited reform. The rise of Chartism (1837–1842) demonstrated the degree to which the lower-middle and working classes desired further reform. Chartists organized massive demonstrations in favor of the People's Charter, a petition that called for the following:

- Universal manhood suffrage
- Annual Parliaments
- Voting by secret ballot
- Equal electoral districts
- Abolition of property qualifications for Members of Parliament
- Payment of Members of Parliament

If enacted into law, the People's Charter would have had the effect of creating a completely democratic House of Commons. But Parliament rejected the Charter on numerous occasions.

In 1867, the new leader of the Conservative (or Tory) Party, Benjamin Disraeli, convinced his party that further reform was inevitable and engineered the passage of the Reform Bill of 1867. The bill doubled the number of people eligible to vote and extended the vote to the lower-middle class for the first time. Additionally, the Conservatives passed a number of laws regulating working hours and conditions, and the sanitary conditions of working-class housing.

In 1884, the Liberals, under William Gladstone, again took the lead, engineering the passage of the Reform Bill of 1884. This bill included the following reforms:

- It extended the right to vote further down the social ladder, thereby enfranchising two-thirds of all adult males.
- It made primary education available to all.
- It made military and civil service more democratic.

The most significant result of the advent of mass politics in Great Britain was competition between Liberals and Conservatives for the newly created votes. In 1879, Gladstone embarked on the first modern political campaign, which came to be known as the Midlothian Campaign, riding the railway to small towns throughout his district to give speeches and win votes. Disraeli and the Conservatives countered with a three-pronged platform of "Church, Monarchy, and Empire."

Review Questions

Multiple Choice

Questions 1–3 refer to the following passage:

> I will not, sir, at present express any opinion as to the details of the Bill; but having during the last twenty-four hours given the most diligent consideration to its general principles, I have no hesitation in pronouncing it a wise, noble, and comprehensive measure, skillfully framed for the healing of great distempers, for the securing at once of the public liberties and of the public repose, and for the reconciling and knitting together of all the orders of the State. [The Ministers'] principle is plain, rational, and consistent. It is this, to admit the middle class to a large and direct share in the representation, without any violent shock to the institutions of our country. . . .
>
> I praise the Ministers for not attempting, under existing circumstances, to make the representation uniform. I praise them for not effacing the old distinction between the towns and the counties, for not assigning members to districts, according to the American practice, by the rule of three. They have done all that was necessary for the removing of a great practical evil, and no more than was necessary.
>
> Thomas Babington Macaulay, Speech on the Reform Bill of 1832, March 2, 1831

1. From the passage, one may infer that Macaulay
   A. believed the bill would be good for Great Britain
   B. thought the bill went too far
   C. opposed the bill
   D. attempted to amend the bill

2. From the passage, one may infer that Macaulay understood the main purpose of the bill to be
   A. the adoption of a constitution for Great Britain
   B. the enfranchisement of the middle class
   C. the enfranchisement of the working class
   D. the creation of democracy in Great Britain

3. From the passages, one may infer that the bill
   A. standardized rules for representation in Great Britain
   B. applied the American system of representation to Great Britain
   C. reformed the rules for representation in Great Britain in a limited way
   D. created a "one man–one vote" system of representation for Great Britain

Short Answer

4. Briefly explain TWO similarities and ONE difference between the unifications of Italy and Germany.

Answers and Explanations

1. **A** is correct because the passage states Macaulay's belief that the bill was "skillfully framed" for "the reconciling and knitting together of all the orders of the State." B is incorrect because the passage contains no notion that the bill went too far. C is incorrect because the passage states that he would not express an opinion on whether it should be passed. D is incorrect because the passage makes no mention of an amendment.

2. **B** is correct because, in the passage, Macaulay states that he understands the framing principle of the bill is "to admit the middle class to a large and direct share in the representation." A is incorrect because the passage makes no mention of creating a constitution for Great Britain. C is incorrect because the passage makes no mention of the working class. D is incorrect because the passage makes no mention of democracy and because the Reform Bill enfranchised only the middle class.

3. **C** is correct because, in the passage, Macaulay praises the architects of the bill for the limited nature of the reforms. A is incorrect because the passage praises the architects of the bill for *not* standardizing the rules of representation. B is incorrect because the passage praises the architects of the bill for *not* importing the American system. D is incorrect because the passage makes no mention of a "one man–one vote" system.

4. Suggested answer:

Thesis: The unifications of Italy and Germany were similar in two ways: (1) both had to overcome significant economic and cultural differences between the north and the south, and (2) both were achieved by, and in the interests of, the aristocratic class. The unifications of Italy and Germany differed in that a genuine class revolt contributed to the unification process only in Italy.

Paragraph Outline:

I. Italy: The northern areas of the peninsula were well developed economically and more sophisticated culturally than the still largely rural and agricultural areas of the south; culturally, the people of the more developed northern region felt little connection to the poor peasants in the south, who often spoke an entirely different dialect.

   Germany: significant cultural barriers existed between the rural, conservative, Protestant north and the urban, liberal, Catholic south; economically, the powerful influence of Hapsburg Austria, which controlled or influenced a large portion of the German Confederation.

II. Italian unification was achieved through the efforts of Count Camillo Benso di Cavour, a conservative aristocrat who united Italy in order to create a constitutional monarchy under Victor Emmanuel II, king of Piedmont. Germany unification was achieved by Otto von Bismarck, a conservative aristocrat who united Germany under William I, king of Prussia.

III. The southern part of the Italian peninsula was originally unified by the efforts of Giuseppe Garibaldi, a Romantic nationalist who had been an early supporter of Mazzini. The southern movement was a genuine revolt of the masses, rather than the political maneuverings of a single kingdom. Garibaldi hoped to establish an Italian republic that would respect the rights of individuals and improve the lot of peasants and workers, but capitulated when given a choice by Cavour between the fulfillment of Italian unification or civil war.

Rapid Review

In the nineteenth century, increased political participation by the masses supported the growth of nationalist ideology and feeling. The failure of the revolutions of 1848 broke the fragile alliance between liberalism and nationalism. Accordingly, the unifications of Italy and Germany were achieved by and for the conservative aristocracy. Meanwhile, the Hapsburg Empire was plagued by a nationalities problem and became Austria-Hungary in 1867. France's defeat led to the fall of the Second Empire in France, and Alexander II turned Russia into a police state. In Great Britain, mass politics provided the impetus for a series of reform bills that would make the country the most democratic of European societies in the nineteenth century.

CHAPTER 20

Mass Politics and Imperialism

IN THIS CHAPTER

Summary: Among the factors leading to the development of European imperialism in the nineteenth century were economic needs created by industrialization, traditional competition between European nations, and the need for European political elites to find ways to win the support of a new political force: the masses. This chapter reviews the growth of European empires beyond Europe, chiefly in Africa, where European powers quickly staked out claims to virtually the entire continent, and Asia, where European control was generally exerted through local elites.

Key Terms:

KEY IDEA

- ✪ **New Imperialism** The expansion of European influence and control in the last decades of the nineteenth century. It was characterized by a shift from indirect commercial influence to active conquest and the establishment of direct political control of foreign lands around the globe, particularly in Africa and Asia.
- ✪ **Scramble for Africa** The rush of European powers to claim interest in and sovereignty over portions of Africa in the first half of the 1880s. It culminated in the Berlin Conference of 1885, at which European powers laid down rules for the official claiming of African territories.
- ✪ **Suez Canal** A canal opened in 1869, built by a French company with Egyptian labor, that connects the Mediterranean Sea through Egypt to the Red Sea and the Indian Ocean. In 1875, Great Britain took advantage of the Egyptian ruler's financial distress and purchased a controlling interest in the canal. Control of the canal led to British occupation and the annexation of Egypt.

- **Sepoy Rebellion of 1857 (sometimes known as the Sepoy Mutiny)** A well-organized anti-British uprising led by military units of Indians who had formerly served the British. It resulted in the British government taking direct control of India and a restructuring of the Indian economy to produce and consume products in order to aid the British economy.
- **Taiping Rebellion** An attempt to overthrow the Manchu rulers of China (1850–1864), whose authority had been undermined by Western interference. Defending their rule from the Rebellion made the Manchus even more dependent on Western support.

Introduction

In the nineteenth century, the development of mass politics helped to make imperialism the defining characteristic of a vigorous and powerful nation-state. In the first part of the nineteenth century, European imperialism (primarily in Africa and Asia) tended to take the form of indirect commercial influence and was, therefore, generally a continuance of Europe's seventeenth- and eighteenth-century economic activity. In the last decades of the nineteenth century, European powers shifted from indirect commercial influence to active conquest and the establishment of direct political control of foreign lands around the globe, particularly in Africa and Asia. This imperial expansion of European influence and control is often referred to as the "New Imperialism."

Causes of the New Imperialism

The causes of the New Imperialism are a matter of debate among historians, but all explanations consist of the following elements to some degree:

- The need for new raw materials in the expanding industrial economy of Europe
- The need for new markets to sell European manufactured goods and to invest newly created capital
- The technological innovations in weaponry and transportation that encouraged European military adventurism
- The rampant nationalism of the nineteenth century that unified European nations and gave them a sense of historical destiny
- The traditional identity of European political elites who competed for fame and glory through conquest
- The need for competing European political elites to win the support of the newly politicized and enfranchised masses

The Scramble for Africa

Two developments spurred an unprecedented "scramble" on the part of European powers to lay claim to vast areas of the African continent: the British takeover of the Suez Canal in Egypt and Belgium's aggressive expansion into the Congo.

The Suez Canal, connecting the Mediterranean Sea through Egypt to the Red Sea and the Indian Ocean, was built by a French company and opened in 1869. In 1875, Great

Britain took advantage of the Egyptian ruler's financial distress and purchased a controlling interest in the canal. By the early 1880s, anti-British and anti-French sentiment was building in the Egyptian army. In the summer of 1882, the British launched a preemptive strike, landing troops in Egypt, defeating Egyptian forces, and setting up a virtual occupation of Egypt. Supposedly temporary, the occupation lasted 32 years. Britain's control of Egypt led to further European expansion in Africa in two ways:

- In order to provide greater security for Egypt, Britain expanded farther south.
- In return for France's acceptance of the British occupation of Egypt, Great Britain supported French expansion into northwest Africa.

A new competition for imperial control of sub-Saharan Africa was initiated by the expansion of Belgian interests in the Congo. In 1876, King Leopold II of Belgium formed a private company and sent explorer Henry Stanley to the Congo River basin to establish trading outposts and sign treaties with local chiefs. Alarmed by the rate at which the Belgians were claiming land in central Africa, the French expanded their claims in western Africa, and Bismarck responded with a flurry of claims for Germany in eastern Africa. This sudden burst of activity led to the Berlin Conference of 1885. There, representatives of European powers established free-trade zones in the Congo River basin and established guidelines for the partitioning of Africa. The guidelines essentially set up two principles:

- A European nation needed to establish enough physical presence to control and develop a territory before it could claim it.
- Claimants must treat the African population humanely.

After the conference, European nations completed the Scramble for Africa until nearly the entire continent was, nominally at least, under European control. Unfortunately, the principle of humane treatment of Africans was rarely followed.

Dominance in Asia

In the era of the New Imperialism, European powers also exerted control over Asia. Here, however, the general method was to rule through local elites.

India: Ruled by Great Britain

In India, the British dominated, initially through the British East India Company, a private trading company that used its economic and military power to influence local politics. Following the Sepoy Rebellion of 1857 (sometimes known as the Sepoy Mutiny), an organized anti-British uprising led by military units of Indians who had formerly served the British, the British government took direct control and restructured the Indian economy to produce and consume products in order to aid the British economy.

A sense of Indian nationalism began to develop as a response to the more intrusive British influence, resulting in the establishment of the Indian National Congress in 1885. The Congress, though really an organization of Hindu elites, promoted the notion of a free and independent India.

Southeast Asia: Dominated by France

In southeast Asia, the French emulated the British strategy of ruling through local elites and fostering economic dependence. During the 1880s and early 1890s, France established the Union of Indochina, effectively dominating in the areas that would become Vietnam, Laos, and Cambodia.

China: Under Increasing European Control

China had been infiltrated by British traders in the 1830s. The British traded opium grown in India to Chinese dealers in exchange for tea, silk, and other goods that were highly prized in Britain. When the Chinese government attempted to end the trade, Great Britain waged and won the Opium War (1839–1842) and forced the Chinese to sign the Treaty of Nanking. The treaty ceded Hong Kong to Great Britain, established several tariff-free zones for foreign trade, and exempted foreigners from Chinese law.

The humiliation of the Manchu rulers and the undermining of the Chinese economy that resulted from foreign interference led to the Taiping Rebellion (1850–1864). Defending their rule from the Rebellion made the Manchus even more dependent on Western support. Chinese nationalism and resistance to foreign influence again manifested itself in the Boxer Rebellion (1899–1900). The combined forces of the European powers were able to suppress the rebellion, but in 1911, a revolution led by Sun Yat-sen succeeded in overthrowing the Manchu dynasty, and a Chinese republic was established.

Japan: Westernization

Japan had been forcibly opened to Western trade by an American fleet commanded by Commodore Matthew J. Perry in 1853. The Japanese government signed a number of treaties granting Western powers effective control of foreign trade. The result was civil war and revolution, which culminated in the Meiji Restoration, during which modernizers, determined to preserve Japanese independence, restored power to the emperor and reorganized Japanese society along Western lines. By 1900, Japan was an industrial and military power. In 1904, the country quarreled with Russia over influence in China and stunned the world with its victory in the Russo-Japanese War.

Review Questions

Multiple Choice

Questions 1–3 refer to the following passage:

This is the entire issue of empire. A people limited in number and energy and in the land they occupy have the choice of improving to the utmost the political and economic management of their own land, confining themselves to such accessions of territory as are justified by the most economical disposition of a growing population; or they may proceed, like the slovenly farmer, to spread their power and energy over the whole earth, tempted by the speculative value or the quick profits of some new market, or else by mere greed of territorial acquisition, and ignoring the political and economic wastes and risks involved by this imperial career.

It must be clearly understood that this is essentially a choice of alternatives; a full simultaneous application of intensive and extensive cultivation is impossible. A nation may either, following the example of Denmark or Switzerland, put brains into agriculture, develop a finely varied system of public education, general and technical, apply the ripest science to its special manufacturing industries, and so support in progressive comfort and character a considerable population upon a strictly limited area; or it may, like Great Britain, neglect its agriculture, allowing its lands to go out of cultivation and its population to grow up in towns, fall behind other nations in its methods of education and in the capacity of adapting to its uses the latest scientific knowledge, in order that it may squander its pecuniary and military resources in forcing bad markets and finding speculative fields of investment in distant corners of the earth, adding millions of square miles and of unassimilable population to the area of the Empire. . . .

No remedy will serve which permits the future operation of these forces. It is idle to attack Imperialism or Militarism as political expedients or policies unless the axe is laid at the economic root of the tree, and the classes for whose interest Imperialism works are shorn of the surplus revenues which seek this outlet.

John A. Hobson, *Imperialism*, 1902

1. From the passage, one may infer that Hobson understood imperialism to be a result of
   A. the strategic requirements of national defense
   B. economic decisions
   C. political necessities
   D. a religious mission

2. From the passage, one may infer that Hobson believed that imperialism was
   A. necessary for a country to thrive economically
   B. beneficial in the long run to industrialized countries
   C. beneficial in the long run for the countries being conquered
   D. detrimental to the long-term economic health of the imperialist country

3. From the passage, one may infer that Hobson argued that imperialism benefitted
   A. the country being conquered
   B. the imperialist country
   C. only certain classes within the imperialist country
   D. only certain classes within the conquered country

Short Answer

4. Identify TWO causes of the New Imperialism and briefly explain how those causal factors might be used to explain the Scramble for Africa.

Answers and Explanations

1. **B** is correct because the passage refers to the economic choice of domestic investment versus quick profits through imperial expansion. A is incorrect because the passage does not refer to the strategic requirements of national defense. C is incorrect because the passage does not refer to politics. D is incorrect because the passage does not refer to any religious mission.

2. **D** is correct because the passage argues that the practice of imperialism produces short-term profits for some classes within the imperialist country, but leads to the neglect of investment necessary for the country's long-term economic health. A is incorrect because the essay does not refer to imperialism as an economic necessity. B and C are incorrect because the passage argues that, in the long term, imperialism is economically harmful.

3. **C** is correct because the passage is analyzing the roots of imperialism (and thus the actions of the imperialist country, not the conquered country) and because the passage refers to "the classes for whose interest imperialism works." A and D are incorrect because the passage is analyzing the roots of imperialism (and thus the actions of the imperialist country, not the conquered country). B is incorrect because the passage states that there are "classes for whose interest Imperialism works," and argues that, more generally, imperialism is bad for all countries concerned.

4. Suggested answer:

Thesis: Two causes of the New Imperialism that help to explain the Scramble for Africa are the need for new raw materials in the expanding industrial economy of Europe and technological innovations in weaponry and transportation.

Paragraph Outline:

I. The need for new raw materials in the expanding industrial economy of Europe helps to explain the Scramble for Africa by providing a *motive* for European expansion into Africa. For example, diamonds in South Africa.

II. Technological innovations in weaponry (such as the breech-loading rifle) and transportation (such as the steam-powered gunboat) help to explain the Scramble for Africa by providing the *means* that encouraged European economic and military adventurism.

Rapid Review

The New Imperialism was the result of a complex set of impulses, which included economic needs created by industrialization, the traditional desire of European nations to compete with one another, and the need for political elites to find ways to win the support of a new political force: the masses. The New Imperialism resulted in the Scramble for Africa, in which European powers laid claim to the entire continent in the last two decades of the nineteenth century. In Asia, the New Imperialism took the form of indirect European control exerted through local elites.

CHAPTER 21

Politics of the Extreme and World War I

IN THIS CHAPTER

Summary: This chapter describes how political parties on both the extreme left and right of the political spectrum gained ground at the turn of the twentieth century, as the gradual reform of liberalism lost its appeal. Also included in this chapter is an explanation of how the great powers of Europe constructed an alliance system that divided Europe into two armed camps, leading to a total war of attrition (World War I) with disastrous consequences.

Key Terms:

- ✪ **Ultranationalists** Political parties which argued that political theories that put class solidarity ahead of loyalty to a nation threatened the very fabric of civilization. Thus, they vowed to fight liberalism and socialism.
- ✪ **Zionism** A movement for the creation of an independent state for Jews, which came into being in 1896 when Theodor Herzl published *The Jewish State*, a pamphlet that urged an international movement to make Palestine the Jewish homeland.
- ✪ **Triple Alliance** A military alliance among Germany, Austria-Hungary, and Italy, forged by Bismarck after the unification of Germany in 1871.
- ✪ **Triple Entente** A military alliance among Britain, France, and Russia, which countered the Triple Alliance.

⚙ **Bolsheviks** A party of revolutionary Marxists, led by Lenin, who seized power in Russia in November 1917.

⚙ **Treaty of Versailles (also Peace of Paris)** The name given to the series of five treaties that made up the overall settlement following World War I.

Introduction

By the beginning of the twentieth century, more people were participating in politics than ever before, but the majority of them were dissatisfied. For those on the left, the pace of reform was too slow and the nature of reform too limited. For those on the right, reforms were unsettling and threatened valued traditions. As a result, political activism on both the left and the right became more extreme. Meanwhile, the great powers of Europe divided themselves into two armed camps and fought what came to be known as World War I, a war of attrition that transformed Europe forever.

Labor Unions Begin in Britain, Then Spread to Other Countries

Europe's working-class population fell into the category of individuals who believed that liberal reform was too slow and too limited; they turned instead to labor unions and socialist parties. In Great Britain, workingmen formed the national Trades Union Congress, an organization that united all the labor unions of the country together for political action, and supported the newly formed Labour Party, a political party that ran working-class candidates in British elections. The working classes of other European countries followed Great Britain's lead, forming unions and supporting socialist parties.

Socialist Parties in Britain, France, and Germany

As Europe's labor movement turned political, it turned to socialists like Karl Marx for leadership. In 1864, Marx helped union organizers found the International Workingmen's Association, often referred to as the First International. The loose coalition of unions and political parties fell apart in the 1870s but was replaced by the Second International in 1889.

While Marx and his communist associates argued for the inevitability of a violent revolution, the character and strength of socialist organizations varied from country to country. In Great Britain, the socialist organization, known as the Fabian Society, counseled against revolution but argued that the cause of the working classes could be furthered through political solutions. The Fabian Society's ultimate goal was a society in which the parts of the economy that were crucial to people's survival and comfort, such as heat and water, should be owned by the state and regulated by experts employed by the government. In France, socialist parties banded together to join the French Socialist Party under the leadership of Jean Jaurès. The fortunes of the French Socialist Party in elections improved steadily in the first years of the twentieth century, and by 1914, it was a major power in French politics.

In Germany the Social Democrats, led by August Bebel, were the most successful socialist party in Europe. The Social Democrats espoused the "revisionist socialism" of Eduard Bernstein, who urged socialist parties to cooperate with bourgeois liberals in order to earn immediate gains for the working class. By 1914, the Social Democrats were the largest political party in Germany.

Women's Suffrage Movements and Feminism

Always left out of liberal reforms and sometimes excluded from labor unions, women of the late nineteenth and early twentieth centuries formed political movements of their own. Feminist groups campaigning for women's rights united in 1878 to convene in Paris for the International Congress of Women's Rights.

In Great Britain, the movement focused mostly on the issue of women's suffrage, or voting rights. The movement went through three distinct phases:

- A pioneering phase from 1866 to 1870, during which suffrage agitation focused on the Reform Act of 1867 and won a number of successes at the level of local government through petitioning and pamphleteering
- A period of relative dormancy from 1870 to 1905
- A period of militancy from 1905 to 1914, during which the National Union of Women's Suffrage Societies, headed by Millicent Garrett Fawcett, campaigned vigorously for women's voting rights, and the Women's Social and Political Union, led by Emmeline Pankhurst and her daughters, Christabel and Sylvia, campaigned, often violently, for a broader notion of women's rights

On the Continent, feminists such as Louise Michel in France and Clara Zetkin in Germany folded their movements into the broader cause of workers' rights and politically supported socialist parties.

Anarchist Activity

People under the more oppressive regimes, where even liberal reform was resisted, turned to anarchism. Theoreticians like Mikhail Bakunin and Pyotr Kropotkin urged the elimination of any form of state authority that oppressed human freedom, and ordinary people enacted the doctrine, first through the method of the "general strike" (massive work stoppages designed to bring the economy to a halt) and later, and more often, through assassination attempts on the lives of government officials. Political assassinations in the first years of the twentieth century included King Umberto I of Italy and President William McKinley of the United States.

Ultranationalism and Anti-Semitism

The international quality of the socialist movement was in direct opposition to the ideology of nationalism that had dominated the second half of the nineteenth century. At the end of the nineteenth and at the beginning of the twentieth centuries, a harder, more extreme version of nationalism came into being. Ultranationalists argued that political theories and parties that put class solidarity ahead of loyalty to a nation threatened the very fabric of civilization, and they vowed to fight them to the death.

Nineteenth-century nationalism had always had a racial component, and ultranationalism quickly merged with the age-old European suspicion of the Jewish people, known as anti-Semitism. The most notorious example of ultranationalist and anti-Semitic political power was the Dreyfus Affair. In 1894, a group of bigoted French army officers falsely accused Alfred Dreyfus a young Jewish captain, of treason. Dreyfus was convicted and sent to Devil's Island prison. The evidence was clearly fabricated, and liberals and socialists quickly came to Dreyfus's defense. His numerous trials (he was eventually exonerated) divided the nation, illustrating how strong ultranationalist and anti-Semitic feelings were in the French establishment.

Zionism

In the face of anti-Semitism, a movement for the creation of an independent state for the Jewish people, known as Zionism, came into being. In 1896, Theodor Herzl published *The Jewish State*, a pamphlet that urged an international movement to make Palestine the Jewish homeland. A year later, the World Zionist Organization was formed, and by 1914, nearly 85,000 Jews, primarily from Eastern Europe, had emigrated to Palestine.

The Causes of World War I

The causes of World War I are still debated by historians, but all explanations include the following to varying degrees:

- The nationalities problem: Ten distinct linguistic and ethnic groups lived within the borders of Austria-Hungary, and all were agitating for either greater autonomy or independence.
- The rise of Germany and the Alliance System: After unification in 1871, Bismarck sought security in the Triple Alliance (Germany, Austria-Hungary, and Italy); Great Britain, France, and Russia countered with the Triple Entente. The Alliance System was supposed to make war between the major powers too costly; instead its assurance of military reprisal limited diplomatic options.
- The Anglo-German rivalry: The unification of Germany and its rise as an industrial and military power generated a heated rivalry with Great Britain.
- The Assassination of the Austrian Archduke: The assassination, on June 28, 1914, of the heir to the Hapsburg throne by a young Bosnian patriot brought the nationalities problem to a crisis point.
- German military planning: Germany was convinced that war with the Triple Entente countries was inevitable. Accordingly, it devised a strategy, known as the Schlieffen Plan, for a two-front war that called for a military thrust westward toward Paris at the first sign of Russian mobilization in the east. The hope was to knock the French out of the war before the Russians could effectively mobilize.

The Beginning of the War: 1914–1915

Key events leading to the beginning of the war and an early stalemate included the following:

- On July 23, 1914, Austria, at Germany's urging, moved to crack down on Serbian nationalism.
- On July 28, 1914, Austria declared war on Serbia. Russia began military mobilization as a show of support for Serbia; that mobilization triggered the Schlieffen Plan.
- On August 4, 1914, the German army invaded Belgium, heading for Paris. In the first 16 months of combat, France suffered roughly half of all its war casualties. Two-thirds of one million men were killed.

- Belgian resistance gave time for British troops to join the battle in late August, but they joined a retreat.
- Russian troops mobilized faster than expected and invaded East Prussia. On August 26, 1914, German Commander Helmuth von Moltke transferred troops from the Western Front to the Eastern Front. The victory by the Germans at the Battle of Tannenberg led to the liberation of East Prussia and began a slow steady German advance eastward. However, the timetable of the Schlieffen Plan was altered, and the Germans were doomed to fight a two-front war.
- On September 6, 1914, French troops met the Germans at the First Battle of Marne.
- October and November 1914 saw a series of local engagements aimed at outflanking the enemy, sometimes known as the Race for the Sea, which extended the front line west until it reached the English Channel.
- The British determination to hold on to the entire French coast stretched the front north through Flanders. In the First Battle of Ypres in October and November 1914, the German advance was halted for good, leading to a stalemate and the beginning of trench warfare.

Total War

When war was declared in 1914, it was met with a joyous enthusiasm all across Europe. Explanations for this reaction include the following:

- A fascination with militarism that pervaded European culture
- Feelings of fraternity or brotherhood that a war effort brought out in people who lived in an increasingly fragmented and divided society
- A sense of Romantic adventurism that cast war as an alternative to the mundane, working life of industrial Europe

Additionally, there were several shared expectations among Europeans as they went to war:

- Recent experience, such as the Franco-Prussian war of 1871, suggested that the war would be brief; most expected it to last about six weeks.
- Each side was confident of victory.
- Each side expected a war of movement, full of cavalry charges and individual heroism.

The reality was a war of nearly five years of trench warfare and the conversion of entire economies to the war effort. As both sides literally dug in, soldiers fought from a network of trenches up to 30 feet deep, often flooded with water and infested with rats and lice. Military commanders, who commanded from rear-guard positions, continued to launch offensive attacks, ordering soldiers "over the top" to the mercy of the machine guns that lined enemy trenches.

Total war also meant changes on the home front, some of which would have lasting consequences:

- Governments took direct control of industries vital to the war effort.
- Labor unions worked with businesses and government to relax regulations on working hours and conditions.
- Class lines were blurred as people from all walks of life worked side by side to aid the war effort.
- Women were drawn into the industrial work force in greater numbers and gained access to jobs that had traditionally been reserved for men.

1916: "The Year of Bloodletting"

In 1916, a war of attrition was fought in trenches in France and Flanders, Belgium, as each side tried to exhaust the resources of the other.

- In February 1916, French troops, led by Marshall Petain, repulsed a German offensive at the Battle of Verdun; 700,000 men were killed.
- From July to November 1916, the British attempted an offensive that has come to be known as the Battle of the Somme; by its end, 400,000 British; 200,000 French; and 500,000 Germans soldiers lay dead.
- On April 6, 1917, America declared war on Germany. Several factors triggered the American entry, including the sinking of American vessels by German U-boats and the Zimmermann Note (a diplomatic correspondence of dubious origin, purporting to reveal a deal between Germany and Mexico).

Russian Revolution and Withdrawal

In March 1917, food shortages and disgust with the huge loss of life exploded into a revolution that forced the tsar's abdication. The new government, dominated by a coalition of liberal reformers and moderate socialists (sometimes referred to as Mensheviks), opted to continue the war effort.

In November 1917, a second revolution brought the Bolsheviks to power. A party of revolutionary Marxists, led by Vladimir Ilyich Ulyanov, who went by the name of Lenin, the Bolsheviks saw the war as a battle between two segments of the bourgeoisie fighting over the power to exploit the proletariat. Accordingly, the Bolsheviks decided to abandon the war and consolidate their revolutionary gains within Russia. They signed the Treaty of Brest-Litovsk with Germany in March 1918, surrendering Poland, Ukraine, Finland, and the Baltic provinces to Germany.

Shortly after the signing of the treaty, Russia was engulfed by civil war. Anti-communist groups, generally called the Whites in contrast to the communist Reds, were led by members of the old tsarist elite intent upon defending their privileges. Both sides received support from foreign governments, and for more than three years, from December 1917 to November 1920, the Bolshevik regime was engaged in a life-and-death struggle, which it ultimately won.

Germany's Disintegration and the Peace Settlement

Germany launched one last great offensive in March 1918 through the Somme toward Paris. The "Allies," as the French, British, and American coalition came to be known, responded by uniting their troops under a single commander, the French General Ferdinand Foch, for the first time. French troops were reinforced by fresh British conscripts and 600,000 American troops. By July 1918, the tide had turned in the Allies' favor for good. German forces retreated slowly along the whole Western Front. By early September, the German high command informed their government that peace had to be made at once. On November 9, 1918, German Kaiser William II abdicated, and two days later representatives of a new German government agreed to terms that amounted to unconditional surrender.

Peace negotiations began in Paris in January 1919 and were conducted by the victors; Germany was forced to accept the terms dictated to it. The French delegation was led by Georges Clemenceau, whose desire was to make sure that Germany could never threaten France again. The U.S. delegation was led by President Woodrow Wilson, who approached the peace talks with bold plans for helping to build a new Europe that could embrace the notions of individual rights and liberty, which he believed characterized the United States Great Britain was led by Prime Minister David Lloyd George, who tried to mediate between the vindictive Clemenceau and the idealistic Wilson.

The result was a series of five treaties that have, collectively, come to be known as the Treaty of Versailles. The overall settlement, sometimes also referred to as the Peace of Paris, contained much that was unprecedented and much that would sow the seeds of further conflict. Among the more significant aspects of the settlement were the following:

- Germany was forced to pay $5 billion annually in reparations until 1921, with no guarantee as to the total amount (the final amount was set at $33 billion in 1921).
- New independent nations were established in Eastern Europe as Hungary, Czechoslovakia, and Yugoslavia were created out of the old Austria-Hungary; Finland, Estonia, Latvia, and Lithuania were created out of the western part of the old Russian Empire; and Poland was created out of lands formerly part of Russia, Germany, and Austria-Hungary.
- Germany, in what came to be known as "the war guilt clause," was forced to accept full blame for the war.
- Germany was stripped of all its overseas colonies.
- The territory of Alsace-Lorraine, taken by Germany during the Franco-Prussian War of 1870–1871, was returned to France.
- The Allies were given the right to occupy German territories on the west bank of the Rhine River for 15 years.
- Germany's armed forces were limited to 100,000 soldiers and saddled with armament limitations.

Review Questions

Multiple Choice

Questions 1–3 refer to the following passage:

In the Second International the German "decisive force" played the determining role. At the [international] congresses, in the meetings of the international socialist bureaus, all awaited the opinion of the Germans. Especially in the questions of the struggle against militarism and war. . . . And what did we in Germany experience when the great historical test came? The most precipitous fall, the most violent collapse. Nowhere has the organization of the proletariat been yoked so completely to the service of imperialism. Nowhere is the state of siege borne so docilely. Nowhere is the press so hobbled, public opinion so stifled, the economic and political class struggle of the working class so totally surrendered as in Germany. . . .

The world war is a turning point. . . . The world war has altered the conditions of our struggle and, most of all, it has changed us. Not that the basic law of capitalist development, the life-and-death war between capital and labor, will experience any amelioration. But now, in the midst of the war, the masks are falling and the old familiar visages smirk at us. The tempo of development has received a mighty jolt from the eruption of the volcano of imperialism. The violence of the conflicts in the bosom of society, the enormousness of the tasks that tower up before the socialist proletariat—these make everything that has transpired in the history of the workers' movement seem a pleasant idyll. Historically, this war was ordained to thrust forward the cause of the proletariat. . . . It was ordained to drive the German proletariat to the pinnacle of the nation.

Rosa Luxemburg, "The War and the Workers," *The Junius Pamphlet*, 1916

1. From the passage, one may infer that European socialists at the Second International
   A. looked to German socialists for guidance in political action
   B. looked to French socialists for guidance in political action
   C. looked to the German government for guidance in political action
   D. were very few in number

2. From the passage, one may infer that, when war broke out in 1914, the socialist organizations in Germany
   A. attempted revolution
   B. supported the government and the war effort
   C. called for widespread work stoppages
   D. united in opposition to the war

3. From the passage, one may infer that Luxemburg looked at the war as
   A. a great opportunity for Germany
   B. the end of European civilization
   C. an event that would end class antagonism
   D. a moment that could ultimately help the socialist cause

Short Answer

4. Briefly explain the role that the Alliance System played in causing World War I.

Answers and Explanations

1. **A** is correct because the passage states that, at the Second International meeting of socialist parties, "all awaited the opinion of the Germans." B is incorrect because the passage makes no mention of French socialists. C is incorrect because the passage refers to socialist groups at the Second International, and because European socialist groups did not look to national governments for guidance. D is incorrect because one cannot tell from the passage how many socialist groups existed in prewar Europe.

2. **B** is correct because the passage indicates that when war broke out, "the organization of the proletariat [joined itself] completely to the service of imperialism," and that "the . . . political class struggle of the working class so totally surrendered . . . in Germany." A is incorrect because the passage makes no reference to any attempt at revolution. C is incorrect because the passage does not refer to a call for work stoppages. D is incorrect because the passage implies that the socialist parties of Germany *failed* to unite in opposition to the war.

3. **D** is correct because the passage says that the "war was ordained to thrust forward the cause of the proletariat. . . . It was ordained to drive the German proletariat to the pinnacle of the nation." A is incorrect because the passage does not refer to an opportunity for Germany. B is incorrect because the passage does not refer to the end of European civilization. C is incorrect because the passage does not predict the end of class antagonism.

4. Suggested answer:

   Thesis: The Alliance System, created to make war more costly and, therefore, less likely, actually helped to cause World War I by making neutrality nearly impossible.

   Paragraph Outline:

   I. Bismarck sought to gain security by creating the Triple Alliance (Germany, Austria-Hungary, and Italy), but this so alarmed Great Britain and its longtime adversaries, France and Russia, that they countered by creating the Triple Entente.

II. The Alliance System was supposed to make war between the major powers too costly; instead its assurance of military reprisal limited diplomatic options and created the specter of two-front war for Germany, convincing Germany that it had to go to war sooner rather than later. Once Germany attacked, all of the countries of the Alliance were honor-bound to join in.

Rapid Review

At the turn of the twentieth century, political gains were made by parties on the extreme left and right of the political spectrum, as the gradual reform of liberalism lost its appeal. The great powers of Europe constructed an alliance system that divided them into two armed camps. From August 1914 to November 1918, the two camps fought a total war of attrition. In the process, the oppressive police state of the Romanovs fell to Marxist revolutionaries in November 1917. The peace settlement that followed the war attempted to weaken and punish Germany.

CHAPTER 22

The Interwar Years and World War II

IN THIS CHAPTER

Summary: In the 1930s, the grim economic conditions of the Great Depression caused the political parties of the center to lose support to socialists on the left and also to fascists on the right. Mussolini's fascists took power in Italy, and Adolf Hitler came to power in Germany and embarked on a policy of rearmament and expansion that led to World War II. This chapter provides a review of these events and the course of World War II, during which 50 to 60 million people lost their lives, including six million Jews murdered in the Holocaust.

Key Terms:

- ✪ **Weimar Republic** The name given to the liberal democratic government established in Germany following World War I.
- ✪ **Spartacists** Marxist revolutionaries in post–World War II Germany, led by Rosa Luxemburg and Karl Liebknecht, who were dedicated to bringing a socialist revolution to Germany.
- ✪ **New Economic Plan (NEP)** A plan instituted by Lenin in the early 1920s that allowed rural peasants and small-business operators to manage their own land and businesses and to sell their products—a temporary compromise with capitalism that worked well enough to get the Russian economy functioning again.
- ✪ **Great Depression** A total collapse of the economies of Europe and the United States, triggered by the American stock market crash of 1929 and lasting most of the 1930s.

- **Blackshirts (*squadristi*)** Italian fascist paramilitary groups, largely recruited from disgruntled war veterans, commanded by Mussolini. They were increasingly relied upon by the Italian government to keep order in the 1920s.
- **National Socialist German Workers' Party (NSDAP, or the Nazi Party)** German political party that began as a small right-wing group—one of the more than 70 extremist paramilitary organizations that sprang up in post–World War I Germany. It was neither socialist nor did it attract many workers; it was a party initially made up of war veterans and misfits. The man responsible for its rise to power was Adolf Hitler.
- ***Anschluss*** The annexation of Austria by Nazi Germany in March 1938.
- **The Holocaust** A genocide in which approximately six million Jews were killed by the Nazi regime and its collaborators.

Introduction

The 1920s were an era of deep uncertainty, as the population of Europe grappled with the experiences and consequences of World War I. In the 1930s, the politics of the extreme flourished, as fascism emerged as an ideology that appealed to the downtrodden. By 1939, Adolf Hitler and his Nazi party controlled Germany, and his systematic repudiation of the Versailles Treaty led to the Second World War, which raged from 1939 to 1945.

Problems and Challenges After World War I

The men who survived the Great War, as World War I was called in the 1920s and 1930s, came home to a world of economic, social, and cultural uncertainty.

Governments had borrowed heavily to finance their war efforts, and interest payments were now coming due. The need to pay enormous sums in veteran and widow war benefits and unemployment benefits further burdened the economies. The inability of economies to meet the reviving demand for goods added inflation to an already grim economic mix. For the first 10 years following the war, Europe experienced a roller-coaster economy, as recessions followed brief periods of prosperity.

Socially, conditions were equally uncertain. Class deference was a casualty of World War I; lingering notions that the wealthier classes were somehow superior to working people were eroded by the experience of working and fighting side by side. Traditional views on gender had also been challenged by the wartime need to suspend restrictions on where and how women worked. In rapid succession, women across Europe gained the right to vote and fought to hold on to the greater freedom they had enjoyed during the war years.

Politically, uncertainty fueled continued radicalization. In France, ultraconservative and socialist parties vied for power. In Great Britain, the wartime coalition government led by David Lloyd George stayed intact and won another term in office, but the Labour Party made great gains at the expense of the Liberals. The various subjects of the British Empire, who had supported Great Britain in the war effort, now began to demand that their loyalty and sacrifice be rewarded, and independence movements coalesced in Ireland and India. In the newly created or reconstituted nations of east-central Europe—Hungary, Poland, and Yugoslavia—liberal democracy failed to take root, and right-wing authoritarian regimes came to power.

The cultural developments of the interwar years also reflected the deep uncertainty of the period. The 1920s have often been referred to as "the Roaring Twenties." The cabaret culture, where men and women mixed easily, seemed to reflect a loosening of social conventions and a pursuit of pleasure after the sacrifices of the war years. But cultural historians have increasingly pointed out that the culture of the interwar years seemed to reflect a deep anxiety for the future. An excellent example is Fritz Lang's film *Metropolis* (1925). Filmmaking became a popular art form in the interwar years, and film stars became celebrities whose lifestyle seemed to epitomize the Roaring Twenties. However, Lang's *Metropolis* depicted a world in which humans are dwarfed by an impersonal world of their own creation. Similarly, T. S. Eliot's epic poem, *The Waste Land* (1922), depicts a world devoid of purpose or meaning.

The Weimar Republic in Germany

The problems and uncertainties of the interwar years were felt most keenly in Germany. The new government, known as the Weimar Republic, was a liberal democracy led by a moderate Social Democrat, Friedrich Ebert. It was a government doomed to failure by several factors:

- Liberal democracy was a form of government largely alien to the German people whose allegiance had been to the kaiser.
- It was a government that was perceived to have been imposed on Germany by its vengeful war enemies.
- It was wrongly blamed for the humiliating nature of the Treaty of Versailles.
- It was faced with insurmountable economic problems, as the general economic difficulties of interwar Europe were compounded by Germany's need to pay the huge war reparations imposed on it.

Almost immediately, the government of the Weimar Republic was challenged by Marxist revolutionaries, known as Spartacists, led by Rosa Luxemburg and Karl Liebknecht, who were dedicated to bringing a socialist revolution to Germany. In order to defeat them, Ebert turned to the old imperial army officers who formed regiments of war veterans known as the *Freikorps* ("Free Corps"). Once the right-wing forces gained the upper hand, they too tried to overthrow the Weimar government in a coup attempt in 1920 that has come to be known as the *Kapp Putsch*. The government was saved, ironically, by the workers of Germany, who forced the right-wing insurgents to step down by staging a general strike. Just as the Weimar government began to stabilize, it found itself unable to pay the reparations demanded of it. When the French occupied the Ruhr Valley in retaliation, German workers again went on strike. The overwhelming uncertainty caused by the situation triggered hyperinflation, which made German currency essentially worthless.

The Soviet Union in Economic Ruins

By the onset of the 1920s, the bloody civil war between the monarchist "Whites" and the Bolshevik-led "Reds" was finally over, and Lenin held uncontested leadership of Russia. But it was a country in ruins, whose people could find neither jobs nor food. In order to deal with the crisis, Lenin launched the New Economic Plan (NEP), which allowed rural peasants and small-business operators to manage their own land and businesses and to sell their products. This temporary compromise with capitalism worked well enough to get the Russian economy functioning again.

In July 1923, Lenin constructed the Soviet Constitution of 1923. On paper it created a federal state, renamed the Union of Soviet Socialist Republics (USSR), but in practice, power continued to emanate from Lenin and the city that he named the capital in 1918, Moscow. Lenin died unexpectedly from a series of strokes in 1924. The man who won the power struggle to succeed him was the Communist Party Secretary Joseph Stalin. From 1924 to 1929, Stalin used a divide-and-conquer strategy combined with his control of the party bureaucracy to gain full control of the party and, thereby, of the Soviet Union. In the autumn of 1924, Stalin announced, in a doctrine that came to be known as "Socialism in One Country," that the Soviet Union would abandon the notion of a worldwide socialist revolution and concentrate on making the Soviet Union a successful socialist state.

In 1928, Stalin ended the NEP and initiated the first of a series of five-year plans, which rejected all notions of private enterprise and initiated the building of state-owned factories and power stations. As an extension of the plan, Stalin pursued the collectivization of agriculture, destroying the culture of the peasant village and replacing it with one organized around huge collective farms. The peasants resisted and were killed, starved, or driven into Siberia in numbers that can only be estimated but which may have been as high as eight million.

Between 1935 and 1939, Stalin set out to eliminate all centers of independent thought and action within the party and the government. In a series of purges, somewhere between seven and eight million Soviet citizens were arrested. At least one million of those were executed, while the rest were sent to work in camps known as *gulags*. The end result was a system that demanded and rewarded complete conformity to the vision of the Communist Party as dictated by Stalin.

The Great Depression

The post–World War I European economy was built on a fragile combination of international loans (mostly from the U.S.), reparations payments, and foreign trade. In October 1929, the New York stock market crashed, with stocks losing almost two-thirds of their value. Unable to obtain further credit, trade dried up. The result was an economic collapse that has come to be known as the Great Depression. Attempts to deal with the problem in traditional ways—by cutting government expenditures, tightening the supply of money, and raising tariffs on imported goods—only made things worse. By 1932, the economies of Europe were performing at levels that were only half those of 1929. Jobs became scarce as the economy contracted, and large segments of the population fell into poverty.

British economist John Maynard Keynes argued that governments needed to increase their expenditures and run temporary deficits in order to "jumpstart" the stagnant economy, but his ideas were only slowly accepted. Europe's economies recovered very slowly, and in the interim, parts of Europe succumbed to a new ideology of the desperate and downtrodden—fascism.

The Rise of Fascism

Historians struggle with definitions of fascism because it has no coherent ideology, and its form varied from nation to nation. But all fascism was a mixture, to one degree or another, of the following ingredients:

- An intense form of nationalism
- A professed belief in the virtues of struggle and youth
- A fanatical obedience to a charismatic leader
- An expressed hatred of both socialism and liberalism

Mussolini and Italian Fascism

The birthplace of fascism was Italy, which became the first country in Europe to have a fascist government. Italy, though a member of the Triple Alliance with Germany and Austria-Hungary, had originally chosen to remain neutral in World War I. But in 1915, Italy entered the war on the side of the Entente in hopes of gaining lands from Austria-Hungary. Italian war veterans returned home disillusioned, as the war experience had turned out to be a nightmare. One such veteran, a former socialist named Benito Mussolini, founded the National Fascist Party in 1919. The new party began to field candidates for the Italian legislature and to establish itself as the party that could save Italy from the threat of socialism. By 1922, squads of fascist "Blackshirts" (*squadristi*), largely recruited from disgruntled war veterans, were doing battle with bands of socialists "Redshirts," and the Italian government was increasingly unable to keep order. In October 1922, Mussolini organized 20,000 fascist supporters and announced his intention to march on Rome. King Victor Emmanuel III responded by naming Mussolini prime minister of the Italian government.

Mussolini quickly moved to consolidate his power by pushing through a number of constitutional changes. A showdown between Mussolini and what parliamentary forces still existed in Italy came in the summer of 1924, when fascists were implicated in the murder of the socialist member of the Italian parliament, Giacomo Matteotti. The masses supported Mussolini, and by early 1926, all opposition parties had been dissolved and declared illegal, effectively making Mussolini dictator of Italy.

Hitler and German Nazism

Understanding the rise of Adolf Hitler and the Nazi Party in Germany requires an understanding of the post–World War I context. Wartime propaganda had led the German public to believe that the war was going well. As a result, Germany's surrender came as an inexplicable shock. The peace settlement seemed unfair and unduly harsh, and there was a growing sense among the German people that Germany must have been betrayed. In that context, the Nazis became popular by telling the German people several things they desperately wanted to hear:

- The Nazis appealed to displaced veterans and young people by telling them that they would build a Germany that had a place for them.
- They promised to get rid of the hated war reparations and to return Germany to military greatness.
- They provided the Germans with someone to blame for defeat by claiming that the Jews had betrayed Germany.
- They appealed to frightened business interests and the Church in Germany by promising to protect them from the socialists.

The so-called National Socialist German Workers' Party (NSDAP), or the Nazi Party, began as a small right-wing group and one of the more than 70 extremist paramilitary organizations that sprang up in postwar Germany. It was neither socialist nor did it attract many workers; it was a party initially made up of war veterans and the unemployed. The man responsible for its rise to power was Adolf Hitler, a failed Austrian art student and war veteran.

Hitler used military attitudes and techniques, as well as expert propaganda, to turn the NSDAP into a tightly knit organization with mass appeal. Hitler and the Nazis made their first bid for power in November 1923 in the "Beer Hall Putsch," when they tried to stage a coup to topple the Bavarian government in Munich. It failed, but Hitler gained national attention in the subsequent trial, during which he publicly decried the terms of the Treaty of Versailles and espoused his views of racial nationalism. Years of reorganization and building of grassroots support produced significant electoral gains in the elections of 1930.

In the elections of 1932, the Nazis won over 35 percent of the vote. Hitler refused to take part in a coalition government, and the German president, the aging military hero Paul von Hindenburg, made the crucial decision to appoint Hitler chancellor of Germany (the equivalent of prime minister). Early in 1933, the German parliament building, the *Reichstag*, burned down. Hitler declared a state of emergency and assumed dictatorial powers. He then used them to eliminate socialist opposition to Nazi rule. In the elections of 1933, Nazis won 288 seats out of 647. With the support of 52 deputies of the Nationalist Party, and in the absence of Communist deputies, who were under arrest, the Nazis were able to rule with a majority. By bullying the members of the *Reichstag* into passing the Enabling Act of March 1933, Hitler was essentially free to rule as a dictator.

Fascist Dictatorships in Spain and Portugal

In both Spain and Portugal, Western-style parliamentary governments faced opposition from the Church, the army, and large landowners. In 1926, army officers overthrew the Portuguese Republic that had been created in 1910, and gradually António de Oliveira Salazar, an economics professor, became dictator.

In Spain, anti-monarchist parties won the election of 1931, and King Alphonso XIII fled as the new Spanish Republic was set up. When a socialist cartel won the election of 1936, General Francisco Franco led a revolt against the Republic from Spanish Morocco, plunging Spain into a bloody civil war. Franco received support from the Spanish monarchy and the Church, while Germany and Italy sent money and equipment. The Republic was defended by brigades of volunteers from around the world (famous writers George Orwell and Ernest Hemingway among them) and eventually received aid from the Soviet Union. The technological might provided by the Germans allowed Franco's forces to overwhelm the defenders of the Republic. Pablo Picasso's 25-foot-long mural *Guernica* (1937), depicting the bombing of the town of Guernica by German planes in 1937, poignantly illustrated the nature of the mismatch. By 1939, Franco ruled Spain as dictator.

Fascism in France

During World War I, France had essentially been administered by the military. At the war's conclusion, Parliament rushed to reassert its dominance, and France became governed by moderate coalitions. But the elections of 1924 swept the *Cartel des Gauches*, a coalition of socialist parties, to power, causing a reaction in the form of a flurry of fascist organizations, with names like *Action française* ("French Action"), the Legion, and the *Jeunesses Patriotes* ("Youth Patriots"). These organizations remained on the political fringe, but they provided extremist opposition and a source of anti-Semitism, which became prominent in the collaboration of the Vichy regime during the German occupation of France in World War II.

Fascism in Great Britain

In Great Britain, small right-wing extremist groups were united in the 1930s under the leadership of Sir Oswald Mosley, who created the British Union of Fascists (BUF). They were united by their hatred of socialism and their anti-Semitism. Although never politically significant in Great Britain, the BUF did mount a serious public disturbance in October 1934 when it battled with socialists and Jewish groups in an incident that has come to be known as the "Battle of Cable Street." More importantly, the existence of the BUF and the initial reluctance of the British government to ban it demonstrate the existence of some sympathy for their authoritarian and anti-Semitic views among powerful people in Britain. Once the war broke out, the BUF was banned and Mosley was jailed.

World War II

Hitler had come to power by promising to repudiate the Treaty of Versailles. In March 1936, he took his first big step by moving his revitalized armed forces into the Rhineland, the area on the west bank of the Rhine River, which the treaty had deemed a demilitarized zone. When that move provoked no substantive response from France or Britain, Hitler embarked on a series of moves to the east that eventually triggered the Second World War:

- In March 1938, Germany annexed Austria without opposition (an event sometimes referred to as the *Anschluss*).
- Hitler then claimed the *Sudetenland*, a region of Czechoslovakia that was home to 3.5 million German speakers.
- Great Britain reacted with what has been called a policy of appeasement, agreeing in the Munich Agreement of September 1938 to allow Hitler to take the *Sudentenland* over Czech objections in exchange for his promise that there would be no further aggression.
- In March 1939, Hitler broke the Munich Agreement by invading Czechoslovakia.
- As Hitler threatened Poland, the hope of Soviet intervention was dashed by the surprise announcement, on August 23, 1939, of a Nazi–Soviet Non-Aggression Pact, guaranteeing Soviet neutrality in return for part of Poland.
- On September 1, 1939, Germany invaded Poland.
- On September 3, 1939, both France and Great Britain declared war on Germany.

In order to understand why Great Britain followed a policy of appeasement and was slow to recognize the pattern of aggressive expansion in Hitler's actions in 1938 and 1939, one has to take into account the following points:

- Great Britain and its allies, unlike Hitler's Germany, had not begun any kind of military buildup and were in no position to back up any ultimatums they might give to Hitler.
- Unlike the Germans, many of whom thought things could get no worse and were eager to avenge the humiliation of defeat in World War I, the British public hoped that they had fought and won the "war to end all wars," and wanted no part of renewed hostilities.
- Many of the British leaders privately agreed with the Germans that the Versailles Treaty had been unprecedented and unwarranted.
- Given British public opinion, a decision to pursue a military response to Hitler's actions would have been political suicide for British leaders.

Blitzkrieg and the "Phony War" (1939–1940)

As Germany invaded Poland, Great Britain and France were not yet in a military position to offer much help. The Poles fought bravely but were easily overrun by the German *blitzkrieg*, or "lightning war," which combined air strikes and the rapid deployment of tanks and highly mobile units. Poland fell to Germany in a month.

Meanwhile, Great Britain sent divisions to France, and the British and French general staffs coordinated strategy. But the strategy was a purely defensive one of awaiting a German assault behind the Maginot Line, a vast complex of tank traps, fixed artillery sites, subterranean railways, and living quarters, which paralleled the Franco-German border but failed to protect the border between France and Belgium. Over the winter of 1939 and 1940, war was going on at sea, but on land and in the air there was a virtual standoff that has come to be termed the "Phony War." During the lull, however, the Soviet Union acted on its agreement with Hitler, annexing territories in Poland and Eastern Europe, including Estonia, Latvia, and Lithuania, and invading Finland.

The Battles of France and Britain (1940)

In April 1940, the Phony War came to an abrupt end as the German *blitzkrieg* moved into Norway and Denmark to prevent Allied intervention in Scandinavia and to secure Germany's access to vital iron ore supplies, and then into Luxembourg, Belgium, and the Netherlands in preparation for an all-out attack on France.

By early June 1940, the German army was well inside France. The Maginot Line proved useless against the mobility of the German tanks, which skirted the Line by going north through the Ardennes Forest. On June 14, 1940, German troops entered Paris. Two days later, the aging General Marshal Pétain assumed control of France and signed an armistice with Germany, according to which the German army, at French expense, would occupy the northern half of France, including the entire Atlantic coast, while Pétain himself governed the rest from the city of Vichy. Not all of France was happy with the deal. General Charles de Gaulle escaped to Britain and declared himself head of a free French government. In France, many joined a Free French movement, which would provide active resistance to German occupation throughout the remainder of the war.

In Great Britain, Prime Minister Neville Chamberlain, who had been the architect of Great Britain's appeasement policy, resigned. King George VI turned to the 65-year-old Winston Churchill, who had been nearly the lone critic of the appeasement policy. Churchill used his oratory skill throughout the war to bolster moral and strengthen the Allies' resolve. The German *blitzkrieg* now drove to the English Channel, trapping the Allied army at the small seaport of Dunkirk. In an episode that has come to be known as "the Miracle of Dunkirk," more than 338,000 Allied troops (224,000 of them British), surrounded on all sides by advancing German units, were rescued by a motley flotilla of naval vessels, private yachts, trawlers, and motorboats. The episode buoyed British spirits, but Churchill was somber, pointing out that "wars are not won by evacuations."

Hitler, and many neutral observers, expected Great Britain to seek peace negotiations, but Churchill stood defiant. The German High Command prepared for the invasion of Great Britain, but the invasion never came. Instead, in one of the most significant moments in the war, Hitler changed his mind and turned on the Soviet Union. Several components make up the explanation for this fateful decision:

- Hitler's racialist view of the world made him wary of the British, whom he considered to be the most closely related race to the Germans.
- Hitler's staff was handicapped by both the lack of time given to them and by their relative lack of experience in mounting amphibious operations.
- A successful invasion of England required air superiority over the English Channel; a combination of daring fighting by the Royal Air Force and a coordinated effort of civilian defense operations all along the coast foiled German attempts to gain it.

A frustrated Hitler responded by ordering a nightly bombing of London in a two-month attempt to disrupt industrial production and to break the will of the British people. In the end, neither was achieved. In mid-October, Hitler decided to postpone the invasion; the Battle of Britain had been won by the British.

The War in North Africa and the Balkans (1941–1942)

In 1941, the war became a global conflict as Italian forces invaded North Africa, attempting to push the British out of Egypt. However, British forces routed the Italians; Germany responded by sending troops into North Africa and the Balkans. Germany had two objectives:

- It coveted the Balkans for their rich supply of raw materials, especially Romanian oil.
- It also wanted control of the Suez Canal in Egypt, which was the vital link between Britain and its resource-rich empire.

The Germans successfully occupied the Balkans, as British efforts to make a last-ditch stand in mainland Greece and on the nearby island of Crete proved in vain. Italian regiments in Libya were reinforced by German divisions under General Erwin Rommel, and the ill-equipped British forces were driven back into Egypt.

German Invasion of the Soviet Union (June to December 1941)

The Nazi–Soviet Non-Aggression Pact had always been a matter of convenience. Both sides knew that war would eventually come; the question was when. Hitler answered the question late in the spring of 1941, launching Operation Barbarossa and sending three million troops into the Soviet Union. Hitler's decision was influenced by several factors:

- His desire to create an empire that dominated all of Europe
- His racialist view of the world, which told him that the "Slavic" peoples of the Soviet Union were an easier target that his "Teutonic cousins," the British
- His need to feed and fuel his war machine with the wheat of Ukraine and the oil of the Caucasus
- His hope that once Germany dominated the continent from the English Channel to the Ural Mountains, the British would have to come to terms with defeat and no invasion of Britain would be necessary

Germany's eastern army succeeded in conquering those parts of the Soviet Union that produced 60 percent of its coal and steel and almost half its grain, and by December, it was within striking distance of Moscow. But as winter set in, the Russian army launched a counterattack against German forces, who were ill-supplied for a winter war. The Russian army suffered millions of casualties but turned back the German invasion.

Hitler's decision to attack the Soviet Union had one other great consequence: it forged the first link in what would become the Grand Alliance between Great Britain, the Soviet Union, and the United States, as Churchill (despite being a staunch anti-communist) pledged his support to the USSR. Publicly, he announced, "Any man or state that fights against Nazidom will have our aid." Privately, he remarked that if Hitler invaded Hell, it would be desirable to find something friendly to say about the devil. The final link in the Grand Alliance would come through a combination of Churchill's persuasion and a Japanese attack.

The American Entry and Its Impact (1942)

Churchill and the American president, Franklin Roosevelt, met in August 1941 on a battleship off the Newfoundland coast. They composed the Atlantic Charter, a document setting forth Anglo-American war aims. It rejected any territorial aggrandizement for either Great Britain or the United States, and it affirmed the right of all peoples to choose their own form of government.

By 1939, a modernized and militarized Japan had conquered the coastal area of China, and its expansionist aims led it to join Germany and Italy as part of what came to be known as the Axis. When war broke out, Japan occupied the part of Indochina that had been under French control and began to threaten the Dutch East Indies. The U.S. responded with an economic embargo on all exports to Japan. On December 7, 1941, Japanese air forces launched a surprise attack in Pearl Harbor, Hawaii, hoping to cripple U.S. naval forces in the Pacific Ocean. The U.S. immediately declared war on Japan, and within a few days, Germany and Italy had declared war on the U.S.

Initially, America's impact on the war was through resources rather than soldiers, but its entry provided the third and final turning point (along with the Battle of Britain and Germany's decision to invade the Soviet Union) in the war. Throughout 1942, American productive capacities were being built up, and the American military force kept growing. In the autumn of 1942, American marines landed on the island of Guadalcanal; it was to be the first of many islands to be recaptured from the Japanese at great cost of human lives.

The Holocaust

In 1941, the embattled Hitler regime embarked on the "Final Solution," the deliberate and methodical extermination of Jewish people in Europe. It began when *Schutzstaffel* (SS) troops under Reinhard Heydrich and Heinrich Himmler began executing Jewish and Slavic prisoners, who had been gathered from around Europe and forced into concentration camps. At first, firing squads were used. Next, the process was speeded up through the use of mobile vans of poison gas. Eventually, large gas chambers were constructed at the camps so that thousands could be murdered at one time. In the end, an estimated six million Jews were murdered, along with an additional seven million people, among whom were Gypsies, homosexuals, socialists, Jehovah's Witnesses, and other targeted groups.

Outside the Nazi inner circle, people and governments were slow to believe and to comprehend what was happening, and even slower to respond:

- Neighbors turned a blind eye when Jews were rounded up and put on trains.
- Collaborating governments from Vichy France to Croatia assisted in various ways with the rounding up and extermination of the Jews.
- British and American commanders refused to divert bombing missions from other targets in order to put the camps out of commission.

The Axis in Retreat (1942–1943)

In June and August 1943, the tide turned against the Axis forces in the Soviet Union, the Mediterranean, and the Pacific. In June 1942, the Germans resumed their offensive in the Soviet Union. By August, they were on the outskirts of Stalingrad on the Volga River. The mammoth Battle of Stalingrad lasted six months; by the time it ended in February 1943, the greater part of a German army had died or surrendered to the Russians, and the remainder was retreating westward.

In October 1942, the British Eighth Army under General Bernard Montgomery halted General Rommel's forces at the Battle of El Alamein, 70 miles west of Alexandria, Egypt, and began a victorious drive westward. In May 1943, Germany's Africa Korps surrendered to the Allies. In November 1943, Allied forces under General Dwight Eisenhower's command landed in Morocco and Algeria and began a drive that pushed all Axis forces in Africa into Tunisia. Seven months later, all Axis forces had been expelled from Africa.

Allied victories in Africa enabled them to advance steadily northward from the Mediterranean into Italy and precipitated the overthrow of Mussolini and the signing of an armistice by a new Italian government. Germany responded by treating its former ally as an occupied country. German resistance made the Allied campaign up the Italian peninsula a long and difficulty one.

Allied Victory (1944–1945)

On "D-Day," June 6, 1944, Allied forces under Eisenhower's command launched an audacious amphibious invasion of German-held France on the beaches of Normandy. The grand assault took the form of an armada of 4,000 ships supported by 11,000 airplanes. By the end of July, Allied forces had broken out of Normandy and encircled the greater part of the German army.

By late August, Paris was liberated, and Hitler's forces were on the retreat. Germany seemed on the point of collapse, but German defensive lines held, and the British people were exposed to a new threat: long-range V-2 rockets fired from the German Ruhr rained down on them for seven months more. The last gasp of the German army came in December 1944 with a sudden drive against thinly held American lines in the Belgian sector. In what has come to be known as the Battle of the Bulge, the Allies checked the German attack and launched a counteroffensive.

In early 1945, Allied troops finally crossed the Rhine River into Germany. In May, they successfully defeated German forces in the Battle of Berlin. On May 1, it was announced that Hitler was dead, and on May 7, the German High Command surrendered unconditionally. In the Pacific, the long and deadly task of retaking the Pacific islands was averted by the dropping of atomic bombs on two Japanese cities: one on Hiroshima on August 6, 1945, and another on Nagasaki on August 9, 1945. Japan surrendered unconditionally on September 2.

Assessment and Aftermath of World War II

World War II was even more destructive than World War I, and civilian casualties, rather than military deaths, made up a significant portion of the 50 to 60 million people who perished in the conflict. Many of Europe's great cities lay in ruins from repeated aerial bombings.

Vast numbers of Europeans were displaced and on the move. Some were trying to get back to homes they were driven from by the war, while others whose homes were destroyed simply had no place to go. Russian prisoners of war were compelled, many against their will, to return to the Soviet Union, where they were greeted with hostility and suspicion by Stalin's regime; many were executed or sent to labor camps. Between 12 and 13 million Germans were moving west. Some were fleeing the vengeance of Soviet troops, while others were driven from their homes in the newly reconstituted Czechoslovakia and other Eastern European countries, and from East Prussia, which had been handed over to Poland.

The war also produced a new power structure in the world. The traditional European powers of Great Britain, France, and Germany were exhausted. Their overseas empires disintegrated rapidly, as they no longer had the resources or the will to keep their imperial holdings against the desires of local inhabitants. In the years immediately following the war, the following countries became independent:

- India gained its independence from Britain.
- Syria and Lebanon broke away from France.
- The Dutch were dismissed from Indonesia.

Finally, it became clear that, in the new world order that emerged from the Second World War, the United States and the Soviet Union stood alone as great powers.

Review Questions

Multiple Choice

Questions 1–3 refer to the following passage:

Fascism, the more it considers and observes the future and the development of humanity quite apart from political considerations of the moment, believes neither in the possibility nor the utility of perpetual peace. It thus repudiates the doctrine of Pacifism—born of a renunciation of the struggle and an act of cowardice in the face of sacrifice. War alone brings up to its highest tension all human energy and puts the stamp of nobility upon the peoples who have courage to meet it. All other trials are substitutes, which never really put men into the position where they have to make the great decision—the alternative of life or death. . . .

Fascism [is] the complete opposite of . . . Marxian Socialism, [according to which] the materialist conception of [the] history of human civilization can be explained simply through the conflict of interests among the various social groups and by the change and development in the means and instruments of production. . . . Fascism, now and always, believes in holiness and in heroism; that is to say, in actions influenced by no economic motive, direct or indirect. And if the economic conception of history be denied, according to which theory men are no more than puppets, carried to and fro by the waves of chance, while the real directing forces are quite out of their control, it follows that the existence of an unchangeable and unchanging class-war is also denied. . . .

Fascism denies, in democracy, the absurd conventional untruth of political equality dressed out in the garb of collective irresponsibility, and the myth of "happiness" and indefinite progress . . . political doctrines pass, but humanity remains, and it may rather be expected that this will be a century of authority . . . a century of Fascism.

Benito Mussolini, *What Is Fascism,* 1932

1. From the passage, one may infer the fascists considered war
   A. a necessary evil
   B. a path to greatness for a nation
   C. to be the cause of Europe's troubles
   D. to be motivated by economic concerns

2. From the passage, one may infer that fascism
   A. is a type of socialism
   B. argues that class conflict is inevitable
   C. believes that people are no more than puppets
   D. rejects the Marxist understanding of history

3. From the passage, one may infer that fascists argued that the state
   A. should be the supreme authority in a nation
   B. should protect individual liberty
   C. should seize the means of production
   D. should guarantee the equality of citizens

Short Answer

4. Briefly describe TWO of the problems facing European countries in the interwar years, and explain how ONE of the problems you identified helps to explain the causes of World War II.

Answers and Explanations

1. **B** is correct because the passage says that war "puts the stamp of nobility upon the peoples who have courage to meet it." A is incorrect because the passage indicates that war is beneficial to a people, not evil. C is incorrect because the passage does not state that war is the source of Europe's troubles. D is incorrect because the passage rejects the notion that people are motivated by economic concerns.

2. **D** is correct because the passage states that fascism is the "complete opposite of . . . Marxian Socialism," and goes on to reject the materialist contention that history is explained through class conflict. A is incorrect because the passage asserts that fascism is the opposite of Marxian socialism and contends that individuals act in ways undetermined by economic and class interest. B is incorrect because the passage *denies* that class conflict is inevitable. C is incorrect because the passage attributes the notion that people are puppets to socialism, not fascism.

3. **A** is correct because the passage indicates that a century of fascism is a century of authority, and because it denies the liberal notions of individual liberty and equality. B is incorrect because the passage does not refer to the protection of individual liberty. C is incorrect because the passage does not refer to a seizure of the means of production. D is incorrect because the passage explicitly denies the liberal notion of equality.

4. Suggested answer:

Thesis: During the interwar years, European countries faced severe economic uncertainty and political radicalization. The political radicalization brought to power governments that desired a second military conflict.

Paragraph Outline:

   I. The post–World War I European economy was built on a fragile combination of international loans (mostly from the United States), reparations payments, and foreign trade. In October 1929, the New York stock market crashed, with stocks losing almost two-thirds of their value. Unable to obtain further credit, trade dried up. The result was an economic collapse that has come to be known as the Great Depression.

   II. Politically, the economic and cultural uncertainty fuelled continued radicalization. In France, ultraconservative and socialist parties vied for power. In Italy and Germany, fascist parties came to power.

   III. The fascist ideology was predicated on militarization and a belief that war tested and ennobled a people. Such an ideology was one factor causing World War II.

Rapid Review

Europe in the 1920s was characterized by a fluctuating economy built on debt and speculation. With the Stock Market Crash of 1929, credit dried up, and the Great Depression ensued. The economic problems added to a climate of social and cultural uncertainty and disillusionment. Political parties of the center lost support to socialists on the left and fascists on the right.

In the late 1930s, Adolf Hitler came to power in Germany and embarked on a policy of rearmament and expansion. France and Great Britain responded initially with a policy of appeasement, but when Hitler invaded Poland in September 1939, the Second World War began. Initial German success in the war was reversed in stages by three crucial turning points:

- Great Britain's victory in the Battle of Britain in 1940
- Hitler's decision to abandon an invasion of Great Britain and invade the Soviet Union instead
- The entry of the United States into the war following the Japanese attack on Pearl Harbor on December 7, 1941

Germany surrendered on May 7, 1945, and Japan followed suit on September 2, 1945, following the dropping of two atomic bombs on the cities of Hiroshima and Nagasaki in August. In the end, between 50 and 60 million people lost their lives in the Second World War, including six million Jews, who were murdered in the Holocaust. The traditional powers of Europe—Great Britain, France, and Germany—gave way to two new superpowers: the United States and the Soviet Union.

CHAPTER 23

The Cold War, Integration, and Globalization

IN THIS CHAPTER

Summary: Following World War II, the Soviet Union solidified its control of Eastern Europe, creating an "Iron Curtain" that divided East and West. The two superpowers, the United States and the Soviet Union, engaged in a global conflict, called the Cold War. This chapter provides a review of the important events of the Cold War and describes the growing economic integration in Western Europe that culminated in the creation of the European Union. This chapter also reviews the sudden end of the Cold War, including the rapid disintegration of the Soviet Union, the destruction of the Iron Curtain, and the reunification of Germany.

Key Terms:

KEY IDEA

- ✪ **Truman Doctrine** A U.S. doctrine (named after President Harry Truman), created in 1947, that established a system of military and economic aid to countries threatened by communist takeover.
- ✪ **Marshall Plan** A plan (named after U.S. Secretary of State George Marshall), launched in 1947, that provided billions of dollars of aid to help the Western European powers rebuild their infrastructures and economies following World War II.
- ✪ **Council for Mutual Economic Assistance** The Soviet Union's response to the Marshall Plan whereby the Soviet Union offered economic aid packages for Eastern European countries.

- ✪ **North Atlantic Treaty Organization (NATO)** A military alliance, formed in 1949, uniting the Western powers against the Soviet Union.
- ✪ **Warsaw Pact** The Soviet Union's response, in 1949, to the formation of NATO, which established a military alliance of the communist countries of Eastern Europe.
- ✪ **Détente** An era of warmer diplomatic relations between the United States and the Soviet Union, for a period lasting from the 1960s into the 1980s. It was characterized by a number of nuclear test-ban treaties and arms-limitation talks between the two superpowers.
- ✪ **Prague Spring** An episode in 1968 when Czechoslovakian communists, led by Alexander Dubcek, embarked on a process of liberalization. Under Dubcek's leadership, the reformers declared that they intended to create "socialism with a human face." Dubcek tried to proceed by balancing reforms with reassurances to the Soviet Union, but on August 21, 1968, Soviet and Warsaw Pact troops invaded and occupied the major cities of Czechoslovakia.
- ✪ **Velvet Revolution** The name for the nearly bloodless overthrow of Soviet communism in Czechoslovakia in 1989.
- ✪ **Globalization** A term that refers to the increasing integration and interdependence of the economic, social, cultural, and even ecological aspects of life in the late twentieth and early twenty-first centuries. The term refers not only to the way in which the economies of the world affect one another, but also to the way that the experience of everyday life is becoming increasingly standardized by the spread of technologies that carry with them social and cultural norms.

Introduction

Following World War II, the Cold War developed between the two new superpowers: the Soviet Union and the United States. In response, Western European nations followed a course of economic integration that culminated in the creation of the European Union. In the decades that followed the collapse of the Soviet Union, Europe experienced both a revival of nationalism and the emergence of globalization.

The Development of Nuclear Weapons

In 1944, German physicists Otto Hahn and Fritz Strassman published a paper (based on work they had done with Lise Meitner, a Jewish physicist who was forced to emigrate due to increasing anti-Semitism in Nazi Germany) that purported to show that vast amounts of energy would be released if a way could be found to split the atom. As World War II raged, the American government secretly funded an effort, known as the Manhattan Project, to build an atomic bomb. In 1945, the project's international team of physicists, led by American physicist Robert Oppenheimer, succeeded in building two atomic bombs. Those bombs were dropped on two Japanese cities: Hiroshima (on August 6, 1945) and Nagasaki (on August 9, 1945). The advent of these nuclear weapons forced Japan's unconditional surrender and created a nuclear arms race between the United States and the Soviet Union.

The Settlement Following World War II

There was no formal treaty at the conclusion of the Second World War. The postwar shape of Europe was determined by agreements reached at two wartime conferences in Tehran, Iran (in December 1943), and Yalta, Crimea, then part of the Soviet Union (in February 1945), and, where agreement could not be reached, by the realities of occupation at the war's end. These were the primary results of the eventual settlement:

- Germany was disarmed and divided into sectors, with Western powers controlling the western sector and the Soviet Union controlling the eastern sector.
- Berlin, which lay in the eastern sector, was itself divided into West Berlin (controlled by the Allies) and East Berlin (controlled by the Soviet Union).
- Poland's border with Germany was pushed westward.
- The United Nations (U.N.) was created with 51 members to promote international peace and cooperation.
- Although the United States and Great Britain called for free elections in the Eastern European nations that were under the control of the Soviet Army, pro-Soviet governments were quickly installed by Stalin.
- By 1946, the world was speaking of an "Iron Curtain" that had descended over Eastern Europe (the phrase was first uttered by Winston Churchill in a speech given in the United States), stretching from the Baltic Sea in the north to the Adriatic Sea in the south and dividing Europe between a communist East and a capitalist West.

The Cold War

The Cold War in Europe

The phrase *Cold War* refers to efforts of the ideologically opposed regimes of the United States and the Soviet Union to extend their influence and control of events around the globe, without engaging in direct military conflict with one another. The first showdown between the superpowers occurred from June 1948 until May 1949, when Soviet troops cut off all land traffic from the west into Berlin in an attempt to take control of the whole city. In response, the Western Powers, led by the United States, mounted what has come to be known as the Berlin Airlift, supplying West Berlin and keeping it out of Soviet control. In 1949, the Western-controlled zones of Germany were formally merged to create the independent German Federal Republic. One month later, the Soviets established the German Democratic Republic in the eastern zone.

In 1947, the United States established the Truman Doctrine, offering military and economic aid to countries threatened by communist takeover. That same year, Truman's secretary of state, George Marshall, launched what has come to be known as the Marshall Plan, contributing billions of dollars of aid to help the Western European powers to rebuild their infrastructures and economies. The Soviet Union soon countered with the Council for Mutual Economic Assistance, an economic aid package for Eastern European countries.

In 1949, the United States established the North Atlantic Treaty Organization (NATO), uniting the Western powers in a military alliance against the Soviet Union. The Soviet Union countered with the Warsaw Pact, a military alliance of the communist countries of Eastern Europe. The one great military imbalance of the postwar period, the United States' possession of the atomic bomb, was countered by the development of a Soviet atomic bomb in 1949. From then on, the two superpowers engaged in a nuclear arms race that saw each develop an arsenal of hydrogen bombs by 1953, followed by huge caches of nuclear warheads mounted on intercontinental ballistic missiles (ICBMs). The overarching strategy of amassing nuclear weapons became appropriately known by its acronym MAD, which stood for "mutual assured destruction." This strategy "reasoned" that neither side would use its nuclear weapons if its own destruction by a retaliatory blast was assured.

The Global Cold War

Once the two superpowers had done what they could to shore up their positions in Europe, their competition spread across the globe. Major events in world history that are directly connected to the Cold War include the following:

- The civil war in China, in which the Soviet-backed communist forces of Mao Zedong defeated, in 1949, the Nationalist forces of Jiang Jieshi, supported by the United States
- The Korean War (1950–1953) between Soviet- and Chinese-supported North Korean communists and U.N.- and U.S.-backed South Koreans, which produced a stalemate at the 38th parallel (the original post–World War II dividing line between North and South Korea) at the cost of some 1.5 million lives
- The Cuban Missile Crisis of October 1963, in which Soviet attempts to install nuclear missiles in Cuba were met with a U.S. blockade of the island, bringing the world to the brink of nuclear war until the Soviets backed down and removed the missiles
- The Vietnam War, in which communist forces, led by Ho Chi Minh, battled an authoritarian, anti-communist government, increasingly reliant on U.S. military aid for its existence (throughout the 1960s until U.S. withdrawal in 1973)

Although it was less in the headlines of world news, the Cold War also had devastating effects in Latin America and Africa, where, for the better part of three decades, local and regional disputes were shaped by the intervention of Soviet and U.S. money, arms, and covert operations. Many of the difficulties faced by these regions today can be traced back to the Cold War.

Détente with the West, Crackdown in the East

Beginning in the late 1960s and lasting into the 1980s, U.S.–Soviet relations entered into a new era that has come to be known as the era of *détente*. In this period, both sides backed away from the notion of a struggle only one side could win. The era of *détente* was characterized by a number of nuclear test-ban treaties and arms-limitation talks between the two superpowers.

However, while Soviet–U.S. relations were thawing during this period, the Soviet Union demonstrated on several occasions that it still intended to rule the Eastern Block with a firm hand. The most dramatic of these events occurred in 1968 in an episode that has come to be known as the Prague Spring. Czechoslovakian communists, led by Alexander Dubcek, embarked on a process of liberalization, stimulated by public demand for greater freedom, economic progress, and equality. Under Dubcek's leadership, the reformers declared that they intended to create "socialism with a human face." Dubcek tried to proceed by balancing reforms with reassurances to the Soviet Union. But on August 21, Soviet and Warsaw Pact troops invaded and occupied the major cities of Czechoslovakia; it was the largest military operation in Europe since the Second World War.

The Soviet regime also continued to demand conformity from its citizens and to punish dissent. A good example is the case Alexander Solzhenitsyn, the acclaimed author who wrote novels that attempted to tell the truth about life in the Soviet Union. For writing novels like *The Cancer Ward* (1966) and *The First Circle* (1968), Solzhenitsyn was expelled, in November 1969, from the Russian Writers' Union. Much to the irritation of the Soviet government, his work was highly acclaimed in the West, and he was awarded the

Nobel Prize in 1970. Following the 1973 publication of his novel *The Gulag Archipelago*, he was arrested. But in a sign that some concessions were being made to Western opinion, he was deported to West Germany rather than exiled to Siberia.

The European Union

The leaders of Western Europe realized almost immediately following World War II they were going to need to function as a whole in order to rival the economic and military power of the two superpowers. Throughout the second half of the twentieth century, Europe embarked on a plan of economic integration that proceeded through several careful stages:

- In 1950, France and West Germany created the French–German Coal and Steel Authority, removing tariff barriers and jointly managing production in that industry.
- In 1952, the Authority expanded to create the six-country European Coal and Steel Community, adding Italy, Belgium, Luxembourg, and the Netherlands.
- In 1957, those six countries signed the Treaty of Rome, establishing the European Economic Community (EEC), sometimes referred to as the Common Market, to begin the process of eliminating tariff barriers and cutting restrictions on the flow of capital and labor.
- In 1967, the EEC merged with other European cooperative bodies to form the European Community (EC), moving toward a broader integration of public institutions.
- Between 1967 and 1986, the EC expanded to 12 countries, adding Denmark, the United Kingdom, and the Republic of Ireland (all in 1973), Greece (in 1981), and Portugal and Spain (both in 1986).
- In 1992, the 12 countries of the EC signed the Maastricht Treaty, changing the name from the EC to European Union (EU), creating the world's largest trading bloc and moving to adopt a common currency (the Euro).
- In 1995, Austria, Finland, and Sweden joined the EU.
- Following the breakup of the Soviet Union, the EU underwent a massive expansion, welcoming countries either newly freed or newly constituted after the breakup of the Soviet Union. The addition of Cyprus, the Czech Republic, Estonia, Hungary, Latvia, Lithuania, Malta, Poland, Slovakia, and Slovenia in 2004, and Bulgaria and Romania in 2007, brought the total membership to 27 countries. The addition of Croatia in 2013 raised that total to 28.

The Disintegration of the Iron Curtain and the Soviet Union

Between 1985 and 1989, the world was stunned as it witnessed the rapid disintegration of the Soviet Union, the destruction of the Iron Curtain, and the reunification of Germany. The causes of these dramatic events were rooted in the nature of the Soviet system, which had for decades put domestic and foreign politics ahead of the needs of its own economy and of its people. The result was an economic system that could no longer function. The trigger for its disintegration was the ascension of a new generation of Soviet leaders.

Gorbachev and the "New Man"

While Western Europe was creating the EC and dreaming of economic and political power that could match those of the superpowers, the big lie of the Soviet economy was coming home to roost. In 1985, Mikhail Gorbachev succeeded a long line of aging Stalinist leaders.

At the age of 54, Gorbachev represented a younger and more sophisticated generation that had spent significant time in the West. Gorbachev believed that the Soviet Union's survival required a restructuring (*perestroika*) of both its economy and its society, and an openness (*glasnost*) to new ideas. Accordingly, Gorbachev challenged the people of the Soviet Union and its satellite countries to take on a new level of responsibility. But such an invitation quickly fanned the fires of autonomy in satellite states.

Poland and Solidarity

There had been growing agitation in Poland since 1980, when workers under the leadership of an electrician named Lech Walesa succeeded in forming a labor union known as "Solidarity." Pressured by numerous strikes, the Polish government recognized the union despite threats of Soviet intervention. By 1981, the movement had become more political, as some of Solidarity's more radical members began calling for free elections. As tensions grew, the Polish military, led by General Wojciech Jaruzelski, responded to the crisis by imposing martial law and a military dictatorship. But with Gorbachev calling for reform, Jaruzelski tried, in November 1987, to gain legitimacy for his rule through a national referendum. However, the majority of voters either voted against or abstained. In August 1988, Jaruzelski ended his military dictatorship and set up a civilian government.

The new government attempted to retain the political monopoly of the Communist Party while simultaneously opening Poland up for Western business. This proved to be impossible, and Walesa and Solidarity took advantage of the new openness to push for political freedom. In January 1989, Solidarity was legalized, and in April, the Communist Party gave up its monopoly on political power. In the first free election in Poland since before World War II, Solidarity triumphed and a noncommunist government was established in September. In December 1990, Walesa was elected president, and Poland began to face the hard task of learning how to live in an unruly democratic society and how to deal with the economic ups and downs of capitalism.

Czechoslovakia and the Velvet Revolution

Seeing Poland and Hungary (which held free elections in the summer and fall of 1989) shed their communist governments without Soviet intervention energized Czech resistance to communist rule. Student-led demonstrations in the fall of 1989 were met with the tear gas and clubs of the police, but the students were soon joined by workers and people from all walks of life. Leading dissidents, like the playwright Václav Havel, began a movement known as the Civic Forum, which sought to rebuild notions of citizenship and civic life that had been destroyed by the Soviet system. Soon Havel and other dissidents were jailed, but they became symbols of defiance and moral superiority.

What followed has come to be known as the Velvet Revolution. Faced with massive demonstrations in Prague (shown around the world on television), and urged by Gorbachev himself to institute democratic reform, Czechoslovakia's communist leaders resigned on November 24. After negotiations and maneuvers by both the Communist Party and the Civic Forum, Havel was chosen president on December 25. Alexander Dubcek, who had led the revolt of 1968, was brought home from exile and named chairman of the Czechoslovakian Parliament.

German Reunification

West Germans had never accepted the division of Germany. The constitution of the German Federal Republic provided legal formalities for reunification. How the East Germans felt about the society of their Western relatives was hard to know. When reunification came, it came suddenly. East German dissidents organized themselves along the lines of the Civic Forum model pioneered in Czechoslovakia. In response to the pressure for reform, the communist regime rescinded its traditional order to shoot anyone trying to escape to West Berlin, and shortly thereafter issued "vacation visas" to those wishing to see their families in the West. There was little expectation of their return.

On November 9, 1989, protesters moved toward the Berlin Wall, and meeting almost no resistance from the soldiers, started to hammer it down. East Germans streamed into West Berlin, where they were embraced by tearful West Germans who gleefully gave them handfuls of cash. The West German chancellor, conservative Helmut Kohl, moved quickly toward reunification. It was a reunification that amounted to East Germany being annexed by the West. Completely swept away in the pace of reunification were the original Civic Forum leaders who were not at all sure that they wished to be reunified with West Germany and its capitalist economy. Key events of the reunification included the following:

- In March 1990, elections were held in East Germany, creating a new government ready to negotiate with West Germany.
- By August 3, the official treaty of reunification was drafted.
- The East German government approved the official treaty of reunification at the beginning of October, and on October 3, 1990, the Germans celebrated Reunification Day.
- On December 2, the first unified national elections resulted in sweeping wins for Kohl, "the Reunification Chancellor," and his party.

Yugoslavia: Fragmentation

Yugoslavia had been a fragile state of six ethnically self-conscious member republics. As the communist regime began to collapse, the ethnic rivalries of Yugoslavia quickly reasserted themselves:

- Albanians in the autonomous province of Kosovo revolted against Serbian rule.
- The Slovenes and Croatians (or Croats), both western Slavs, agitated for independence from Serbia.
- In 1989, the communist regime began to collapse, and the stronger republics were moving toward independence. A fragile multiparty system was put into place.

The Soviet Union Comes Apart

Caught between the hardliners who wished to slow down reform and a population that wanted it to come faster, Gorbachev's popularity began to slip. Determined to go forward, Gorbachev persuaded the Communist Party to give up its monopoly on political power and called for free elections. Sensing collapse, Party members resigned in large numbers.

The various "republics" that made up the Soviet Union now emulated the satellite states and began to agitate for independence. Lithuania led the way, declaring the restoration of Lithuanian independence in March 1990. Others soon followed suit, including the Russian Republic, led by the charismatic deputy, Boris Yeltsin. Gorbachev was faced with a crisis. In the spring of 1991, Gorbachev proposed a compromise. He suggested that all the republics sign a Treaty of the Union, declaring them all to be independent but also members of a loose confederation. In August 1991, just as the treaty was about to take effect, hardliners tried to oust Gorbachev. For three days, there was confusion about who was in charge and what the military would do. Yeltsin seized the moment, positioning himself between the parliament building and military tanks. The military backed off and the coup attempt failed, but it was Yeltsin who was now the favorite. Gorbachev resigned late in 1991, and the Soviet Union, as the world had known it, disintegrated. Most of the republics chose to join a loose confederation known as the Commonwealth of Independent States (CIS), whereas a few, especially the Baltic states, opted for independence.

Nationalism and Globalization

Following the collapse of the Soviet Union, nationalism, which had been driven underground, again came to the surface in Eastern Europe:

- In Czechoslovakia, resurgent nationalism split the country in half, as the Slovak region split off to form the republic of Slovakia, leaving the Czechs to form the Czech Republic.
- In Azerbaijan, Azerbaijanis and Armenians fought for dominance.
- In the Russian Republic, Chechens began a guerilla war against Russian troops when their demands for independence were refused.
- In Yugoslavia, the fragile, multiparty system fell apart. Serbians and Slovenes fought over land and power; ethnic groups in Croatia, Bosnia-Herzegovina, and Macedonia followed suit as the situation degenerated into a vicious, multisided war with acts of genocide committed on both sides.

While politics in the post–Cold War era often seemed to regress, the unity of the world's economies, societies, and cultures continued to move forward. Near the end of the twentieth century, the term *globalization* became prominent to describe the increasing integration and interdependence of the economic, social, cultural, and even ecological aspects of life. The term refers not only to the way in which the economies of the world affect one another, but also to the way that the experience of everyday life is becoming increasingly standardized by the spread of technologies that carry with them social and cultural norms.

Review Questions

Multiple Choice

Questions 1–3 refer to the following passage:

In a great number of countries, far from the Russian frontiers and throughout the world, Communist fifth columns are established and work in complete unity and absolute obedience to the directions they receive from the Communist center. Except in the British Commonwealth and in the United States where Communism is in its infancy, the Communist parties or fifth columns constitute a growing challenge and peril to Christian civilization. . . .

I do not believe that Soviet Russia desires war. What they desire is the fruits of war and the indefinite expansion of their power and doctrines. But what we have to consider here today while time remains, is the permanent prevention of war and the establishment of conditions of freedom and democracy as rapidly as possible in all countries. . . . From what I have seen of our Russian friends and allies during the war, I am convinced that there is nothing they admire so much as strength, and there is nothing for which they have less respect than for weakness, especially military weakness. For that reason the old doctrine of a balance of power is unsound.

Winston S. Churchill, "Iron Curtain" speech, March 5, 1946

1. From the passage, one may infer that Churchill believed that
   A. communism was an immediate threat in the United States
   B. the Russian frontier was in danger of falling to communist forces
   C. communists in European countries were obedient to the communist government of the Soviet Union
   D. communism posed a growing challenge to Asia

2. From the passage, one may infer that Churchill thought the goal of the Soviet Union was
   A. the expansion of its power and influence wherever possible
   B. a global revolution of the proletariat
   C. a third world war
   D. control of all of Asia
3. From the passage, one may infer that Churchill argued that
   A. a third world war was inevitable
   B. securing the rule of democratic governments in Europe required a strong military presence throughout Europe
   C. a balance of power must be created between the West and the Soviet Union
   D. the United States should join the British Commonwealth in order to prevent the spread of communism

Short Answer

4. Briefly explain TWO ways in which people were able to reconstruct civic life in the police-states that had been formed under Soviet-style communism, and illustrate each with an example.

Answers and Explanations

1. **C** is correct because the passage states the belief that "Communist fifth columns are established and work in complete unity and absolute obedience to the directions they receive from the Communist center" (that is, the Soviet Union). A is incorrect because the passage states that communism was "in its infancy" in the United States. B is incorrect because the Russian frontier was already a part of the Soviet Union at the time of the speech, and because the reference in the passage is to places *far from* the Russian frontier. D is incorrect because the passage states that communism posed a growing threat "to Christian civilization," that is, to Europe and the United States.

2. **A** is correct because the passage states Churchill's belief that the government of the Soviet Union wanted "the indefinite expansion of their power and doctrines." B is incorrect because the passage makes no mention of a global revolution of the proletariat. C is incorrect because the passage says that Churchill does *not* believe that the Soviet Union wants war. D is incorrect because the passage makes no mention of Asia.

3. **B** is correct because the passage implies that military weakness would encourage the expansionist aims of the Soviet Union. A is incorrect because the passage does not refer to the inevitability of war. C is incorrect because the passage states Churchill's belief that "the old doctrine of a balance of power is unsound." D is incorrect because the passage does not urge the United States to join the British Commonwealth.

4. Suggested answer:

   Thesis: During the 1980s, people within the police-states of Soviet-dominated Eastern Europe were able to reconstruct spaces for normal civic life in several ways, including the development and expansion of a labor union movement and the development of "civic forums."

   Paragraph Outline:

   I. In Poland in the 1980s, workers under the leadership of an electrician named Lech Walesa succeeded in forming a labor union known as Solidarity. Pressured by numerous strikes, the Polish government recognized the union despite threats of Soviet intervention.

II. In Czechoslovakia in the 1980s, people from all walks of life created a movement that became known as the Civic Forum, which, by commandeering public spaces like libraries and churches for town meetings, began to rebuild notions of citizenship and civic life that had been destroyed by the Soviet system.

Rapid Review

Following World War II, the Soviet Union solidified its control of Eastern Europe, creating an "Iron Curtain" that divided East from West. The two superpowers, the United States and the Soviet Union, engaged in a conflict, called the Cold War, which had global implications. The advent of nuclear weapons forced Japan's unconditional surrender but subsequently created a nuclear arms race between the United States and the Soviet Union. Meanwhile, Western European nations followed a course of economic integration that culminated in the creation of the European Union. Between 1985 and 1989, systemic economic problems and a bold attempt at reform led to the rapid disintegration of the Soviet Union, the destruction of the Iron Curtain, and the reunification of Germany. In the decades that followed, two major trends affected life in Europe: the revival of nationalism and the emergence of globalization.

STEP **5**

Build Your Test-Taking Confidence

AP European History
Practice Test 1—Section I

ANSWER SHEET

1 (A) (B) (C) (D)
2 (A) (B) (C) (D)
3 (A) (B) (C) (D)
4 (A) (B) (C) (D)
5 (A) (B) (C) (D)
6 (A) (B) (C) (D)
7 (A) (B) (C) (D)
8 (A) (B) (C) (D)
9 (A) (B) (C) (D)
10 (A) (B) (C) (D)
11 (A) (B) (C) (D)
12 (A) (B) (C) (D)
13 (A) (B) (C) (D)
14 (A) (B) (C) (D)
15 (A) (B) (C) (D)
16 (A) (B) (C) (D)
17 (A) (B) (C) (D)
18 (A) (B) (C) (D)
19 (A) (B) (C) (D)

20 (A) (B) (C) (D)
21 (A) (B) (C) (D)
22 (A) (B) (C) (D)
23 (A) (B) (C) (D)
24 (A) (B) (C) (D)
25 (A) (B) (C) (D)
26 (A) (B) (C) (D)
27 (A) (B) (C) (D)
28 (A) (B) (C) (D)
29 (A) (B) (C) (D)
30 (A) (B) (C) (D)
31 (A) (B) (C) (D)
32 (A) (B) (C) (D)
33 (A) (B) (C) (D)
34 (A) (B) (C) (D)
35 (A) (B) (C) (D)
36 (A) (B) (C) (D)
37 (A) (B) (C) (D)
38 (A) (B) (C) (D)

39 (A) (B) (C) (D)
40 (A) (B) (C) (D)
41 (A) (B) (C) (D)
42 (A) (B) (C) (D)
43 (A) (B) (C) (D)
44 (A) (B) (C) (D)
45 (A) (B) (C) (D)
46 (A) (B) (C) (D)
47 (A) (B) (C) (D)
48 (A) (B) (C) (D)
49 (A) (B) (C) (D)
50 (A) (B) (C) (D)
51 (A) (B) (C) (D)
52 (A) (B) (C) (D)
53 (A) (B) (C) (D)
54 (A) (B) (C) (D)
55 (A) (B) (C) (D)

AP European History Practice Test 1 Exam:
Section I
(Multiple-Choice)

Directions: The multiple-choice section consists of 55 questions to be answered in **55 minutes**. The sets of questions below refer to the attached primary source, secondary source, or historical issue. For each question, select the one answer that best answers or completes the question and fill in the letter that corresponds to your choice on the answer sheet supplied.

Questions 1–3 relate to the following passage:

At last it seems to me that I have come to understand why man is the most fortunate of all creatures and consequently worthy of all admiration. . . . The nature of all other beings is limited. . . . Imagine! The great generosity of God! The happiness of man! To man it is allowed to be whatever he chooses to be!

Pico della Mirandola, *Oration on the Dignity of Man*, 1486

1. From the passage, one may infer that Pico was participating in which cultural movement?

   A. The Renaissance
   B. The Reformation
   C. The Scientific Revolution
   D. The Enlightenment

2. From the passage, one may infer that Pico believed that humankind was unique because

   A. human beings have a soul
   B. human beings know that they will die
   C. it is possible for human beings to go to heaven
   D. the potential of the human being is unlimited

3. From the passage, one may infer that Pico rejected the notion

   A. that man was a unique kind of creature
   B. that God intended man to strive to achieve
   C. that man is unworthy of admiration
   D. that humans are God's equals

Questions 4–6 relate to the following petition:

The Scribbling-Machines have thrown thousands of your petitioners out of employ, whereby they are brought into great distress, and are not able to procure a maintenance for their families, and deprived them of the opportunity of bringing up their children to labour. . . . The number of Scribbling-Machines extending about seventeen miles south-west of Leeds exceed all belief, being no less than *one hundred and seventy!* And as each machine will do as much work in twelve hours, as ten men can in that time do by hand, . . . [And, as the machines do] as much work in one day as would otherwise employ twenty men, . . . [a] full four thousand men are left to shift for a living how they can, and must of course fall to the Parish, if not timely relieved. . . . How are those men, thus thrown out of employ to provide for their families; and what are they to put their children apprentice to, that the rising generation may have something to keep them at work, in order that they may not be like vagabonds strolling about in idleness? . . . Many more evils we could enumerate, but we would hope, that the sensible part of mankind, who are not biased by interest, must see the dreadful tendency of their continuance; a depopulation must be the consequence; trade being then lost, the landed interest will have no other satisfaction but that of being *last devoured*.

Leeds Woolen Workers Petition, 1786

4. This document can be used as evidence for

   A. the spread of revolutionary ideas among the British working class in the eighteenth century
   B. the rise of the Luddite movement in Britain in the eighteenth century
   C. the replacing of traditional laborers by machines in the industrialization of Britain in the eighteenth century
   D. an increase in the use of child labor in eighteenth-century Britain

5. The sentiments expressed by the Leeds woolen workers illustrate which of the following historical trends?

   A. The social effects of industrialization
   B. The rise of nationalism
   C. Imperial expansion
   D. Cultural changes in a material age

6. The authors of this document made which of the following assumptions?

   A. The introduction of machines did not increase economic productivity.
   B. The economic well-being of the city and region was tied to its inhabitants having employment.
   C. Having large families was economically advantageous.
   D. The working class was lazy and tended toward idleness.

Questions 7–9 relate to the following excerpt from a poem:

Take up the White Man's burden—
Send forth the best ye breed—
Go bind your sons to exile
To serve your captives' need;
To wait in heavy harness,
On fluttered folk and wild—
Your new-caught, sullen peoples,
Half-devil and half-child.

…

Take up the White Man's burden—
The savage wars of peace—
Fill full the mouth of Famine
And bid the sickness cease;
And when your goal is nearest
The end for others sought…
Watch sloth and heathen Folly
Bring all your hopes to naught.

Rudyard Kipling, *The White Man's Burden*, 1899

7. Based on this poem, Kipling's conception of the British imperial mission could best be summed up as
   A. a difficult but necessary task
   B. a ruthless exercise of power
   C. a glorious, religious responsibility
   D. a hopeless task with no purpose

8. The poem describes which kind of attitude toward the native peoples who were under the rule or influence of the British Empire?

   A. They are "exiled sons" of the British race.
   B. While "savage," they fight wars for the sake of a lasting peace.
   C. They are ready for conversion to Christianity.
   D. They are the product of a less-civilized and less-developed civilization.

9. It is generally acknowledged that Kipling fashioned *White Man's Burden* to address the subject of the American colonization of the Philippines, which the United States had recently won from Spain in the Spanish-American War. With that information in mind, what message can Kipling be said to be offering the Americans in this excerpt?

   A. A reminder of the responsibility of advanced civilizations to bring the benefits of modern civilization to less-developed peoples
   B. A warning to avoid the war and hardships of imperialism
   C. An exhortation to Christianize the heathen peoples of the world
   D. An ironic presentation of the sheer folly of imperialism

Questions 10–12 refer to the engraving below:

William Hogarth, *Marriage à la Mode (The Marriage Contract), Plate 1*, 1745

10. The scene depicted in the engraving refers to which manifestation of social change in the eighteenth century?

   A. The marriage of older men to younger women
   B. The liquidation of art collections by a cash-poor aristocracy
   C. The combining, through marriage, of aristocratic status and bourgeois wealth
   D. The movement to allow Protestant churchmen to marry

11. The engraving is an example of which of the following developments in eighteenth-century art?

   A. Artists' abandonment of realistic representation
   B. Artists' criticism of social practices through satire
   C. Artists' creation of flattering portraits for rich patrons
   D. The continued development of landscape

12. Which of the following is an accurate summation of the kind of commentary Hogarth was attempting?

   A. The practice of selling art to foreigners leads to cultural bankruptcy.
   B. The practice of painting flattering portraits of the rich will be the death of true art.
   C. The practice of economically motivated marriages of convenience is morally repugnant and bound to bring misery.
   D. The marrying of aristocratic status to bourgeois wealth will solidify the future of the realm.

Questions 13–14 refer to the following quotation:

The various modes of worship which prevailed in the Roman world were all considered by the people as equally true; by the philosopher as equally false; and by the magistrate as equally useful.

Edward Gibbon, *The Decline and Fall of the Roman Empire*, 1776–1788

13. The interpretation of the state of religious belief in ancient Rome by the eighteenth-century English historian Edward Gibbon might be offered as evidence for

   A. the clergy's monopoly on academic scholarship in eighteenth-century Britain
   B. the hatred of all things Roman by British scholars in the eighteenth century
   C. the spread of religious skepticism among the educated elite of Britain in the eighteenth century
   D. the lack of sources available to the eighteenth-century scholar for the study of ancient Roman civilization

14. Gibbon's interpretation of the state of religious worship in ancient Rome could be summarized as

   A. In ancient Rome, religious worship was decentralized and tended to vary with one's social position.
   B. In ancient Rome, religious worship was the source of much social tension and turmoil.
   C. In ancient Rome, religious worship was homogeneous and highly centralized.
   D. In ancient Rome, religious worship was revolutionized by the introduction of Christianity.

Questions 15–17 refer to the following map:

15. The map above was constructed by drawing a thin line for each voyage recorded in British trade ship logs between 1750 and 1800. As a result, the darker shaded areas record the most heavily travelled routes. Which of the following conclusions could be drawn from the evidence provided by this map?

    A. British ships did not sail along the west coast of Africa during this period.
    B. British ships did not sail the Atlantic Ocean during this period.
    C. British ships did not sail the Pacific Ocean during this period.
    D. British ships did not sail in the Indian Ocean during this period.

16. The information provided by the map could be used as evidence to support which of the following assertions?

    A. British ships frequented a northwest passage through North American waters into the Pacific Ocean.
    B. China was a frequent destination of British trade ships.
    C. British trade ships frequented the Mediterranean Sea during this period.
    D. A Triangle of Trade connected Britain, North America, and the west coast of Africa.

17. The information provided by the map could be used as evidence to support which of the following assertions?

    A. British trade ships of this period reached trade ports in India by sailing southward around the horn of Africa and into the Indian Ocean.
    B. British trade ships of this period transported slaves from western Africa to the New World.
    C. British trade ships of this period reached India by sailing west through the Mediterranean Sea and through the Suez Canal into the Indian Ocean.
    D. British trade ships of this period did not travel to India.

Questions 18–20 refer to the following passage:

The history of all hitherto existing societies is the history of class struggles. . . . The modern bourgeois society that has sprouted from the ruins of feudal society has not done away with class antagonisms. It has but established new classes, new conditions of oppression, new forms of struggle in place of the old ones. Our epoch, the epoch of the bourgeoisie, possesses, however, this distinctive feature: it has simplified the class antagonisms. Society as a whole is more and more splitting up into two great hostile camps, into two great classes, directly facing each other: Bourgeoisie and Proletariat.

Karl Marx and Friedrich Engels, The Communist Manifesto, 1848

18. Marx and Engels would be most inclined to view which of the following developments as a significant event in European history?

    A. The War of the Roses
    B. The French Revolution of 1789 to 1793
    C. The Seven Years' War
    D. Britain's Glorious Revolution of 1688

19. *The Communist Manifesto* can be understood as an example of the influence of which mode of modern European thinking?

    A. The Oxford Movement
    B. Materialism and economic determinism
    C. Hegelian idealism
    D. The rationalism of the Scottish Enlightenment

20. A follower of Marx and Engels's view of history would argue that an all-out war between the bourgeoisie and the proletariat classes was

    A. a destructive development that could be avoided through the study of philosophy
    B. a possibility which should be encouraged in order to foster progress
    C. an inevitable result of fundamental economic change
    D. an example of history repeating itself

Questions 21–23 refer to the following quotation:

1848 was the decisive year of German, and so of European, history: it recapitulated Germany's past and inspired Germany's future. . . . Never has there been a revolution so inspired by a limitless faith in the power of ideas; never has a revolution so discredited the power of ideas in its result. The success of the revolution discredited conservative ideas; the failure of the revolution discredited liberal ideas. After it, nothing remained but the idea of Force, and this idea stood at the helm of German history from then on. For the first time since 1521, the German people stepped on to the centre of the German stage only to miss their cue once more. German history reached its turning-point and failed to turn. This was the fateful essence of 1848.

A. J. P. Taylor, The Course of German History, 1945

21. The subject of Taylor's analysis in this quotation is

    A. the industrial revolution in the context of German history
    B. the failure of the revolutions of 1848
    C. the rise of the Nazi Party in Germany
    D. the importance of the revolutions of 1848 in modern German history

22. From the quotation, one may infer that Taylor argues that the most important effect of the political revolutions of 1848 was

    A. the failure to bring about a change in the ruling class
    B. the demonstration of the power of ideas
    C. the discrediting of both conservative and liberal political ideology
    D. the creation of the idea of a modern police force

23. Why might it be important to note that Taylor was writing his analysis in 1945?

    A. A historian writing at the end of World War II might be inclined to look for, and find, the origins of perceived German belligerence.
    B. A historian writing in 1945 would be dead now, and therefore, his analysis is irrelevant.
    C. Historical analysis written in 1945 is "out of date," and one should look for a more recent book.
    D. A historian writing at the end of World War II would be looking for the origins of the Cold War.

Questions 24–26 refer to the following passage:

Perestroika [Restructuring] is an urgent necessity arising from the profound processes of development in our socialist society. This society is ripe for change. It has long been yearning for it. Any delay in beginning *perestroika* could have led to an exacerbated internal situation in the near future, which, to put it bluntly, would have been fraught with serious social, economic, and political crises.

Mikhail Gorbachev, *Perestroika: New Thinking for Our Country and the World,* 1987

24. From the passage, one may infer that Gorbachev argued that

    A. a restructuring of the socialist society of the Soviet Union was inevitable
    B. a restructuring of the socialist society of the Soviet Union would exacerbate the current situation
    C. a restructuring of the socialist society of the Soviet Union was necessary in order to avoid a crisis
    D. a restructuring of socialist society was necessary in order to avoid the collapse of the Soviet Union

25. From the passage, one may infer that Gorbachev believed that

    A. the problems that required *perestroika* were the fault of capitalist enemies of socialism
    B. the problems that required *perestroika* were internal to the development of socialist society
    C. a socialist society could not work
    D. a socialist society could not coexist with capitalism

26. From the passage, one may infer that Gorbachev argued that

    A. the need for *perestroika* had come upon Soviet society suddenly
    B. the need for *perestroika* had been exaggerated
    C. the need for *perestroika* was long in the making
    D. the time for *perestroika* had passed

Questions 27–29 refer to the following passage:

"It's come! It's posted at the district mayor's office," a passerby shouted at me as he ran. I reached the *Rue Drout* in one leap. . . . I read the message at a glance. . . . "The First Day of Mobilization Will Be Sunday, August 2 [1914]." . . . It was an announcement to a million and a half Frenchmen. . . . War! . . . Dead tired but exhilarated, I got back to [my newspaper's office] and burst into the office of Georges Clemenceau, our chief. "What is Paris saying?" he asked me. "It's singing, sir!" "It will be all right then[," Clemenceau replied].

Roland Doregelès, *After 50 Years*, c. 1965

27. From the passage, one may infer that Doregelès recalled that

   A. mobilization for war in 1914 was greeted with great skepticism in Paris
   B. mobilization for war in 1914 was greeted with great skepticism all across Europe
   C. mobilization for war in 1914 was greeted with great enthusiasm all across Europe
   D. mobilization for war in 1914 was greeted with great enthusiasm in Paris

28. From the passage, one may infer that Doregelès

   A. shared Paris's excitement about the advent of war
   B. was disgusted that his city should be excited about the advent of war
   C. was frightened that his city should be excited about the advent of war
   D. had grave doubts about France's ability to win the coming war

29. From the passage, one may infer that Clemenceau

   A. was disgusted to hear that Paris was reacting with joy at the advent of war
   B. had grave doubts about France's ability to win a war against Germany
   C. would one day serve as prime minister of France
   D. was relieved to hear that Paris was reacting with joy at the advent of war

Questions 30–31 refer to the following passage:

For the catastrophe of 1914 the Germans are responsible. . . . Germany, in this matter, was unfortunate enough to allow herself (in spite of her skill at dissimulation) to be betrayed into an excess of candour by her characteristic tendency to go to extremes. *Deutschland über alles. Germany above everything!* . . . There you have the ultimate framework of an old but childish race.

Georges Clemenceau, *Grandeur and Misery of Victory*, 1930

30. From the passage, one may infer that Clemenceau

   A. blamed Germany for the Great Depression
   B. blamed Germany for World War I
   C. blamed Germany for World War II
   D. blamed Germany for the Franco-Prussian War

31. From the passage, one may infer that Clemenceau believed

   A. that the lyrics from the popular song *Deutschland über alles* (which eventually became the German national anthem) were the reason Germany started the war
   B. that the lyrics from the popular song *Deutschland über alles* (which eventually became the German national anthem) were evidence of Germany's aggressive attitude
   C. that the reason Germany lost the war was that it was betrayed from within
   D. that Germany provided the ultimate framework for modern warfare

Questions 32–33 refer to the following quotation:

What is tolerance? . . . We are full of weakness and errors; let us mutually pardon our follies. This is the last law of nature. . . . Of all religions, the Christian ought doubtless to inspire the most tolerance, although hitherto the Christians have been the most intolerant of all men.

Voltaire, *Letters on the English Nation*, 1733

32. From the passage, one may infer that Voltaire was participating in what cultural movement?

    A. The Scientific Revolution
    B. The Reformation
    C. The Enlightenment
    D. The Romantic Movement

33. From the quotation, one can infer that

    A. Voltaire was an atheist
    B. tolerance was a value of the Enlightenment
    C. Voltaire believed tolerance violated the laws of nature
    D. Voltaire believed tolerance was uniquely English

Questions 34–36 refer to the following passage:

For a long time, educated Germans answered it in the positive, initially by laying claim to a special German mission, then, after the collapse of 1945, by criticizing Germany's deviation from the West. Today, the negative view is predominant. Germany did not, according to the now prevailing opinion, differ from the great European nations to an extent that would justify speaking of a "unique German path." And, in any case, no country on earth ever took what can be described as the "normal path."

Heinrich August Winkler, *Germany: The Long Road West*, Volume 1, 2006

34. From this passage, one may infer that

    A. the notion of a unique German path in history has never been the prevailing public opinion in Germany
    B. Winkler advocates a Marxist view of German history
    C. there has been a longstanding debate in Germany about the existence of a unique German path in history
    D. the question of a unique German path in history has been answered once and for all

35. From this passage, one may infer that, prior to 1945,

    A. there was significant belief in a unique German mission in history
    B. almost no one believed in a unique German mission in history
    C. the historian Heinrich August Winkler argued that there was a unique German mission in history
    D. the historian Heinrich August Winkler opposed the notion that there was a unique German mission in history

36. From this passage, one may infer that the belief that Germany had a unique mission in history

    A. resulted from Germany's defeat in World War II
    B. was unaffected by Germany's defeat in World War II
    C. was proven correct by Germany's defeat in World War II
    D. was discredited by Germany's defeat in World War II

Questions 37–39 refer to the following poster from Great Britain during World War II:

37. From the poster, one may infer that

   A. the wartime needs of Britain led to the conscription of women into the military
   B. the wartime economy of Britain required women to do factory work
   C. women working in factories with men led to social change in Britain
   D. wartime needs led to women joining the industrial workforce of Great Britain for the first time

38. From the poster, one may infer that

   A. women were put in charge of factories in Great Britain during World War II
   B. women made up a significant portion of the British military during World War II
   C. women were happy to join the industrial workforce in Great Britain during World War II
   D. women were involved in the production of munitions during World War II

39. From the poster, one may infer that some propaganda in Great Britain during World War II

   A. focused predominately on minority groups
   B. had the same goals as German propaganda
   C. aimed at making women feel like they were an important part of the war effort
   D. gave an unrealistic picture of the opportunities open to women

Questions 40–42 refer to the following passage:

Having by our late labours and hazards made it appear to the world how high a rate we value our freedom, and God having so far owned our cause, as to deliver the enemies thereof into our hands: We do now hold ourselves bound in mutual duty to each other, to take the best care we can for the future, to avoid both the danger of returning into a slavish condition, and the chargeable remedy of another war. . . . In order whereunto we declare:

1. That matters of Religion, and the ways of God's worship are not at all entrusted by us to any human power . . .

2. That the matter of [compelling] and constraining any of us to serve in the wars is against our freedom . . .

3. That in all laws made, or to be made, every person may be bound alike. . . .

Leveller Army Officers, *An Agreement of the People*, 1647

40. From the passage, one may infer that the authors of the passage recently fought in

 A. the Seven Years' War
 B. the American War for Independence
 C. the English Civil War
 D. the Battle of Agincourt

41. From the passage, one may infer that the authors of the passage

 A. fought for religious freedom
 B. defended the monarchy in the English Civil War
 C. fought to establish a republic
 D. fought for independence from England

42. From the passage, one may infer that the authors of the passage

 A. meant to form a ruling body of England
 B. meant to establish equality under the law in England
 C. were demanding an end to hostilities
 D. were slaves demanding their freedom

Questions 43–45 refer to the following passage:

We have, by this perpetual and irrevocable edict, established and proclaimed:

"First, that the recollection of everything done be one party or the other . . . during all the preceding period of troubles, remain obliterated and forgotten, as if no such things had ever happened. . . .

"We ordain that the Catholic Apostolic and Roman religion shall be restored and reestablished in all places and localities of this our kingdom and countries subject to our sway, where the exercise of the same has been interrupted, in order that it may be peaceably and freely exercised, without any trouble or hindrance. . . .

"And in order to leave no occasion for troubles or differences between our subjects, we have permitted, and herewith permit, those of the said religion called Reformed to live and abide in all the cities and places of this our kingdom and countries of our sway, and without being annoyed, molested, or compelled to do anything in the matter of religion contrary to their consciences. . . ."

Henry IV of France, *The Edict of Nantes,* 1598

43. From the passage, one may infer that

    A. Henry IV was a Catholic
    B. Henry IV was a Protestant
    C. prior to 1598, France had been free of religious conflict
    D. prior to 1598, France was stricken with religious conflict

44. From the passage, one may infer that Henry IV decided

    A. to ban the Catholic Church in France
    B. that the Catholic Church should exist in France
    C. that the Catholic Church is the one true Church
    D. that the Catholic Church caused too much trouble and hindrance in France

45. From the passage, one may infer that Henry IV

    A. was banning Protestants from France
    B. intended for Protestants to be able to live peacefully in his kingdom
    C. was converting to Catholicism
    D. was converting to Protestantism

Questions 46–48 refer to the following passage:

The assumption by a government of the office of Reliever-general to the poor is necessarily forbidden by the principle that a government cannot rightly do anything more than protect. In demanding from a citizen contributions for the mitigation of distress . . . the state is . . . reversing its function. . . . To enforce the fundamental law—to take care that every man has freedom to do all that he wills, provided he infringes not the equal freedom of any other man. . . . [But that] is quite a separate thing from insuring him satisfaction. . . .

 The poverty of the incapable, the distresses that come upon the imprudent, the starvation of the idle, and those shoulderings aside of the weak by the strong . . . are the decrees of a large, farseeing benevolence. . . . When regarded not separately, but in connection with the interests of universal humanity, these harsh fatalities are seen to be full of the highest beneficence.

Herbert Spencer, *Social Statistics: Survival of the Fittest Applied to Humankind*, 1851

46. From the passage, one may infer that Spencer was an advocate of which nineteenth-century political philosophy?

    A. Conservatism
    B. Anarchism
    C. Liberalism
    D. Socialism

47. From the passage, one may infer that Spencer

    A. opposed the use of tax money to provide aid to the poor
    B. challenged the government's right to tax the people
    C. believed that the government should do more than merely protect its people
    D. believed that working people should unite for a common cause

48. From the passage, one may infer that Spencer advocated which social philosophy?

    A. Utopian socialism
    B. Social conservatism
    C. Romanticism
    D. Social Darwinism

Questions 49–52 refer to the following passage:

The principle which regulates the existing social relations between the two sexes—the legal subordination of one sex to the other—is wrong in itself, and now one of the chief hindrances to human improvement. . . . The masters of all other slaves rely, for maintaining obedience on fear. . . . The masters of women wanted more than simple obedience, and they turned their whole force of education to effect their purpose. All women are brought up from the very earliest years in the belief that their ideal of character is the very opposite of that of men; not self-will and government by self-control, but submission and yielding to the control of others. . . . If the general principle of social and economic science is . . . true, we ought to act as if we believed it, and not to ordain that to be born a girl instead of a boy . . . shall decide the person's position through all life."

John Stuart Mill, *The Subjection of Women*, 1869

49. From the passage, one may infer that Mill was an advocate of which nineteenth-century political philosophy?

    A. Socialism
    B. Conservatism
    C. Anarchism
    D. Liberalism

50. From the passage, one may infer that Mill advocated

    A. the abolition of slavery
    B. the maintenance of a patriarchal social organization
    C. the reform of women's education
    D. an end to arranged marriages

51. From the passage one may infer that Mill sub-scribed to which view of human nature?

    A. People are born evil and corrupt.
    B. People are generally good and will do the right thing most times.
    C. Men and women have natures that are sub-stantially different from one another.
    D. People are born *tabula rasa*—a blank slate.

52. From the passage, one may infer that Mill advocated

    A. the abolition of marriage
    B. equal opportunity for women
    C. social engineering of a better society
    D. social Darwinism

Questions 53–55 refer to the following passage:

As with a Commander of the Army, or leader of any enterprise, so it is with the mistress of the house. Her spirit will be seen through the whole establishment; and just in proportion as she performs her duties intelligently and thor-oughly, so will her domestics follow in her path. Of all of those acquirements, which more particularly belong to the feminine character, there are none which take a higher rank, in our estimation, than such as enter into a knowledge of household duties; for on these are perpetually dependent the happiness, comfort, and well-being of the family.

Isabella Beeton, *Book of Household Management*, 1861

53. From the passage, one may infer that the subject of Beeton's book was

    A. the role of women in army regiments
    B. the running of a school for domestic servants
    C. the running of a school for girls
    D. the role of a woman in running her own domestic household

54. From the passage, one may infer that Beeton believed that

    A. women were better suited than men for the task of household management
    B. women were better suited than men to run schools
    C. men were better suited than women for the task of household management
    D. men were better suited than women to run schools

55. From the passage, one may infer that Beeton believed that

    A. women held considerable power and respon-sibility in the public sphere of social life
    B. women were denied power and responsibility in the public sphere of social life
    C. women held considerable power and respon-sibility within the domestic sphere of social life
    D. women were denied power and responsibil-ity within the domestic sphere of social life

AP European History Practice Test 1 Exam:
Section II
(Short-Answer)

Directions: The short-answer section consists of four questions to be answered in **45 minutes**. Briefly answer all parts of the following four questions.

1. Briefly explain TWO ways in which the Scientific Revolution had an impact on European intellectual culture.

2. Answer Parts A, B, and C.

   A) Briefly explain ONE similarity between the French Revolution (1789–1799) and the Russian Revolution (1917–1924).

   B) Briefly explain ONE difference between the French Revolution (1789–1799) and the Russian Revolution (1917–1924).

   C) Briefly analyze ONE factor that accounts for the difference you identified in part B.

3. Answer Parts A and B.

   A) Briefly explain ONE aspect of the Romantic Movement.

   B) Briefly explain TWO reasons for the rise of the Romantic Movement.

Question 4 is based on the following passage:

It is a truth which admits not a doubt, that the comforts and well-being of the poor cannot be permanently secured without some regard on their part, or some effort on the part of the legislature, to regulate the increase of their numbers, and to render less frequent among them early and improvident marriages. The operation of the system of poor laws has been indirectly contrary to this. They have rendered restraint superfluous, and have invited imprudence, by offering it a portion of the wages of prudence and industry.

David Ricardo, *Principles of Political Economy and Taxation*, 1817

4. Answer Parts A and B.

   A) Briefly explain ONE reason that the passage can be identified with classical liberalism.

   B) Briefly describe TWO factors that explain the rise to prominence of classical liberalism at the time at which the passage was written.

AP European History Practice Test 1 Exam:
Section III
(Document-Based)

Directions: The document-based section consists of one question to be answered in **60 minutes**. The following question is based on documents 1–7 provided below. (The documents have been edited for the purpose of this exercise.) The historical thinking skills that this question is designed to test include contextualization, synthesis, historical argumentation, and the use of historical evidence. Your response should be based on your knowledge of the topic and your analysis of the documents.

Write a well-integrated essay that does the following:

- States an appropriate thesis that addresses all parts of the question
- Supports that thesis with evidence from at least six of the seven documents and your knowledge of European history beyond these documents
- Analyzes most of the documents in terms of their purpose, point of view, argument, limitations, format, intended audience, and/or social context
- Places your argument in the context of appropriate broader regional, national, or global developments

Question: Compare and contrast the ideologies presented below concerning the proper form and role of government in society.

Document 1

Source: Samuel Smiles, *Self-Help*, 1859

"Even the best institutions can give man no active aid. Perhaps the utmost they can do is to leave him free to develop himself and improve his individual condition. But in all times men have been prone to believe that their happiness and well-being were to be secured by means of institutions rather than by their own conduct. Hence the value of legislation as an agent in human advancement has always been greatly over-estimated."

Document 2

Source: Joseph de Maistre, *Essay on the Generative Principle of Political Constitutions*, 1809

"One of the greatest errors of a century which professed them all was to believe that a political constitution could be created and written *a priori*, whereas reason and experience unite in proving that a constitution is a divine work and that precisely the most fundamental and essentially constitutional of a nation's laws could not possibly be written."

Document 3

Source: John Stuart Mill, *On Liberty*, 1859

". . . [T]he sole end for which mankind are warranted, individually or collectively, in interfering with the liberty of action of any of their number, is self-protection. That the only purpose for which power can be rightfully exercised over any member of a civilised community, against his will, is to prevent harm to others."

Document 4

Source: Prince Clement von Metternich, secret memorandum to Emperor Alexander I of Russia, 1820

"Presumption makes of every man the guide of his own belief, the arbiter of laws according to which he is pleased to govern himself, or to allow someone else to govern him and his neighbors; it makes him, in short, the sole judge of his own faith, his actions and the principles according to which he guides them. . . . Placed beyond the passions which agitate society, it is in the days of trial chiefly that [monarchs] are called upon to despoil realities of their false appearances, and to show themselves as they are, fathers invested with the authority belonging by right to the heads of families, to prove that, in the days of mourning, they know how to be just, wise, and therefore strong, and that they will not abandon the people whom they ought to govern to be the sport of factions, to error and it consequences, which must involve the loss of society."

Document 5

Source: Karl Marx and Friedrich Engels, *The Communist Manifesto*, 1848

"The proletariat will use its political supremacy to wrest, by degrees, all capital from the bourgeoisie, to centralize all instruments of production in the hands of the State, i.e., of the proletariat organized as the ruling class; and to increase the total productive forces as rapidly as possible."

Document 6

Source: Eduard Bernstein, *Evolutionary Socialism*, 1909

"I set myself against the notion that we have to expect shortly a collapse of the bourgeois economy, and that social democracy should be induced by the prospect of such an imminent, great, social catastrophe to adapt its tactics to that assumption. . . . [T]he conquest of political power necessitates the possession of political rights; and the most important problem of tactics which German social democracy has at this moment to solve, appears to me to be to devise the best way for the extension of the political and economic rights of the German working classes."

Document 7

Source: Peter Kropotkin, *Anarchism: Its Philosophy and Ideal*, 1898

"When we ask for the abolition of the State and its organs we are always told that we dream of a society composed of men better than they are in reality. But no; a thousand times no. All we ask is that men should not be made worse than they are."

AP European History Practice Test 1 Exam:
Section IV
(Long-Essay)

Directions: The long essay section consists of one question to be answered in **35 minutes**. Write an essay that responds to ONE of the following two questions.

Question 1: Analyze the major social effects of the Industrial Revolution.

Question 2: Explain the ways in which the development of mass politics contributed to the New Imperialism of the late nineteenth century.

Answers and Explanations for AP European History Practice Test 1

Section I: Multiple-Choice Questions

1. **A.** The reference to the pride and confidence in the abilities of man and the date of publication both tell you that this is a passage from a Renaissance thinker. B is incorrect because such pride would be frowned upon by advocates of the Protestant Reformation. C is incorrect because the passage does not refer to knowledge about the natural world and because the Scientific Revolution was a seventeenth-century phenomenon. D is incorrect because the Enlightenment was an eighteenth-century development.

2. **D.** The passage says that humans are the most fortunate creatures because, unlike other creatures whose nature is limited, a man is "allowed to be whatever he chooses to be!" A is incorrect because the passage does not mention a soul. B is incorrect because the passage does not mention man's foreknowledge of death. C is incorrect because the passage does not mention heaven.

3. **C.** The passage explicitly says that man is worthy of admiration, thus one can easily infer that Pico rejects the notion that man is *un*worthy of admiration. A is incorrect because the passage states that man alone has an unlimited potential; thus, one may infer that Pico accepts, rather than rejects, the notion that man is unique. B is incorrect because one may infer from the passage that God, having given man an unlimited nature, intended him to strive to achieve, and because striving to achieve is a value of Renaissance humanists like Pico. D is incorrect because one cannot infer anything from the passage about humans' ability to become the equal of God.

4. **C.** The petitioners are clearly objecting to the elimination of their traditional laboring jobs by the introduction of machines. A is incorrect because the petitioners are asking for a return to *traditional* modes of work. B is incorrect because there is no evidence in this document that the Leeds woolen workers were resorting to the violent destruction of machines that characterized the Luddite movement. D is incorrect because there is no evidence in the document for an increase in the use of child labor; rather, the document expresses concern about the loss of apprenticeship opportunities.

5. **A.** The replacing of workers and traditional labor techniques by machines was a prominent social effect of industrialization. B is incorrect because the document makes no reference to nationalist concerns. C is incorrect because the document makes no reference to the empire or its expansion. D is incorrect because the concerns of the document are about a specific social effect—the elimination of jobs, not broader cultural issues.

6. **B.** The document makes the argument that unemployment would lead to the depopulation of the region, which in turn would cause the collapse of the local economy. A is incorrect because the document explicitly acknowledges that productivity is increased by the introduction of machines. C is incorrect because the document makes no reference to the size of families. D is incorrect because the document is an appeal for continued work and mentions "idleness" only as an undesirable outcome of unemployment.

7. **A.** The metaphor of a burden and images of a "heavy harness" and "savage wars of peace" all indicate difficult but necessary work. B is incorrect because none of the images in the poem implies ruthlessness. C is incorrect because the excerpt contains no images that are glorious or religious. D is incorrect because, though the excerpt does refer to hopes coming to naught, the overall theme of a burden implies an important purpose that justifies the effort.

8. **D.** Phrases like "half-devil, half-child," and "sloth and heathen" imply that these are peoples of a backward or less-developed civilization. A and B are incorrect because both of the lines they refer to are describing the British imperialists, not the people over whom the British are ruling. C is incorrect because nothing in the excerpt suggests that the natives are "ready" for conversion.

9. **A.** The excerpt contains both a message of responsibility and a warning about great costs. B is incorrect because the excerpt exhorts the Americans to "take up the . . . burden," not avoid it. C is incorrect because the excerpt does not call for the Christianizing of other civilizations. D is incorrect because the poem is devoid of irony; it considers the burden of imperial rule to be heavy but not folly.

10. **C.** Hogarth was commenting on the phenomenon of cash-strapped aristocrats marrying their sons to daughters of wealthy bourgeois businessmen in order to ensure a combination of wealth and status in the next generation of the family. A is incorrect because the engraving depicts two fathers haggling over the details of marrying their son and daughter. B is incorrect because the subject of the engraving is not the sale of art. D is incorrect because the subject of the engraving is not churchmen marrying.

11. **B.** Hogarth was criticizing the practice of economically motivated marriage through a satirically humorous depiction. A is incorrect because the scene is depicted realistically. C is incorrect because the depiction of the aristocrats in the scene is not flattering. D is incorrect because the image is not a landscape.

12. **C.** The sight of two fathers treating their children as economic assets while the clergyman leers at the bride-to-be shows Hogarth's moral repugnance. The mutual lack of interest shown by the future bride and groom foreshadows the misery that will follow (and which Hogarth depicts in the rest of this series of engravings). A is incorrect because the subject of the engraving is not the sale of art to foreigners. B is incorrect because portrait painting and patronage are not the subject of the engraving. D is incorrect because the scene depicted does not inspire confidence in the future of the realm.

13. **C.** There was a spread of religious skepticism among the educated elite in Britain in the eighteenth century, and the possibility of a skeptical and flexible attitude toward religion is implied in Gibbon's interpretation. A is incorrect because Gibbon was not a clergyman, and the clergy did not have a monopoly on scholarship in eighteenth-century Britain. B is incorrect because the excerpt implies no hatred of Roman religious attitudes. D is incorrect because one can tell nothing about the sources available from the excerpt.

14. **A.** Gibbon's interpretation refers to various attitudes toward religious worship that correlated with the social position of the worshiper. B is incorrect because Gibbon makes no reference to social tension or turmoil. C is incorrect because Gibbon refers to various kinds of religious worship, which implies the opposite of homogeneity and centralization. D is incorrect because Gibbon makes no reference to the introduction of Christianity in this excerpt.

15. **C.** There are no lines on the map that indicate British sailing routes in the Pacific Ocean. A, B, and D are incorrect because there are lines on the map that indicate British sailing routes along the west coast of Africa, in the Atlantic Ocean, and in the Indian Ocean.

16. **D.** The dark shaded lines connecting Britain, North America, and the west coast of Africa indicate the existence of such a Triangle of Trade. A is incorrect because no lines travel through North American waters to the Pacific Ocean. B is incorrect because there are very few lines connecting Britain and China. C is incorrect because there are no lines indicating British trade voyages in the Mediterranean during this period.

17. **A.** The heavy blue shading shows a high frequency of British trade ship voyages southward, around the horn of Africa, and to India via the Indian Ocean. B is incorrect because the map offers no evidence for assertions about the cargo that ships carried. The map shows that no British trade ships sailed west through the Mediterranean Sea, and because the map indicates that there is no Suez Canal during this period. D is incorrect because the map clearly

provides evidence for numerous voyages to India by British ships during this period.

18. **B.** Marx and Engels viewed the French Revolution as a significant effect of the economic change that created a powerful bourgeoisie. A, C, and D are incorrect because they are merely political struggles between members of a stable ruling aristocracy.

19. **B.** Marx and Engels's belief that all history is the struggle of economic classes is materialist, and their belief in the inevitability of historical events as a reaction to economic change is an example of economic determinism. A is incorrect because the Oxford Movement was a movement of High Church Anglicans in England whose members argued for the return to lost Christian traditions of faith. C is incorrect because, while Marx makes use of the Hegelian dialectic, he turns it on its head, emphasizing materialist, economic causes, instead of the role of ideas, in history. D is incorrect because the economic ideas of the thinkers of the Scottish Enlightenment, such as Adam Smith, emphasized the importance of individual self-interest and action, whereas Marx emphasized the importance of economic classes.

20. **C.** Marx and Engels's view of history was that class conflict and the events that manifested from it were the inevitable consequences of economic change. A and B are incorrect because the economic determinism that characterized Marx and Engels's thought convinced them that class warfare was inevitable, not a possibility which could be avoided. D is incorrect because the excerpt does not say anything about history repeating itself, and because Marx and Engels did not believe that history repeated itself.

21. **D.** The quotation is discussing the discrediting of political ideology in modern German history as a result of the revolutions of 1848 and their failure to bring about significant change. A is incorrect because the quotation does not discuss industrialization. B is incorrect because the quotation is not offering an analysis of the reasons why the revolutions failed but of the effects of that failure on modern German history. C is incorrect because the quotation does not analyze

the rise of the Nazi Party in Germany (even though there is an implied connection).

22. **C.** The quotation suggests that the most important long-term effect was the rise of "Force" as the only viable option in German political history, due to the discrediting of both the conservative and liberal political ideologies in the course of the revolutions of 1848. A is incorrect because, although the quotation notes that no change in who ruled was brought about *in* 1848, the thrust of the quotation is about the long-term effects of the revolutions of 1848 on German history. B is incorrect because, although the quotation notes that the early stages of the revolutions demonstrated the power of ideas, it argues that the long-term effect is a discrediting of that power. D is incorrect because the "Force" alluded to in the quotation is not a police force.

23. **A.** It is important to note the post–World War II context of a historical analysis that purports to find the roots of a German fascination with "Force" as a political ideology. B is incorrect because it is not the status of the historian, but the quality of his logic and evidence that one should consider. C is incorrect because, although the statement is in some general sense true, it is not particularly important to the reading of Taylor's analysis. D is incorrect because, though the statement may be true, it is not at all relevant to Taylor's analysis, which does not purport to find the roots of the Cold War.

24. **C.** The passage quotes Gorbachev as saying that *perestroika* (restructuring) was urgently necessary because delay would have exacerbated (worsened) the situation and led to crises. A is incorrect because the passage does not say that restructuring was inevitable. B is incorrect because the passage does not say that restructuring would exacerbate the situation, but rather that *delay* in restructuring would. D is incorrect because the passage does not go as far as to say that delay in restructuring would have caused the collapse of the Soviet Union.

25. **B.** In the passage Gorbachev states that the need for *perestroika* arose from the process of development in the socialist society in which he and his audience lived. A is incorrect because the passage

makes no mention of capitalist enemies. C is incorrect because *perestroika* was meant to allow a socialist society to develop successfully, and because the passage makes no mention the failure of socialism. D is incorrect because the passage makes no mention of capitalism.

26. **C.** The passage quotes Gorbachev as saying that the time for *perestroika* was ripe and that people had yearned for change for a long time. A is incorrect because the passage says that people had yearned for change for a long time, and because it says nothing about a sudden crisis. B is incorrect because the document says nothing about the need for *perestroika* being exaggerated. D is incorrect because the document says the time for *perestroika* is ripe, not that it has passed.

27. **D.** Doregelès recalled that the people of Paris (thereby indicating that it is the reaction of the people of that city) were singing (a sign of enthusiasm). A is incorrect because Doregelès recalled that the people of Paris were singing (a sign of enthusiasm, not skepticism). B and C are incorrect because Doregelès recalled that the people of *Paris* were singing; one can infer nothing, therefore, about the rest of Europe.

28. **A.** Doregelès says that he was "exhilarated" (excitedly happy) by what he had seen and experienced. B is incorrect because nothing in the passage indicates that Doregelès was disgusted. C is incorrect because nothing in the passage indicates that Doregelès was frightened. D is incorrect because the passage gives no indication about how Doregelès thought France would fare in the war.

29. **D.** The passage tells us that Clemenceau reacted by saying, "It will be all right then," indicating that Clemenceau had some concern that the French public would react poorly. A is incorrect because nothing in the passage indicates that Clemenceau was disgusted. B is incorrect because there is nothing in the passage that indicates what Clemenceau thought of France's chances in the war. C is incorrect because nothing in the passage indicates that Clemenceau would serve as Prime Minister of France.

30. **B.** World War I began in 1914, and the passage clearly states that Clemenceau blames Germany for it. A is incorrect because the Great Depression began in 1929. C is incorrect because World War II began in 1939. D is incorrect because the Franco-Prussian War began in 1870.

31. **B.** The passage indicates that Clemenceau believes that the chauvinistic lyrics of *Deutschland über alles* reveal the German aggressiveness that caused the war. A is incorrect because the passage does not offer an argument or an opinion about the *reasons* Germany started the war. C is incorrect because the meaning of *betrayed* in the passage is "unwittingly revealed" and refers to Germany's intentions, not the outcome of the war. D is incorrect because the phrase *ultimate framework* refers to the German "race," not to modern warfare.

32. **C.** The date locates the passage in the eighteenth century (the century of the Enlightenment), the phrase *law of nature* is a key phrase from the Enlightenment, and Voltaire is a famous Enlightenment *philosophe*. A is incorrect because the Scientific Revolution was a seventeenth-century phenomenon, and because Voltaire is associated with the Enlightenment. B is incorrect because the Reformation is a sixteenth-century phenomenon, and because Voltaire is associated with the Enlightenment. D is incorrect because the Romantic Movement is an eighteenth-century phenomenon, and because Voltaire is associated with the Enlightenment.

33. **B.** Voltaire is known to be an Enlightenment *philosophe*, and the quotation asserts the necessity of tolerance. A is incorrect because, although it criticizes the behavior of Christians, it says nothing about Voltaire's religious beliefs (or lack thereof). C is incorrect because the quotation asserts that the imperfection of men is a natural law; it does not say that tolerance violates the laws of nature. D is incorrect because, although the quotation is from a letter praising English society, it does not say that tolerance is uniquely English.

34. **C.** The passage indicates that German public opinion on the existence of a unique German path in history shifted in 1945 and has shifted again "today" (when Winkler was writing in 2006); all of that indicates a long-standing debate. A is incorrect because the passage indicates that

the prevailing public opinion until "today" held that there was some sort of unique German path in history. B is incorrect because there is nothing Marxist about the existence of public belief in a unique German path in history. D is incorrect because the passage says nothing to indicate that Winkler believed that the question has been answered "once and for all."

35. **A.** In the first sentence of the passage, Winkler asserts that there was significant public belief in a special German mission. B is incorrect because, in the first sentence of the passage, Winkler asserts that there was significant public belief in a special German mission. C and D are incorrect because Winkler was not asserting or opposing anything in 1945; he wrote in 2006.

36. **D.** The passage indicates that Germany's defeat in World War II ("the collapse of 1945") led to a shift from asserting that Germany had a unique mission in history to a claim that Germany was unique in the way it had "deviated" from the rest of Western civilization. A is incorrect because the passage clearly indicates that public opinion on the existence of a unique German mission was changed by the collapse of 1945. B is incorrect because the passage clearly indicates that German public opinion on the question of its uniqueness was substantively affected by the collapse of 1945. C is incorrect because the passage indicates that public opinion was changed by the collapse of 1945, not "proven to be correct."

37. **B.** One can infer from this World War II–era poster that the wartime economy required women to do factory work. A is incorrect because the poster does not indicate that women were being conscripted. C is incorrect because the poster indicates nothing about the consequences of women and men working together in factories. D is incorrect because nothing in the poster indicates that this was the first time that women were part of Great Britain's industrial workforce.

38. **D.** The prevalence of tanks and aircraft seeming to emanate from the factory in the poster allow you to infer that women were used in the production of munitions in Great Britain during World War II. A is incorrect because one may infer nothing from the poster about who is "in

charge" of the factories. B is incorrect because one may infer nothing from the poster about the proportions of men and women in the military. C is incorrect because one may infer nothing from the poster about the emotional state of the women working in factories.

39. **C.** It is clear that the goal of the poster was to make women feel like they were important to the war effort. A is incorrect because women were not a minority group in Great Britain during World War II. B is incorrect; although its assertion that British and German propaganda had similar goals is probably true, it cannot be inferred from this British poster alone. D is incorrect because factory work during the war was available to women (and because the poster asserts nothing more than that).

40. **C.** The phrase "late labours and hazards," the reference to the delivering of the enemies of God into their hands, the date (1647), and the term "Leveller" all allow one to infer that that the authors recently fought in the English Civil War. A is incorrect because the Seven Years' War was fought from 1756 to 1763. B is incorrect because the American War for Independence was fought from 1775 to 1782. D is incorrect because the Battle of Agincourt was fought in 1451.

41. **A.** The demand articulated by the passage, "That matters of Religion, and the ways of God's worship are not at all entrusted by us to any human power," allows one to infer that the authors of the passage fought for religious freedom. B is incorrect because the Levellers fought on the Parliamentary side, not the side of the monarchy, and because supporters of the monarchy would not be demanding any of the things the Levellers do in the passage. C is incorrect because nothing in the passage mentions the establishment of a republic. D is incorrect because the Levellers were English, and because the passage mentions nothing about independence.

42. **B.** The phrase, "That in all laws made, or to be made, every person may be bound alike," allows one to infer that the authors of the passage meant to establish equality under the law in England. A is incorrect because nothing in the passage indicates that the Levellers were

demanding to form a ruling body of England. C is incorrect because, at the time the passage was written, hostilities in the English Civil War had already ceased, and because nothing in the passage indicates a demand for the cessation of hostilities. D is incorrect because the authors were army officers, not slaves (the word *slavish* in the phrase, "the danger of returning into a slavish condition," is used as an analogy).

43. **D.** One can infer from the phrase, "the recollection of everything done by one party or the other . . . during all the preceding period of troubles," that Henry is trying to put an end to religious conflict in France. A and B are incorrect because one can infer nothing about Henry IV's own religion from the document. C is incorrect because the phrase, "the recollection of everything done by one party or the other . . . during all the preceding period of troubles," clearly indicates that there had been religious conflict in the period prior to 1598.

44. **B.** The reference to the restoration of the Catholic Church anywhere where it had been interrupted allows one to infer that Henry IV was assuring the existence of the Catholic Church in France. A is incorrect because the reference to the restoration of the Catholic Church anywhere where it had been interrupted shows that Henry IV was not abolishing the Catholic Church. C is incorrect because nothing in the passage allows one to infer that Henry IV believed or asserted that the Catholic Church was the one true Church. D is incorrect because nothing in the passage allows one to infer that Henry IV believed or asserted that the Catholic Church had caused too much trouble and hindrance.

45. **B.** The phrase, "herewith permit, those of the said religion pretended Reformed to live and abide in all the cities and places of this our kingdom and countries of our sway," allows one to infer that Henry IV intended for Protestants to be able to live peacefully in his kingdom. A is incorrect because the phrase, "herewith permit, those of the said religion pretended Reformed to live and abide in all the cities and places of this our kingdom and countries of our sway," shows that Henry IV

intended for Protestants to be able to live peacefully in his kingdom, not be banned from it. C and D are incorrect because nothing in the passage allows one to infer anything about Henry IV's religious conversion.

46. **C.** The statement in the passage, "To enforce the fundamental law—to take care that every man has freedom to do all that he wills, provided he infringes not the equal freedom of any other man," allows one to infer that Spencer was an advocate of nineteenth-century liberalism. A is incorrect because the passage makes no reference to the nineteenth-century conservative belief in the value of traditional customs and institutions. B is incorrect because nothing in the passage refers to the nineteenth-century anarchist belief that the government was the enemy of liberty. D is incorrect because nothing in the passage makes reference to the nineteenth-century socialist belief that competition should be replaced by cooperation.

47. **A.** The passage makes it clear that Spencer believed that to use tax money to aid the poor exceeded the bounds of the proper role of government and would do harm to the "universal interests of humanity." B is incorrect because the passage does not challenge the right of the government to tax its people. C is incorrect because the passage explicitly says that the government "cannot rightly do anything more than protect." D is incorrect because the passage makes no reference to people uniting.

48. **D.** The last paragraph of the passage articulates the basic belief of social Darwinism, that weeding out of the weak makes for a stronger, more prosperous society. A is incorrect because nothing in the passage makes any reference to the creation of the cooperative society called for by utopian socialism. B is incorrect because nothing in the passage refers to the upholding of traditional social customs called for by social conservatism. C is incorrect because nothing in the passage refers to the cultivation of emotion and sentiment called for by Romanticism.

49. **D.** The passage's reference to "hindrances to human improvement" allows one to infer that

Mill was an advocate of nineteenth-century liberalism. A is incorrect, because nothing in the passage makes reference to the nineteenth-century socialist belief that competition should be replaced by cooperation. B is incorrect because the passage makes no reference to the nineteenth-century conservative belief in the value of traditional customs and institutions. C is incorrect because nothing in the passage refers to the nineteenth-century anarchist belief that the government was the enemy of liberty.

50. **C.** The passage indicates that the cause of women's submission to men is the nature of women's early education; thus, one may infer that Mill advocated educational reform to reverse the condition. A is incorrect because the subject of the passage is the subjection of women; the word "slavery" is used metaphorically. C is incorrect because a patriarchal social hierarchy is based on the subjection of women; Mill's passage is dedicated to ending the subjection of women. D is incorrect because there is no reference to the institution of marriage in the passage.

51. **D.** The passage's notion that early education determines a person's character is consistent with a *tabula rasa*, or blank slate, theory of human nature. A is incorrect because nothing in the passage refers to a corrupt or evil nature of human beings. B is incorrect because nothing in the passage implies that people are generally good or will do the right thing most of the time. C is incorrect because the passage indicates that the differences between the nature of women and men are a product of differing early educations.

52. **B.** Mill's call, in the last sentence of the passage, for an end to a system by which gender decides a person's opportunity in life allows one to infer that Mill advocated for equal opportunity for women. A is incorrect because the passage does not refer to the institution of marriage. C is incorrect because the passage does not mention social engineering. D is incorrect because the passage does not advocate the benefits of unbridled competition the way a social Darwinist passage would.

53. **D.** The references to the "mistress of the house" and "household duties," along with the title, allow one to infer that the subject is the role of a woman in running her own domestic household. A is incorrect because the reference to a commander of the army is a metaphor. B is incorrect because the "domestics" referred to are household servants. C is incorrect because the topic of the passage is clearly the management of a household, not a school.

54. **A.** The passage's reference to the importance of "acquirements, which more particularly belong to the feminine character" allow one to infer that Beeton believed that women were better suited than men for the task of household management. B and D are incorrect because the topic of the passage is not the running of a school. C is incorrect because the passage's reference to the importance of "acquirements, which more particularly belong to the feminine character" allow one to infer that Beeton believed that women, not men, were better suited than men for the task of household management.

55. **C.** The reference in the passage to a mistress of the house being the "leader" of an establishment, and her assertion that the "happiness, comfort, and well-being of the family" were dependent on her doing her job well, allow one to infer that Beeton believed that women held considerable power and responsibility within the domestic sphere of social life (within the confines of the household). A and B are incorrect because the passage makes no reference to the public sphere of life (outside the confines of the household). D is incorrect because the reference in the passage to the mistress of the house being the "leader" of an establishment and her assertion that the "happiness, comfort, and well-being of the family" were dependent on her doing her job well allow one to infer that Beeton believed that women held considerable power and responsibility within the domestic sphere of social life (within the confines of the household), not that they were denied such power and responsibility.

Section II: Short-Answer Questions

Strategies

Remember the strategies discussed in Chapter 5 for the short-answer questions:

Step 1. Compose a topic sentence that responds to the question and gives you something specific to support and illustrate.

Step 2. Support and illustrate the assertion in the topic sentence with specific examples.

Question 1

Briefly explain TWO ways in which the Scientific Revolution had an impact on European intellectual culture.

> **Topic Sentence for first part of answer:** The Scientific Revolution established the dominance in European intellectual culture of an approach to knowledge of the natural world that combined skepticism and empiricism.
>
> **Body of paragraph that presents specific examples that support and illustrate the assertion of the topic sentence:** In *Starry Messenger*, published in 1610, Galileo explicitly rejected the approach of medieval scholars by refusing to recognize the authority of ancient texts. Instead, he offered a radical alternative by describing the methods by which he had constructed a telescope to assist him in the direct observation of the heavens, and by then presenting and illustrating those results through descriptions and sketches of his observations of the moon, the Milky Way, and the moons of Jupiter. Galileo's approach became the accepted method of societies of gentleman scientists across Europe, including the Royal Society of London and the Royal Academy of Sciences in Paris, both established in the 1660s.
>
> **Topic sentence for the second part of answer:** A second effect of the Scientific Revolution on European intellectual culture was to firmly establish a belief in the existence of natural laws in the universe, a belief which formed the basis of the Enlightenment.
>
> **Body of paragraph that presents specific examples that support and illustrate the assertion of the topic sentence:** In his *Principia Mathematica* (1687), Isaac Newton not only provided the correct calculations for planetary motion, he set out "definitions" and "laws of motion" by which the trajectory of any moving object in the universe could be

calculated and predicted. In other words, Newton had shown that, through the rigorous application of empirical observation and reason, man could discern the laws that God had created to govern the natural world. His eighteenth-century successors, the *philosophes*, argued that the same process could lead to knowledge of the natural laws that govern human behavior. In *Wealth of Nations* (1776), for example, Adam Smith argued that man's natural tendency to follow his own self-interest produced natural laws that governed human economic activity like "an invisible hand." It was therefore in accordance with natural law that a civil government should protect the property of an individual and not interfere in the workings of the economy.

Question 2

Part A: Briefly explain ONE similarity between the French Revolution (1789–1799) and the Russian Revolution (1917–1924).

> **Topic Sentence:** In both the French Revolution and the Russian Revolution, an aristocracy and an established church that were resistant to change were toppled by those who felt excluded from power.
>
> **Body of paragraph that presents specific examples that support and illustrate the assertion of the topic sentence:** In France in 1789, the representatives of the First and Second Estates (the aristocracy and the clergy) resisted calls from the bourgeois representatives of the Third Estate to curb their power and privilege. By the end of the revolution in 1799, both the aristocracy and the clergy had irretrievably lost those powers and privileges. In Russia in 1917, an aristocratic governing class around Tsar Nicholas II and the Russian Orthodox Church, both of which had long resisted calls for greater participation from other segments of society, found themselves faced with an insurrection fostered by a sophisticated, underground network of socialist organizations. By the end of 1917, both the aristocracy and the Church had irretrievably lost those powers and privileges.

Part B: Briefly explain ONE difference between the French Revolution (1789–1799) and the Russian Revolution (1917–1924).

> **Topic Sentence:** In Russia, revolution led to the permanent abolition of the monarchy; in France, the monarchy was restored episodically in the nineteenth century.

Body of paragraph that presents specific examples that support and illustrate the assertion of the topic sentence: The abdication of Nicholas II of Russia in March 1917 marked the end of the Russian monarchy. Despite the efforts of Russian monarchists and of other European powers, the socialist insurgents and the Communist Party they eventually formed ruled Russia continuously until 1989. In France, the execution of Louis XVI on January 21, 1793, marked the beginning of a long period of political instability in which the French monarchy enjoyed periods of precarious restoration between 1815 and 1848.

Part C: Briefly analyze ONE factor that accounts for the difference you identified in part B.

Topic Sentence: One factor that helps to explain the different fortunes of the monarchy after the French Revolution and the Russian Revolution is the state of organized, socialist opposition.

Body of paragraph that presents specific examples that support and illustrate the assertion of the topic sentence: By 1917, the long-term existence in Russia of a repressive police state under the Romanov tsars had created a strong, highly organized, underground network of socialist opposition to both aristocratic and bourgeois rule. When the terrific toll of World War I created a vacuum of legitimate political authority in Russia, the Socialist Party network was ready to fill it. In France during the French Revolution, socialism was nothing but a budding idea and had produced no organized opposition. Instead, the power struggle was between the aristocracy and the bourgeoisie. In 1815, monarchy was reimposed with the help of the victorious aristocratic-led coalition that defeated Napoleon in 1815. In 1830, bourgeois factions deposed Charles X but thought it in their interests to retain a monarchy, with the pliant Louis-Philippe taking the throne.

Question 3

Part A: Briefly explain ONE aspect of the Romantic Movement.

Topic Sentence: One aspect of the Romantic Movement was its insistence on the importance of the cultivation of the senses, sentiment, and emotion.

Body of paragraph that presents specific examples that support and illustrate the assertion of the topic sentence: Two examples of that aspect of the Romantic Movement are the works of Jean-Jacques Rousseau and Johann Wolfgang von Goethe. The roots of Romanticism are often traced back to the works of Rousseau because, in *Emil* (1762), he argued that humans are born essentially good and virtuous but are easily corrupted by society, and that the early years of a child's education should be spent developing the senses, sentiment, and emotion. Goethe's *The Sorrows of Young Werther* (1774) glorified the "inner emotional experience" of the sensitive, emotional individual.

Part B: Briefly explain TWO factors that account for the rise of the Romantic Movement.

Topic Sentence: Two factors that help to account for the rise of the Romantic Movement are the emphasis on reason that dominated the writings of the Enlightenment *philosophes* and the changes wrought by the process of industrialization.

Body of paragraph that presents specific examples that support and illustrate the assertion of the topic sentence: The works of Rousseau and Goethe explicitly assert the need for the cultivation of the senses, sentiment, and emotion as a remedy for the ruthless and soulless rationalism of the Enlightenment. Meanwhile, many of the Romantics explicitly offered the solace of nature as a remedy for the dehumanizing effects of factory work and urban living conditions, both of which they saw as arising from the excessive emphasis on reason in European society. For example, the works of the English poets William Wordsworth and Samuel Taylor Coleridge extolled the almost mystical qualities of the lake country of northwest England.

Question 4

It is a truth which admits not a doubt, that the comforts and well-being of the poor cannot be permanently secured without some regard on their part, or some effort on the part of the legislature, to regulate the increase of their numbers, and to render less frequent among them early and improvident marriages. The operation of the system of poor laws has been indirectly contrary to this. They have rendered restraint superfluous, and have invited imprudence, by offering it a portion of the wages of prudence and industry.

David Ricardo, *Principles of Political Economy and Taxation*, 1817

Part A: Briefly explain ONE reason that the passage can be identified with classical liberalism.

Topic Sentence: Ricardo's notion that state intervention on behalf of the poor ("the poor laws") would only serve to increase the number of poor people identifies the passage with classical liberalism.

Body of paragraph that presents specific examples that support and illustrate the assertion of the topic sentence: Classical liberalism asserted that there were laws of nature that governed economic markets and that any attempt by the state or society to interfere with the workings of those laws would only make matters worse. Specifically, Ricardo is writing in the tradition of Adam Smith, who argued in *Wealth of Nations* (1776) that there was an "invisible hand" that guided the economic activity of societies.

Part B: Briefly describe TWO factors that explain the rise to prominence of classical liberalism at the time at which the passage was written.

Topic Sentence: Two factors that help explain the rise to prominence of classical liberalism in 1817 are the wide-ranging influence of the Enlightenment and the emergence of a fully commercial economy in Great Britain (where Ricardo wrote).

Body of paragraph that presents specific examples that support and illustrate the assertion of the topic sentence: By 1815, Enlightenment works such as John Locke's *Essay on Human Understanding* and *Second Treatise of Government* (both 1689) and Adam Smith's *Wealth of Nations* (1776), which propounded the existence of laws of nature and the need for constitutions that synchronized human law with natural law, provided a treasure trove of ideas that could be applied to new economic questions. By the second decade of the nineteenth century, such ideas were mined by a new generation of thinkers who were confronted both by the world's most productive economy and a whole set of unprecedented social problems that came with it. Thinkers like Ricardo and Jeremy Bentham (who espoused utilitarianism, a strain of liberalism that argued that all human laws and institutions ought to be judged by their usefulness in promoting "the greatest good for the greatest number" of people) saw in classical liberalism an approach to social problems that embraced a tradition of rational scientific thought that could be adapted to new problems.

Section III: Document-Based Question

Strategies

Remember the five steps to a history essay of high quality described in Chapter 6:

Step 1. As you read the documents, determine what they have in common and how you can group them.

Step 2. Compose a thesis that explains how these documents are linked in the way you have chosen.

Step 3. Compose your topic sentences and make sure that they add up logically to your thesis.

Step 4. Support and illustrate your thesis with specific examples that contextualize the documents.

Step 5. *If you have time*, compose a one-paragraph conclusion that restates your thesis.

Grouping the Documents

A question about politics or political ideology almost always lends itself to the construction of a spectrum. Begin by grouping the documents according to ideology. Outline the shared aspects of each group of documents and explain how those shared characteristics identify a particular ideology. Construct a spectrum and organize the groups along it. Finally, note the differences in the documents within each group to note the variation possible in each ideology. For speed and brevity, refer to the documents by their number.

Creating Your Outline

A possible outline to an answer to this DBQ looks like this:

Thesis: The documents illustrate a spectrum of political ideologies that run from conservatism through liberalism to socialism.

Topic Sentence A: Documents #2 and #4 are examples of conservatism.

Specific Examples: In #2, de Maistre illustrates the conservative belief that written constitutions are unnatural. In #4, Metternich illustrates the conservative belief that traditional monarchy is the natural, time-tested and, therefore, proper form of government, and that monarchs must be not yield to calls for reform.

Topic Sentence B: Documents #1 and #3 are examples of liberalism.

　Specific Examples: In #1, Smiles illustrates the early liberal belief that only individual effort can better a person's social and economic position. In #3, Mill illustrates the liberal position that the only legitimate role for government is to protect individual liberty. (Note: later in his career, Mill would speak for the utilitarian position that there is a role for government in improving social conditions.)

Topic Sentence C: Documents #5 and #6 are examples of socialism.

　Specific Examples: In #5, Marx and Engels establish the position of scientific socialism, which argues that capitalism demands the exploitation of the working class, will inevitably crash, and that the workers should seize political power through violent revolution. In #6, Bernstein provides a corrective in the form of revisionism, arguing that capitalism's collapse is not imminent and that the workers should participate in politics.

Topic Sentence D: Document #7 is an example of anarchism and does not fit well on the spectrum.

　Specific Example: Kropotkin illustrates the position of anarchism that government corrupts humanity and must be disrupted and if possible destroyed. Because it is anti-political, it does not fit neatly on a political spectrum.

Conclusion: The documents form a political spectrum from conservatism through liberalism to socialism, with anarchism rejecting the notion of a political spectrum.

Section IV: Long-Essay Question

Strategies

Choose the question for which you can quickly write a clear thesis and three topic sentences that you can illustrate and support with several specific examples. Then follow the five-step formula to constructing a history essay of high quality. Here are the five steps described in Chapter 7:

Step 1. Find the action words in the question, and determine what the question wants you to do.

Step 2. Compose a thesis that responds to the question and gives you something specific to support and illustrate.

Step 3. Compose your topic sentences, and make sure that they add up logically to your thesis.

Step 4. Support and illustrate your thesis with specific examples.

Step 5. *If you have time,* compose a one-paragraph conclusion that restates your thesis.

And remember the pitfalls to avoid:

- **Avoid long sentences with multiple clauses.** Your goal is to write the clearest sentence possible; most often the clearest sentence is a relatively short sentence.
- **Do not get caught up in digressions.** No matter how fascinating or insightful you find some idea or fact, if it doesn't directly support or illustrate your thesis, don't put it in.
- **Skip the mystery.** Do not ask a lot of rhetorical questions, and do not go for a surprise ending. The readers are looking for your thesis, your argument, and your evidence; give it to them in a clear, straightforward manner.

Creating Your Outline: Question 1

Question 1: Analyze the major social effects of the Industrial Revolution.

Thesis: The Industrial Revolution produced a Western European society that was more urban, less family oriented, and filled with uncertainty.

Topic Sentence A: The rise of the centralized factory system that characterized the Industrial Revolution produced a Western European society that was much more urban.

　Specific Examples: In the eighteenth century, the majority of the British population lived in the countryside. By end of the nineteenth century, the majority of the British population lived in cities. Examples include the rise of Manchester, Sheffield, and Birmingham from small villages to industrial cities.

Topic Sentence B: The Industrial Revolution created a Western European society that was less family oriented.

　Specific Examples: Eldest sons and daughters moved to cities to seek factory work. With the rise of industrial cities came the rise of working-class slums. Fathers, wives, and children often worked in different factories.

Topic Sentence C: The Industrial Revolution destroyed the certainties of traditional society.

Specific Examples: In the agricultural economy, there was no such thing as unemployment. As more and more machines were introduced, the demand for labor went down, and unemployment became a cyclical phenomenon. The rise of the workhouses and poor houses in Great Britain were responses to that unemployment.

Conclusion: The Industrial Revolution replaced the traditional, rural, family-oriented society of certainty with a new urban, individualized society of uncertainty.

Creating Your Outline: Question 2

Question 2: Explain the ways in which the development of mass politics contributed to the New Imperialism of the late nineteenth century.

Thesis: The development of mass politics contributed to the development of the New Imperialism of the late nineteenth century by creating a large group of nationalistic voters whose support had to be won by political elites.

Topic Sentence A: The second half of the nineteenth century saw a development of a large group of new voters.

Specific examples: In Great Britain, reform bills of 1867 and 1884 created nearly universal manhood suffrage. In France, Louis-Napoleon granted universal manhood suffrage in 1848. In Germany, Bismarck promised universal manhood suffrage (though never provided it) in return for popular support of his policies.

Topic Sentence B: The newly politicized masses were enthusiastically nationalist.

Specific Examples: Support for the Crimean War and the occupation of Egypt in Great Britain. Plebiscites for the Second Empire, making Louis-Napoleon emperor in France. Support for the Franco-Prussian War in Germany.

Topic Sentence C: Politicians discovered that imperialism appealed to the newly politicized masses.

Specific Examples: Disraeli made the Conservatives the party of "Church, monarchy, and *empire*" in Great Britain. Louis-Napoleon's decision to end the republic and proclaim the Second Empire in France. Bismarck's "blood and iron" unification of Germany. The popularity of the Scramble for Africa.

Conclusion: The rise of a large, nationalistic constituency that politicians had to win over contributed to the New Imperialism of the late nineteenth century.

AP European History
Practice Test 2—Section I

ANSWER SHEET

1 Ⓐ Ⓑ Ⓒ Ⓓ
2 Ⓐ Ⓑ Ⓒ Ⓓ
3 Ⓐ Ⓑ Ⓒ Ⓓ
4 Ⓐ Ⓑ Ⓒ Ⓓ
5 Ⓐ Ⓑ Ⓒ Ⓓ
6 Ⓐ Ⓑ Ⓒ Ⓓ
7 Ⓐ Ⓑ Ⓒ Ⓓ
8 Ⓐ Ⓑ Ⓒ Ⓓ
9 Ⓐ Ⓑ Ⓒ Ⓓ
10 Ⓐ Ⓑ Ⓒ Ⓓ
11 Ⓐ Ⓑ Ⓒ Ⓓ
12 Ⓐ Ⓑ Ⓒ Ⓓ
13 Ⓐ Ⓑ Ⓒ Ⓓ
14 Ⓐ Ⓑ Ⓒ Ⓓ
15 Ⓐ Ⓑ Ⓒ Ⓓ
16 Ⓐ Ⓑ Ⓒ Ⓓ
17 Ⓐ Ⓑ Ⓒ Ⓓ
18 Ⓐ Ⓑ Ⓒ Ⓓ
19 Ⓐ Ⓑ Ⓒ Ⓓ

20 Ⓐ Ⓑ Ⓒ Ⓓ
21 Ⓐ Ⓑ Ⓒ Ⓓ
22 Ⓐ Ⓑ Ⓒ Ⓓ
23 Ⓐ Ⓑ Ⓒ Ⓓ
24 Ⓐ Ⓑ Ⓒ Ⓓ
25 Ⓐ Ⓑ Ⓒ Ⓓ
26 Ⓐ Ⓑ Ⓒ Ⓓ
27 Ⓐ Ⓑ Ⓒ Ⓓ
28 Ⓐ Ⓑ Ⓒ Ⓓ
29 Ⓐ Ⓑ Ⓒ Ⓓ
30 Ⓐ Ⓑ Ⓒ Ⓓ
31 Ⓐ Ⓑ Ⓒ Ⓓ
32 Ⓐ Ⓑ Ⓒ Ⓓ
33 Ⓐ Ⓑ Ⓒ Ⓓ
34 Ⓐ Ⓑ Ⓒ Ⓓ
35 Ⓐ Ⓑ Ⓒ Ⓓ
36 Ⓐ Ⓑ Ⓒ Ⓓ
37 Ⓐ Ⓑ Ⓒ Ⓓ
38 Ⓐ Ⓑ Ⓒ Ⓓ

39 Ⓐ Ⓑ Ⓒ Ⓓ
40 Ⓐ Ⓑ Ⓒ Ⓓ
41 Ⓐ Ⓑ Ⓒ Ⓓ
42 Ⓐ Ⓑ Ⓒ Ⓓ
43 Ⓐ Ⓑ Ⓒ Ⓓ
44 Ⓐ Ⓑ Ⓒ Ⓓ
45 Ⓐ Ⓑ Ⓒ Ⓓ
46 Ⓐ Ⓑ Ⓒ Ⓓ
47 Ⓐ Ⓑ Ⓒ Ⓓ
48 Ⓐ Ⓑ Ⓒ Ⓓ
49 Ⓐ Ⓑ Ⓒ Ⓓ
50 Ⓐ Ⓑ Ⓒ Ⓓ
51 Ⓐ Ⓑ Ⓒ Ⓓ
52 Ⓐ Ⓑ Ⓒ Ⓓ
53 Ⓐ Ⓑ Ⓒ Ⓓ
54 Ⓐ Ⓑ Ⓒ Ⓓ
55 Ⓐ Ⓑ Ⓒ Ⓓ

AP European History Practice Test 2 Exam:
Section I
(Multiple Choice)

Directions: The multiple-choice section consists of 55 questions to be answered in **55 minutes**. Each set of questions below refers to the written passage or figure that precedes it. Select the best answer for each question, and fill in the corresponding letter on the answer sheet supplied.

Questions 1–3 refer to the passage below.

Albeit the king's Majesty justly and rightfully is and ought to be the supreme head of the Church of England, and so is recognized by the clergy of this realm in their convocations, yet nevertheless, for corroboration and confirmation thereof, and for increase of virtue in Christ's religion within this realm of England, and to repress and extirpate all errors, heresies, and other enormities and abuses heretofore used in the same, be it enacted, by authority of this present Parliament, that the king, our sovereign lord, his heirs and successors, kings of this realm, shall be taken, accepted, and reputed the only supreme head in earth of the Church of England, called *Anglicans Ecclesia*; and shall have and enjoy, annexed and united to the imperial crown of this realm, as well the title and style thereof, as all honors, dignities, preeminences, jurisdictions, privileges, authorities, immunities, profits, and commodities to the said dignity of the supreme head of the same Church belonging and appertaining; and that our said sovereign lord, his heirs and successors, kings of this realm, shall have full power and authority from time to time to visit, repress, redress, record, order, correct, restrain, and amend all such errors, heresies, abuses, offenses, contempts, and enormities, whatsoever they be, which by any manner of spiritual authority or jurisdiction ought or may lawfully be reformed, repressed, ordered, redressed, corrected, restrained, or amended, most to the pleasure of Almighty God, the increase of virtue in Christ's religion, and for the conservation of the peace, unity, and tranquility of this realm; any usage, foreign land, foreign authority, prescription, or any other thing or things to the contrary hereof notwithstanding.

English Parliament, Act of Supremacy, 1534

1. From the passage, one may infer that the English Parliament wished to argue that the Act of Supremacy would

   A. give the English king a new position of authority
   B. give the position of head of the Church of England to Henry VIII alone and exclude his heirs
   C. establish Calvinism as the one true theology in England
   D. end various forms of corruption plaguing the Church in England

2. The passage can be used as evidence for which of the following historical trends of the time period?

   A. The consolidation of the power of the monarchy
   B. The increased power of the Catholic Church
   C. The increased piety of the nobility
   D. The increasing religiosity of the masses

3. From the passage and its historical context, one may infer that the Act was, in part,

   A. an attempt to prevent the spread of Protestantism in England
   B. a solution to Henry VIII's financial difficulties
   C. an attempt to legitimize Henry VIII's only heir
   D. an attempt to ally England with the Holy Roman Emperor

Questions 4–6 refer to the passage below.

Florence is more beautiful and five hundred forty years older than your Venice. . . . We have round about us thirty thousand estates, owned by nobleman and merchants, citizens and craftsman, yielding us yearly bread and meat, wine and oil, vegetables and cheese, hay and wood, to the value of nine thousand ducats in cash. . . . We have two trades greater than any four of yours in Venice put together—the trades wool and silk. . . . Our beautiful Florence contains within the city . . . two hundred seventy shops belonging to the wool merchant's guild, from whence their wares are sent to Rome and the Marches, Naples and Sicily, Constantinople . . . and the whole of Turkey. It contains also eighty-three rich and splendid warehouses of the silk merchant's guild.

Benedetto Dei, "Letter to a Venetian," 1472

4. From the passage, one may argue that wealth in Renaissance Italy was measured in

   A. the size of landed estates
   B. the number of estates owned by an individual
   C. the monetary value of goods
   D. the amount of gold held

5. From the passage, one may infer that the economy of Renaissance Florence was primarily based on

   A. banking
   B. the export of agricultural goods
   C. war and conquest
   D. the manufacture and export of wool and silk products

6. The passage may be used as evidence for the existence of which of the following Renaissance cultural characteristics?

   A. Pride in the mastery of the military arts
   B. Chivalry
   C. Civic pride
   D. Patronage of the arts

Questions 7–9 refer to the passage below.

First we must remark that the cosmos is spherical in form, partly because this form being a perfect whole requiring no joints, is the most complete of all, partly because it makes the most capacious form, which is best suited to contain and preserve everything; or again because all the constituent parts of the universe, that is the sun, moon and the planets appear in this form; or because everything strives to attain this form, as appears in the case of drops of water and other fluid bodies if they attempt to define themselves. So no one will doubt that this form belongs to the heavenly bodies. . . .

That the earth is also spherical is therefore beyond question, because it presses from all sides upon its center. Although by reason of the elevations of the mountains and the depressions of the valleys a perfect circle cannot be understood, yet this does not affect the general spherical nature of the earth. . . .

As it has been already shown that the earth has the form of a sphere, we must consider whether a movement also coincides with this form, and what place the earth holds in the universe. . . . The great majority of authors of course agree that the earth stands still in the center of the universe, and consider it inconceivable and ridiculous to suppose the opposite. But if the matter is carefully weighed, it will be seen that the question is not yet settled and therefore by no means to be regarded lightly. Every change of place which is observed is due, namely, to a movement of the observed object or of the observer, or to movements of both. . . . Now it is from the earth that the revolution of the heavens is observed and it is produced for our eyes. Therefore if the earth undergoes no movement this movement must take place in everything outside of the earth, but in the opposite direction than if everything on the earth moved, and of this kind is the daily revolution. So this appears to affect the whole universe, that is, everything outside the earth with the single exception of the earth itself. If, however, one should admit that this movement was not peculiar to the heavens, but that the earth revolved from west to east, and if this was carefully considered in regard to the apparent rising and setting of the sun, the moon and the stars, it would be discovered that this was the real situation."

Nicolas Copernicus, *The Revolutions of the Heavenly Bodies*, 1543

7. The passage may be used as evidence that Copernicus differed from the traditional, Aristotelian natural philosophers of his day because he suggested that

   A. the cosmos is spherical
   B. the Earth is spherical
   C. the cosmos is geostatic
   D. the Earth is not stationary

8. From the passage, one may say that Copernicus's argument for a spherical cosmos was based on

   A. observation and induction
   B. ancient textual authority
   C. experimentation
   D. deduction from first principles

9. From the passage, one could argue that Copernicus was working in

   A. the Aristotelian tradition
   B. the natural magic tradition
   C. the skeptical tradition
   D. the Platonic/Pythagorean tradition

Questions 10–11 refer to the passage below.

About the year 1645, while I lived in London . . . I had the opportunity of being acquainted with diverse worthy persons, inquisitive into natural philosophy, and other parts of human learning; and particularly of what has been called the "New Philosophy" or "Experimental Philosophy." We did by agreements . . . meet weekly in London on a certain day, to treat and discourse of such affairs. . . . Our business was (precluding matters of theology and state affairs), to discourse and consider of Philosophical Enquiries, and such as related thereunto: as physic, anatomy, geometry, astronomy, navigation, statics, magnetics, chemics, mechanics, and natural experiments; with the state of these studies, as then cultivated at home and abroad. We then discoursed of the circulation of the blood, the valves in the veins, the *venae lactae*, the lymphatic vessels, the Copernican hypothesis, the nature of comets and new stars, the satellites of Jupiter, the oval shape (as it then appeared) of Saturn, the spots in the sun, and its turning on its own axis, the inequalities and selenography of the moon, the several phases of Venus and Mercury, the improvement of telescopes, and grinding of glasses for that purpose, the weight of air, the possibility, or impossibility of vacuities, and nature's abhorrence thereof, the Torricellian experiment in quicksilver, the descent of heavy bodies, and the degrees of acceleration therein; and divers other things of like nature. Some of which were then but new discoveries, and others not so generally known and embraced, as now they are. . . .

   We barred all discourses of divinity, of state affairs, and of news, other than what concerned our business of Philosophy. These meetings we removed soon after to the Bull Head in Cheapside, and in term-time to Gresham College, where we met weekly at Mr. Foster's lecture (then Astronomy Professor there), and, after the lecture ended, repaired, sometimes to Mr. Foster's lodgings, sometimes to some other place not far distant, where we continued such enquiries, and our numbers increased.

Dr. John Wallis, *Account of Some Passages of his Life*, 1700

10. The passage may be used as evidence for the development of

    A. an independent society for the study of natural philosophy in the seventeenth century
    B. the study of natural philosophy in the royal courts in the seventeenth century
    C. new universities for the study of natural philosophy in the seventeenth century
    D. the study of natural philosophy in the Church in the seventeenth century

11. From the passage, one may infer that the main interest of Wallis's group was

    A. undermining of the traditional worldview
    B. creating of a secular science to challenge the Church
    C. ascertaining the state of the New Philosophy in England and abroad
    D. the regulation of new knowledge so as not to undermine traditional values

Questions 12–14 refer to the passage below.

[T]he the end and measure of this power, when in every man's hands in the state of nature, being the preservation of all of his society, that is, all mankind in general, it can have no other end or measure, when in the hands of the magistrate, but to preserve the members of that society in their lives, liberties, and possessions, and so cannot be an absolute, arbitrary power over their lives and fortunes, which are as much as possible to be preserved, but a power to make law, and annex such penalties to them, as may tend to the preservation of the whole by cutting off those parts, and those only, which are so corrupt that they threaten the sound and healthy, without which no severity is lawful. And this power has its original only from compact, and agreement, and the mutual consent of those who make up the community. . . .

Whensoever, therefore, the legislative shall transgress this fundamental rule of society; and either by ambition, fear, folly or corruption, endeavor to grasp themselves, or put into the hands of any other, an absolute power over the lives, liberties, and estates of the people; by this breach of trust they forfeit the power the people had put into their hands for quite contrary ends.

John Locke, *Second Treatise of Government*, 1690

12. From the passage, one may infer that Locke argued that society and its legitimate government held power over the members of society by virtue of

A. divine right
B. the consent of those members of society
C. a covenant between the members of society
D. conquest

13. Based on the passage, one could argue that Locke was an advocate of

A. divine right monarchy
B. absolutism
C. constitutionalism
D. socialism

14. From the passage, one may infer that Locke believed a government loses its legitimacy when

A. it is weak and can be overthrown
B. when the people wish to change governors
C. when it becomes corrupt
D. it tries to exercise absolute power

Questions 15 and 16 refer to the image below.

"England is not a free people, till the poor that have no land,
have a free allowance to dig and labour the commons . . ."
Gerrard Winstanley, 1649

15. From the illustration, one may infer that Gerrard Winstanley and his Diggers were resisting

    A. the king in the English Civil War
    B. Parliament in the English Civil War
    C. the enclosure movement
    D. the institution of the three-field agricultural system

16. From the illustration, one may infer that the Parliamentarian regime that was victorious in the English Civil War in 1649

    A. supported the efforts of Winstanley and the Diggers to return to old customs
    B. was determined to drive Winstanley and the Diggers off of all common land
    C. rewarded Winstanley and the Diggers for their previous support by awarding them use of the commons
    D. were indifferent to Winstanley and his movement

Questions 17–19 refer to the passage below.

In a word, whoever will deign to consult common sense upon religious opinions, and will bestow on this inquiry the attention that is commonly given to any objects we presume interesting, will easily perceive that those opinions have no foundation; that Religion is a mere castle in the air. . . .

Savage and furious nations, perpetually at war, adore, under diverse names, some God, conformable to their ideas. . . . Madmen everywhere be seen who, after meditating upon their terrible God, imagine that to please him they must do themselves all possible injury. . . . The gloomy ideas more usefully formed of the Deity, far from consoling them under the evils of life, have everywhere disquieted their minds, and produced follies destructive to their happiness.

How could the human mind make any considerable progress, while tormented with frightful phantoms, and guided by men interested in perpetuating its ignorance and fears? . . . Occupied solely by his fears, and by unintelligible reveries, he has always been at the mercy of his priests, who have reserved for themselves the right of thinking for him and directing his actions. . . .

Let men's minds be filled with true ideas; let their reason be cultivated. . . . To discover the true principles of morality, men have no need of theology, of revelation, or of gods.

Baron d'Holbach, *Good Sense*, 1772

17. From the passage, one could best characterize d'Holbach's theological stance as

A. atheist
B. deist
C. Protestant
D. Catholic

18. The passage may be used as evidence that d'Holbach was participating in

A. the later stages of the Protestant Reformation
B. the new political ideas of the early Enlightenment
C. the phase of the Enlightenment that called for "enlightened despotism"
D. the later, radical phase of the Enlightenment

19. The passage can be identified as part of the eighteenth-century cultural movement known as the Enlightenment because

A. it defends atheism
B. it affirms the core Enlightenment ideals of reason and freedom of thought
C. it offers a rational proof of the existence of God
D. it uses satire to undermine orthodox ideas

Questions 20 and 21 refer to the passage below.

The National Assembly, after having heard the report of the ecclesiastical committee, has decreed and do decree the following as constitutional articles:

Title I

IV. No church or parish of France nor any French citizen may acknowledge upon any occasion, or upon any pretext whatsoever, the authority of an ordinary bishop or of an archbishop whose see shall be under the supremacy of a foreign power, nor that of his representatives residing in France or elsewhere. . . .

Title II

I. Beginning with the day of publication of the present decree, there shall be but one mode of choosing bishops and parish priests, namely that of election.

II. All elections shall be by ballot and shall be decided by the absolute majority of the votes.

III. The election of bishops shall take place according to the forms and by the electoral body designated in the decree of December 22, 1789, for the election of members of the departmental assembly.

XXI. Before the ceremony of consecration begins, the bishop elect shall take a solemn oath, in the presence of the municipal officers, of the people, and of the clergy, to guard with care the faithful of his diocese who are confided to him, to be loyal to the nation, the law, and the king, and to support with all his power the constitution decreed by the National Assembly and accepted by the king.

Civil Constitution of the Clergy, July 12, 1790

20. From the passage, one may infer that the authors of the passage intended

A. to reform the church of France along Protestant lines

B. to make the clergy of France subservient to the French government

C. to ensure that the clergy of France would be completely abolished

D. to make the clergy of France subservient to the Pope in Rome

21. Which of the following groups in France in 1790 would have been most likely to oppose the proclamations of this document?

A. Members of the National Assembly

B. Supporters of the king

C. Existing archbishops

D. Simple parish priests who cared deeply about their parishioners

Questions 22–24 refer to the passage below.

From this moment until that in which the enemy shall have been driven from the soil of the Republic, all Frenchmen are in permanent requisition for the service of the armies. The young men shall go to battle; the married men shall forge arms and transport provisions; the women shall make tents and clothing and shall serve in the hospitals; the children shall turn old linen into lint; the aged shall betake themselves to the public places in order to arouse the courage of the warriors and preach the hatred of kings and the unity of the Republic. . . .

The Committee of Public Safety is charged to take all necessary measures to set up without delay an extraordinary manufacture of arms of every sort which corresponds with the ardor and energy of the French people. It is, accordingly, authorized to form all the establishments, factories, workshops, and mills which shall be deemed necessary for the carrying on of these works, as well as to put in requisition, within the entire extent of the Republic, the artists and workingmen who can contribute to their success.

The representatives of the people sent out for the execution of the present law shall have the same authority in their respective districts, acting in concert with the Committee of Public Safety; they are invested with the unlimited powers assigned to the representatives of the people to the armies.

The Levée en Masse, August 23, 1793

22. This passage established

    A. the French Republic
    B. the Committee of Public Safety
    C. war against the Coalition
    D. mass conscription

23. The passage can be used as one example of the way in which the Committee of Public Safety

    A. revamped the economy of the new French Republic
    B. successfully harnessed the human resources of the new French Republic
    C. reformed the religious rituals of the Church in the new French Republic
    D. brought about its own destruction

24. It could be argued that the passage represents a turning point in the history of warfare in modern European history because

    A. it represented the introduction of weaponry produced by large-scale industrialization
    B. it advocated the total extinction of a nation's enemies
    C. it was war run by a committee
    D. it advocated total war

Questions 25–27 refer to the passage below.

Many things combine to make the hand spinning of wool, the most desirable work for the cottager's wife and children. A wooden wheel costing 2 s[hillings] for each person, with one reel costing 3 s[hillings] set up the family. The wool-man either supplies them with wool by the pound or more at a time, as he can depend on their care, or they take it on his account from the chandler's shop, where they buy their food and raiment. No stock is required, and when they carry back their pound of wool spun, they have no further concern in it. Children from five years old can run at the wheel, it is a very wholesome employment for them, keeps them in constant exercise, and upright; persons can work at it till a very advanced age.

But from the establishment of the [mechanical] spinning machines in many counties where I was last summer, no hand work could be had, the consequence of which is the whole maintenance of the family devolves on the father, and instead of six or seven shillings a week, which a wife and four children could add by their wheels, his weekly pay is all they have to depend upon. . . .

I then walked to the Machines, and with some difficulty gained admittance: there I saw both the Combing Machine and Spinning Jenny. The Combing Machine was put in motion by a Wheel turned by four men, but which I am sure could be turned either by water or steam. The frames were supplied by a child with Wool, and as the wheel turned, flakes of ready combed Wool dropped off a cylinder into a trough, these were taken up by a girl of about fourteen years old, who placed them on the Spinning Jenny, which has a number of horizontal beams of wood, on each of which may be fifty bobbins. One such girl sets these bobbins all in motion by turning a wheel at the end of the beam, a wire then catches up a flake of Wool, spins it, and gathers it upon each bobbin. The girl again turns the wheel, and another fifty flakes are taken up and Spun. This is done every minute without intermission, so that probably one girl turning that wheel, may do the work of One Hundred Hand Wheels at the least. About twenty of these sets of bobbins, were I judge at work in one room. Most of these Manufactories are many stories high, and the rooms much larger than this I was in. Struck with the impropriety of even so many as the twenty girls I saw, without any woman presiding over them, I enquired of the Master if he was married, why his Wife was not present? He said he was not a married man, and that many parents did object to send their girls, but that the poverty of others, and not having any work to set them to, left him not at any loss for hands. I must do all the parties the justice to say, that these girls appeared neat and orderly: yet at best, I cannot but fear the taking such young persons from the eyes of their parents, and thus herding them together with only men and boys, must bring up a dissolute race of poor.

Observations . . . on the Loss of Woollen Spinning, c. 1794

25. The changes described by the passage reflect

    A. the shift from cottage industry organization to the mill system
    B. the shift from agricultural work to industrial manufacturing
    C. the shift from single country markets to international trade
    D. the shift from individual labor to labor organized into trade unions

26. From the passage, one may infer that

    A. the work took very little time
    B. a family could make enough spinning to support the entire household
    C. the initial investment in equipment was quickly recouped
    D. the work was done only by girls

27. From the passage, one may infer that one of the moral objections to mill work in the wool spinning industry was

    A. the lack of religious instruction provided to the young workers in the mills
    B. that it promoted petty theft from desperate workers
    C. that it broke down traditional gender roles by employing women and girls in a trade
    D. that large numbers of young girls worked for unmarried men without parental supervision

Questions 28–30 refer to the passage below.

After as careful an examination of the evidence collected as I have been enabled to make, I beg leave to recapitulate the chief conclusions which that evidence appears to me to establish. As to the extent and operation of the evils which are the subject of this inquiry [the results indicate]:

That the various forms of epidemic, endemic, and other disease caused, or aggravated, or propagated chiefly amongst the labouring classes by atmospheric impurities produced by decomposing animal and vegetable substances, by damp and filth, and close and overcrowded dwellings prevail amongst the population in every part of the kingdom, whether dwelling in separate houses, in rural villages, in small towns, in the larger towns—as they have been found to prevail in the lowest districts of the metropolis. . . .

That the ravages of epidemics and other diseases do not diminish but tend to increase the pressure of population. . . . [In] the districts where the mortality is greatest the births are not only sufficient to replace the numbers removed by death, but to add to the population.

That the younger population, bred up under noxious physical agencies, is inferior in physical organization and general health to a population preserved from the presence of such agencies.

That the population so exposed is less susceptible of moral influences, and the effects of education are more transient than with a healthy population.

That these adverse circumstances tend to produce an adult population short-lived, improvident, reckless, and intemperate, and with habitual avidity for sensual gratifications.

Sir Edwin Chadwick, Inquiry into the Sanitary Condition of the Poor, 1842

28. From the passage, one may infer that one of the chief sources of disease in the poor areas of mid-nineteenth-century Britain was

   A. a diet deficient in important nutrients and vitamins
   B. overcrowded living conditions and poor sanitation
   C. a new wave of the Black Death
   D. unsafe working conditions

29. According to Chadwick's report, the effect of rampant epidemic and disease on population pressure was

   A. a decrease in population pressure due to high mortality rates
   B. nonexistent, because high mortality rates balanced out high birth rates
   C. an increase in population pressure due to higher birth rates
   D. nonexistent, because population pressure and rates of epidemic and disease are unrelated

30. From the passage, one may infer that mid-nineteenth-century reformers in Britain believed that unsanitary living conditions

   A. produced a population of poor moral quality
   B. had no effect on the morality of the population
   C. caused disease
   D. improved moral values, as people had to struggle harder in their daily life

Questions 31 and 32 refer to the image below.

THE LIFE

AND

HISTORY OF SWING,

THE

KENT RICK-BURNER.

WRITTEN BY HIMSELF.

See page 21.

LONDON:
PRINTED AND PUBLISHED BY R. CARLILE,
62, FLEET-STREET.
1830.

Price Threepence.

31. The image most likely refers to which of these events in 1830?

 A. The death of King George IV of England and the ascension of William IV
 B. The Swing Riots in Britain
 C. The July Revolution in France
 D. The Irish Potato Famine

32. From the image, one may infer that it depicted a conflict between

 A. factory owners and industrial workers
 B. naval officers and sailors
 C. agricultural and industrial interests
 D. landlords and agricultural laborers

Questions 33 and 34 refer to the passage below.

Europe no longer possesses unity of faith, of mission, or of aim. Such unity is a necessity in the world. Here, then, is the secret of the crisis. It is the duty of every one to examine and analyze calmly and carefully the probable elements of this new unity. . . .

It was not for a material interest that the people of Vienna fought in 1848; in weakening the empire they could only lose power. It was not for an increase of wealth that the people of Lombardy fought in the same year; the Austrian Government had endeavored in the year preceding to excite the peasants against the landed proprietors, as they had done in Gallicia; but everywhere they had failed. They struggled, they still struggle, as do Poland, Germany, and Hungary, for country and liberty; for a word inscribed upon a banner, proclaiming to the world that they also live, think, love, and labor for the benefit of all. They speak the same language, they bear about them the impress of consanguinity, they kneel beside the same tombs, they glory in the same tradition; and they demand to associate freely, without obstacles, without foreign domination, in order to elaborate and express their idea; to contribute their stone also to the great pyramid of history. It is something moral which they are seeking; and this moral something is in fact, even politically speaking, the most important question in the present state of things. It is the organization of the European task. . . . The nationality of the peoples . . . can only be founded by a common effort and a common movement; . . . nationality ought only to be to humanity that . . . of a human group called by its geographical position, its traditions, and its language, to fulfil a special function in the European work of civilization.

Giuseppe Mazzini, *On Nationality*, 1852

33. From the passage, one may infer that Mazzini argued that the proper definition of a nation was

    A. a kingdom with long-standing borders
    B. a people with shared geography, language, and traditions
    C. a people strong enough to avoid foreign domination
    D. a people with a unified political ideology

34. Mazzini could best be described as influenced by which two ideological movements of the mid-nineteenth century?

    A. Conservatism and nationalism
    B. Socialism and nationalism
    C. Romanticism and nationalism
    D. Anarchism and socialism

Questions 35–37 refer to the passage below.

Yesterday Deputy Bamberger compared the business of government with that of a cobbler who measures shoes, which he thereupon examines as to whether they are suitable for him or not and accordingly accepts or rejects them. I am by no means dissatisfied with this humble comparison . . . . The profession of government in the sense of Frederick the Great is to serve the people, and may it be also as a cobbler; the opposite is to dominate the people. We want to serve the people. But I make the demand on Herr Bamberger that he act as my co-shoemaker in order to make sure that no member of the public goes barefoot, and to create a suitable shoe for the people in this crucial area. . . .

   For it is an injustice on the one hand to hinder the self-defense of a large class of our fellow citizens and on the other hand not to offer them aid for the redress of that which causes the dissatisfaction. That the Social Democratic leaders wish no advantage for this law, that I understand; dissatisfied workers are just what they need. Their mission is to lead, to rule, and the necessary prerequisite for that is numerous dissatisfied classes. They must naturally oppose any attempt of the government, however well-intentioned it may be, to remedy this situation, if they do not wish to lose control over the masses they mislead. . . .

   The whole problem is rooted in the question: does the state have the responsibility to care for its helpless fellow citizens, or does it not? I maintain that it does have this duty. . . . It would be madness for a corporate body or a collectivity to take charge of those objectives that the individual can accomplish; those goals that the community can fulfill with justice and profit should be relinquished to the community. [But] there are objectives that only the state in its totality can fulfill. . . . Among the last mentioned objectives [of the state] belong national defense [and] the general system of transportation. . . . To these belong also the help of persons in distress and the prevention of such justified complaints. . . . That is the responsibility of the state from which the state will not be able to withdraw in the long run.

Otto von Bismarck, "Reichstag Speech on the Law for Workers' Compensation," 1884

35. This passage most clearly shows the influence of which of the following trends in Europe in the second half of the nineteenth century?

    A. The birth of constitutionalism
    B. The blending of nationalism with liberalism
    C. The birth of popular nationalism
    D. The blending of nationalism with conservatism

36. In the passage, Bismarck is attempting to portray his government as

    A. servants of the people
    B. absolute rulers
    C. leaders who deserve to be followed
    D. loyal opposition to the party in power

37. The role of the state described by Bismarck could be best described as

    A. fulfilling all social objectives that are worthy of being fulfilled
    B. fulfilling no social objectives but rather leaving them to private individuals and the community
    C. fulfilling social objectives that have been demanded by the people
    D. fulfilling social objectives that it alone can fulfill

Questions 38–40 refer to the image below.

38. In the image, Giuseppe Garibaldi is depicted as fitting the "boot of Italy" onto the leg of King Victor Emmanuel II of Piedmont-Sardinia. From the image, one may infer that the cartoonist

    A. opposed Italian unification
    B. favored Italian unification
    C. believed Garibaldi to have had a significant role in bringing about the unification of Italy
    D. believed that Count Cavour was most responsible for Italian unification

39. From the image, one may infer that the date of the image is

    A. before June 1848
    B. after June 1848
    C. after October 1860
    D. before October 1860

40. From the image, one may infer that the cartoonist

    A. viewed the unification of Italy as coming to fruition
    B. viewed the unification of Italy as doubtful
    C. viewed the unification of Italy as a positive development
    D. viewed the unification of Italy as a negative development

Questions 41 and 42 refer to the passage below.

Confidential—For Your Excellency's personal information and guidance

The Austro-Hungarian Ambassador yesterday delivered to the [German] Emperor [Wilhelm II] a confidential personal letter from the Emperor Francis Joseph [of Austria-Hungary], which depicts the present situation from the Austro-Hungarian point of view, and describes the measures which Vienna has in view. A copy is now being forwarded to Your Excellency. . . .

His Majesty desires to say that he is not blind to the danger which threatens Austria-Hungary and thus the Triple Alliance as a result of the Russian and Serbian Pan-Slavic agitation. . . . His Majesty will, furthermore, make an effort at Bucharest, according to the wishes of the Emperor Franz Joseph, to influence King Carol to the fulfilment of the duties of his alliance, to the renunciation of Serbia, and to the suppression of the Rumanian agitations directed against Austria-Hungary.

Finally, as far as concerns Serbia, His Majesty, of course, cannot interfere in the dispute now going on between Austria-Hungary and that country, as it is a matter not within his competence. The Emperor Franz Joseph may, however, rest assured that His Majesty will faithfully stand by Austria-Hungary, as is required by the obligations of his alliance and of his ancient friendship.

> Theobald von Bethmann-Hollweg (chancellor of Germany),
> telegram to the German ambassador at Vienna, July 6, 1914

41. The best description of the context of Bethmann-Hollweg's telegram is

   A. Germany's collaboration with Austria-Hungary during Germany's unification process
   B. the Balkan Question and the Triple Alliance
   C. Germany's rearmament in violation of the Treaty of Paris
   D. Germany's negotiations with Austria-Hungary and Italy to create the Triple Alliance

42. From the passage, one may infer that Bethmann-Hollweg's telegram is often referred to as Germany's "blank check" because

   A. it pledged Germany to join the Triple Alliance and support Austria-Hungary against the Triple Entente
   B. it was understood to give Austria an unlimited scope of response to the assassination of Franz Ferdinand, to Serbia, and Pan-Slavism within the Austro-Hungarian Empire
   C. it pledged Germany's unlimited support to Franz Joseph in his efforts to succeed the recently assassinated Franz Ferdinand
   D. it offered nothing in terms of real support to Franz Joseph and Austria-Hungary

Questions 43–45 refer to the passage below.

How has the war affected women? How will it affect them? Women, as half the human race, are compelled to take their share of evil and good with men, the other half. The destruction of property, the increase of taxation, the rise of prices, the devastation of beautiful things in nature and art—these are felt by men as well as by women. Some losses doubtless appeal to one or the other sex with peculiar poignancy, but it would be difficult to say whose sufferings are the greater, though there can be no doubt at all that men get an exhilaration out of war which is denied to most women. . . .

Men and women must take counsel together and let the experience of the war teach them how to solve economic problems by co-operation rather than conflict. Women [drawn into the workforce] have been increasingly conscious of the satisfaction to be got from economic independence, of the sweetness of earned bread, of the dreary depression of subjection. They have felt the bitterness of being "kept out"; they are feeling the exhilaration of being "brought in." They are ripe for instruction and organization in working for the good of the whole. . . .

It would be wise to remember that the dislocation of industry at the outbreak of the war was easily met . . . because there was an untapped reservoir of women's labor to take the place of men's. The problems after the war will be different, greater, and more lasting. . . .

Because it will obviously be impossible for all to find work quickly (not to speak of the right kind of work), there is almost certain to be an outcry for the restriction of work in various directions, and one of the first cries (if we may judge from the past) will be to women: "Back to the Home!" This cry will be raised whether the women have a home or not. We must understand the unimpeachable right of the man who has lost his work and risked his life for his country, to find decent employment, decent wages and conditions, on his return to civil life. We must also understand the enlargement and enhancement of life which women feel when they are able to live by their own productive work, and we must realize that to deprive women of the right to live by their work is to send them back to a moral imprisonment (to say nothing of physical and intellectual starvation), of which they have become now for the first time fully conscious. And we must realize the exceeding danger that conscienceless employers may regard women's labor as preferable, owing to its cheapness and its docility. . . . The kind of man who likes "to keep women in their place" may find he has made slaves who will be used by his enemies against him.

Helena Swanwick, "The War in Its Effect upon Women," 1916

43. From the passage, one may infer that the context for Swanick's essay was

   A. possible social changes likely to occur with the coming of World War II
   B. effects of social changes that had occurred over a decade of warfare
   C. effects of social change being felt during the so-called Inter-War Years
   D. social changes that were being experienced during World War I

44. From the passage, one may infer that its author believed that women who had been drawn into the workforce would, at the war's conclusion,

   A. never be able to readjust to life at home
   B. revolt against traditional social rules
   C. face pressure to return to the home
   D. be paid better than men because of the experience they had gained

45. From the passage, one may infer that Swanick surmised that some employers would be tempted to see women as

   A. cheap and manageable alternatives to returning male labor
   B. unsuitable for a return to home life
   C. fair game for military service in the next war
   D. willing and able to work alongside men

Questions 46–47 refer to the passage below.

ARTICLE I: Germany, Austria-Hungary, Bulgaria and Turkey for the one part, and Russia for the other part, declare that the state of war between them has ceased. They are resolved to live henceforth in peace and amity with one another. . . .

ARTICLE III: The territories lying to the west of the line agreed upon by the contracting parties, which formerly belonged to Russia, will no longer be subject to Russian sovereignty; the line agreed upon is traced on the map submitted as an essential part of this treaty of peace. The exact fixation of the line will be established by a Russo-German commission.

Treaty of Brest-Litovsk, March 14, 1918

46. The Treaty of Brest-Litovsk can best be described as the result of

   A. the Bolsheviks' need to end the Russian war effort in order to consolidate their revolutionary gains
   B. corruption on the part of Bolshevik leaders and collaboration with Russian business interests
   C. the breaking up of the Triple Entente
   D. French and British aid being given to the so-called White Russians who opposed the Bolshevik government

47. The result of Article III of the treaty was

   A. the surrender of the western part of the German Empire to the Russian Empire
   B. the surrender of the eastern part of the German Empire to the Russian Empire
   C. the surrender of the western part of the Russian Empire to the German Empire
   D. the surrender of the eastern part of the Russian Empire to the German Empire

Questions 48 and 49 refer to the passage below.

Apart from the desire to produce beautiful things, the leading passion of my life has been and is hatred of modern civilization. What shall I say of it now, when the words are put into my mouth, my hope of its destruction—what shall I say of its supplanting by Socialism?

What shall I say concerning its mastery of and its waste of mechanical power, its commonwealth so poor, its enemies of the commonwealth so rich, its stupendous organization—for the misery of life! Its contempt of simple pleasures which everyone could enjoy but for its folly? Its eyeless vulgarity which has destroyed art, the one certain solace of labor? All this I felt then as now, but I did not know why it was so. The hope of the past times was gone, the struggles of mankind for many ages had produced nothing but this sordid, aimless, ugly confusion; the immediate future seemed to me likely to intensify all the present evils by sweeping away the last survivals of the days before the dull squalor of civilization had settled down on the world.

This was a bad lookout indeed, and, if I may mention myself as a personality and not as a mere type, especially so to a man of my disposition, careless of metaphysics and religion, as well as of scientific analysis, but with a deep love of the earth and the life on it, and a passion for the history of the past of mankind.

William Morris, How I Became a Socialist, 1896

48. From the passage, one may infer that, by 1896, Morris had dedicated himself to

   A. the spread of mechanical power in industry
   B. the transformation of Britain into a commonwealth
   C. the triumph of socialism
   D. the spread of liberal democracy

49. From the passage, one may infer that Morris

   A. chose to become a socialist because he was appalled by the great waste of resources and general misery caused by modern society
   B. chose to become a socialist because of the persuasiveness of Marx's arguments
   C. rejected socialism because it produced nothing but ugly confusion
   D. rejected socialism because of a deep love of the Earth and the life on it

Questions 50 and 51 refer to the passage below.

The situation is critical in the extreme. In fact it is now absolutely clear that to delay the uprising would be fatal.

With all my might I urge comrades to realize that everything now hangs by a thread; that we are confronted by problems which are not to be solved by conferences or congresses (even congresses of Soviets), but exclusively by peoples, by the masses, by the struggle of the armed people. . . .

Who must take power? That is not important at present. Let the Revolutionary Military Committee do it, or "some other institution" which will declare that it will relinquish power only to the true representatives of the interests of the people, the interests of the army, the interests of the peasants, the interests of the starving.

All districts, all regiments, all forces must be mobilized at once and must immediately send their delegations to the Revolutionary Military Committee and to the Central Committee of the Bolsheviks with the insistent demand that under no circumstances should power be left in the hands of Kerensky [and his colleagues], . . . not under any circumstances; the matter must be decided without fail this very evening, or this very night.

Vladmir Illyich Lenin, "Call to Power," 1917

50. From the passage, one may infer that the immediate context for Lenin's "Call to Power" was

   A. Russia's entrance into World War I
   B. the onset of the February Revolution
   C. Russia's exit from World War I
   D. the onset of the October Revolution

51. From the passage, one may infer that Lenin believed that

   A. the Russian military had to launch a new offensive
   B. Kerensky had to move immediately against the Bolsheviks
   C. the Bolshevik faction could wait no longer to seize power
   D. only the Russian military could effectively govern Russia

Questions 52 and 53 refer to the passage below.

In order to make the title of this discourse generally intelligible, I have translated the term "Protoplasm," which is the scientific name of the substance of which I am about to speak, by the words "the physical basis of life." I suppose that, to many, the idea that there is such a thing as a physical basis, or matter, of life may be novel—so widely spread is the conception of life as something which works through matter. . . . Thus the matter of life, so far as we know it (and we have no right to speculate on any other), breaks up, in consequence of that continual death which is the condition of its manifesting vitality, into carbonic acid, water, and nitrogenous compounds, which certainly possess no properties but those of ordinary matter.

Thomas Henry Huxley, "The Physical Basis of Life," 1868

52. From the passage, one may infer that Huxley argued that "life" was

   A. a force that works through matter
   B. essentially a philosophical notion
   C. merely a property of a certain kind of matter
   D. a supernatural phenomenon

53. From the passage, one may infer that Huxley's view is representative of the nineteenth-century ideology known as

   A. anarchism
   B. materialism
   C. conservatism
   D. romanticism

Questions 54 and 55 refer to the passage below.

As a Jew, I have never believed in collective guilt. Only the guilty were guilty.

Children of killers are not killers but children. I have neither the desire nor the authority to judge today's generation for the unspeakable crimes committed by the generation of Hitler.

But we may—and we must—hold it responsible, not for the past, but for the way it remembers the past. And for what it does with the memory of the past. In remembering, you will help your own people vanquish the ghosts that hover over its history. Remember: a community that does not come to terms with the dead will continue to traumatize the living.

We remember Auschwitz and all that it symbolizes because we believe that, in spite of the past and its horrors, the world is worthy of salvation; and salvation, like redemption, can be found only in memory.

Elie Wiesel, "Reflections of a Survivor," 1987

54. From the passage, one may infer that Wiesel believed that the current generation of Germans

A. shared their ancestors' guilt for the Holocaust
B. had a responsibility to remember the Holocaust
C. shared in the responsibility for the Holocaust
D. had no responsibility where the Holocaust was concerned

55. From the passage, one may infer that Wiesel asserted that remembering the Holocaust

A. was necessary for the German people to become reconciled to their own history
B. hindered the healing process for the German people
C. would ensure that it never occurred again
D. would allow the Jews to forgive the German people

AP European History Practice Test 2 Exam:
Section II
(Short-Answer)
Four Questions
50 minutes/20%

Directions: Briefly answer all parts of the following four questions.

1. Briefly explain TWO ways in which the economy of Europe changed from a system of locally and agriculturally based economies to a system of more interconnected economies based on capital.

2. Answer Parts A and B.

   A) Briefly give TWO possible explanations for the rise of the New Imperialism at the end of the nineteenth century.

   B) Briefly explain which of the possible explanations (given in A) is more plausible.

3. Answer Parts A and B.

   A) Briefly explain TWO effects that the development of separate sphere ideology had on women in the nineteenth century.

   B) Briefly explain ONE reason for the emergence of a separate sphere ideology in the nineteenth century.

Question 4 is based on the following passage:

Détente does not and cannot abolish the class struggle. No one can expect that under conditions of détente the communists will reconcile themselves to capitalist exploitation or that the monopolists will become revolutionaries. Thus the strict observance of the principle of non-interference in the affairs of other states, respect for their independence and sovereignty—this is the indispensable condition for détente.

We do not hide the fact that we see in détente the road to the creation of more favorable conditions of peaceful socialist and communist construction. This only goes to show that socialism and peace are inseparable.

Leonid Brezhnev, excerpts from a speech at the CPSU Congress, February 29, 1976

4. Answer Parts A and B.

   A) Briefly explain ONE reason why the passage can be identified with developments in the Cold War.

   B) Briefly describe TWO factors that explain Brezhnev's willingness to enter into détente with the United States during this period.

AP European History Practice Test 2 Exam:
Section III
(Document-Based)
One Question
55 minutes/25%

Directions: The following question is based on documents 1–7 provided below. (The documents have been edited for the purpose of this exercise.) The historical thinking skills that this question is designed to test include contextualization, synthesis, historical argumentation, and the use of historical evidence. Your response should be based on your knowledge of the topic and your analysis of the documents.

Write a well-integrated essay that does the following:

- States an appropriate thesis that directly addresses all parts of the question.
- Supports that thesis with evidence from all or all but one of the documents *and* your knowledge of European history beyond or outside of the documents.
- Analyzes the majority of the documents in terms of such features as their intended audience, purpose, point of view, format, argument, limitations, and/or social context as appropriate to your argument.
- Places your argument in the context of broader regional, national, or global processes.

Question: Compare and contrast the views presented below concerning the value of empire in the nineteenth century.

Document 1

Source: William Rathbone Gregg, "Shall We Retain Our Colonies?" 1851

[Formerly,] our colonies were customers who could not escape us, and vendors who could sell to us alone.

But a new system has risen up, not only differing from the old one, but based upon radically opposite notions of commercial policy. We have discovered that under this system our colonies have cost us, in addition to the annual estimate for their civil government and their defense, a sum amounting to many millions a year in the extra price we have paid for their produce beyond that which other countries could have supplied to us. . . . [T]hey yield us nothing and benefit us in nothing as colonies that they would not yield us and serve us were they altogether independent.

Document 2

Source: Benjamin Disraeli, "Crystal Palace Speech," 1872

Gentlemen, there is another and second great object of the Tory party. If the first is to maintain the institutions of the country, the second is, in my opinion, to uphold the empire of England. . . .

[W]hat has been the result of this attempt during the reign of Liberalism for the disintegration of empire? It has entirely failed. But how has it failed? Through the sympathy of the colonies with the mother country. They have decided that the empire shall not be destroyed, and in my opinion no minister in this country will do his duty who neglects any opportunity of reconstructing as much as possible our colonial empire, and of responding to those distant sympathies which may become the source of incalculable strength and happiness to this land. Therefore, gentlemen, with respect to the second great object of the Tory party also—the maintenance of the Empire—public opinion appears to be in favour of our principles. . . .

It cannot be far distant, when England will have to decide between national and cosmopolitan principles. The issue is not a mean one. It is whether you will be content to be a comfortable England, modelled and moulded upon continental principles and meeting in due course an inevitable fate, or whether you will be a great country—an imperial country—a country where your sons, when they rise, rise to paramount positions, and not merely obtain the esteem of their countrymen, but command the respect of the world. . . .

Document 3

Source: William Ewart Gladstone, "England's Mission," 1878

The honour to which the recent British policy is entitled is this: that from the beginning . . . to the end, the representatives of England, instead of taking the side of freedom, emancipation, and national progress, took, in every single point where a practical issue was raised, the side of servitude, of reaction, and of barbarism. . . .

Since [the Tory] accession to office, we have taken to ourselves . . . the Fiji Islands; the Transvaal Republic, in the teeth, it is now alleged, of the wishes of more than four-fifths of the enfranchised population; [and] the island of Cyprus. . . . [W]e have begun to protrude our military garrisons into our Indian frontier: in order to warn Russia how justly indignant we shall be if she should take . . . any corresponding step. . . .

I hold that to . . . overlook the proportions between our resources and our obligations, and above all to claim anything more than equality of rights in the moral and political intercourse of the world is not the way to make England great, but to make it morally and materially little.

Document 4

Source: John G. Paton, "Letter on New Hebrides Mission," 1883

For the following reasons we think the British government ought now to take possession of the New Hebrides group of the South Sea islands, of the Solomon group, and of all the intervening chain of islands from Fiji to New Guinea:

1. Because she has already taken possession of Fiji in the east, and we hope it will soon be known authoritatively that she has taken possession of New Guinea at the northwest, adjoining her Australian possessions, and the islands between complete this chain of islands lying along the Australian coast.

2. The sympathy of the New Hebrides natives are all with Great Britain, hence they long for British protection, while they fear and hate the French, who appear eager to annex the group, because they have seen the way the French have treated the native races in New Caledonia, the Loyalty Islands, and other South Sea islands.

   . . .

3. All the men and all the money used in civilizing and Christianizing the New Hebrides have been British. Now fourteen missionaries and the Dayspring mission ship, and about 150 native evangelists and teachers are employed in the above work on this group, in which over £6000 yearly of British and British-colonial money is expended; and certainly it would be unwise to let any other power now take possession and reap the fruits of all this British outlay.

Document 5

Source: Jules François Camille Ferry, "Speech before the French Chamber of Deputies," 1884

The policy of colonial expansion is a political and economic system . . . that can be connected to three sets of ideas: economic ideas; the most far-reaching ideas of civilization; and ideas of a political and patriotic sort.

In the area of economics, I am placing before you, with the support of some statistics, the considerations that justify the policy of colonial expansion, as seen from the perspective of a need, felt more and more urgently by the industrialized population of Europe and especially the people of our rich and hardworking country of France: the need for outlets [exports]. . . .

Gentlemen, we must speak more loudly and more honestly! We must say openly that indeed the higher races have a right over the lower races. . . . I repeat, that the superior races have a right because they have a duty. They have the duty to civilize the inferior races. . . .

I say that French colonial policy, the policy of colonial expansion, the policy that has taken us under the Empire [Napoleon III's Second Empire], to Saigon, to Indochina, that has led us to Tunisia, to Madagascar—I say that this policy of colonial expansion was inspired by . . . the fact that a navy such as ours cannot do without safe harbors, defenses, supply centers on the high seas.

Document 6

Source: German newspaper advertisement, June 24, 1890

The diplomacy of the English works swiftly and secretly. What they created burst in the face of the astonished world on June 18th like a bomb—the German-English African Treaty. With one stroke of the pen—the hope of a great German colonial empire was ruined! Shall this treaty really be? No, no and again no! The German people must arise as one and declare that this treaty is unacceptable!... The treaty with England harms our interests and wounds our honor; this time it dares not become a reality! We are ready at the call of our Kaiser to step into the ranks and allow ourselves dumbly and obediently to be led against the enemy's shots, but we may also demand in exchange that the reward come to us which is worth the sacrifice, and this reward is: that we shall be a conquering people which takes its portion of the world itself!

Document 7

Source: Captain F. D. Lugard, *The Rise of Our East African Empire*, 1893

It is sufficient to reiterate here that, as long as our policy is one of free trade, we are compelled to seek new markets; for old ones are being closed to us by hostile tariffs, and our great dependencies, which formerly were the consumers of our goods, are now becoming our commercial rivals. It is inherent in a great colonial and commercial empire like ours that we go forward or go backward. To allow other nations to develop new fields, and to refuse to do so ourselves, is to go backward; and this is the more deplorable, seeing that we have proved ourselves notably capable of dealing with native races and of developing new countries at less expense than other nations. . . .

A word as to missions in Africa. Beyond doubt I think the most useful missions are the medical and the industrial, in the initial stages of savage development. A combination of the two is, in my opinion, an ideal mission. . . . The "medicine man" is credited, not only with a knowledge of the simples and drugs which may avert or cure disease, but owing to the superstitions of the people, he is also supposed to have a knowledge of the charms and *dawa* which will invoke the aid of the Deity or appease His wrath, . . . The value of the industrial mission, on the other hand, depends, of course, largely on the nature of the tribes among whom it is located, . . . [W]hile improving the status of the native, [Industrial missions] will render his land more productive, and hence, by increasing his surplus products, will enable him to purchase from the trader the cloth which shall add to his decency, and the implements and household utensils which shall produce greater results for his labor and greater comforts in his social life.

AP European History Practice Test 2 Exam:
Section IV
(Long-Essay)
One Question
35 minutes/15%

Directions: Write an essay that responds to ONE of the following two questions.

Question 1: Compare the political effects of nationalism on European civilization from 1789 to 1848 with the political effects of nationalism on European civilization from 1866 to 1945.

Question 2: Compare the context in which scientific work was done in the seventeenth century with the context in which scientific work was done in the nineteenth century.

Section I: Multiple-Choice Questions

1. **D.** The passage refers to forms of corruption when it states that the act would firmly establish the king's "power and authority . . . to visit, repress, redress, record, order, correct, restrain, and amend all such errors, heresies, abuses, offenses" in the realm. A is incorrect because the passage states that the king is already "justly and rightfully . . . the supreme head of the Church of England," and that the purpose of the act is "for corroboration and confirmation" of that fact. B is incorrect because the passage clearly states that the position of head of the Church of England is established for both Henry VIII and "his heirs and successors, kings of this realm." C is incorrect because the passage makes no reference to Calvinist theology and because the Church of England under Henry VIII did not espouse a Calvinist theology.

2. **A.** The passage is evidence of a monarch, with the aid of his Parliament, consolidating his power at the expense of the Church and its clergy. B is incorrect because the passage indicates that the act is establishing power in the English monarchy at the expense of the Catholic Church. C is incorrect because the passage does not refer to any increase in piety on the part of the nobility. D is incorrect because the passage does not refer to any increase in religiosity on the part of the masses.

3. **B.** The passage states that the act establishes Henry VIII's right to "have and enjoy . . . all . . . profits, and commodities . . . of the same Church," which went a long way toward solving his financial difficulties. A is incorrect because the passage makes no mention of preventing the spread of Protestantism and was, by establishing the Church of England's independence from Rome, advancing the Protestant cause in England. C is incorrect because the passage makes no mention of legitimizing an heir and because Henry VIII had no male heir in 1534. D is incorrect because the passage makes no

mention of an alliance with the Holy Roman Emperor.

4. **C.** The author boasts of the monetary value of the goods ("nine thousand ducats in cash") produced on the estates of Florence. A is incorrect because the passage does not mention the size of the estates in Florence. B is incorrect because the passage does not mention the number of estates owned by any individuals. D is incorrect because the passage does not mention gold.

5. **D.** The passage refers to the large number of exports of wool and silk products. A is incorrect because the passage does not refer to banking. B is incorrect because the passage indicates that the production of agricultural products on the estates of Florence is for local consumption. C is incorrect because the passage does not refer to war and conquest.

6. **C.** The passage illustrates the author's great pride in the achievements of his city. A is incorrect because the passage does not refer to the mastery of military arts. B is incorrect because the passage does not refer to the code of chivalry, which was a characteristic of medieval culture, not Renaissance culture. D is incorrect because, despite the fact that patronage of the arts was a Renaissance value, the passage does not mention it.

7. **D.** The passage argues that perception of motion is relative to the observer, and therefore it is possible that the Earth is in motion. A and B are incorrect because Copernicus's assertion that the cosmos and the Earth are spherical is in agreement with the traditional, Aristotelian natural philosophers. C is incorrect because Copernicus is suggesting that the cosmos might not be geostatic.

8. **A.** The argument in the passage rests on observation (that the sun and moon are spherical and that water droplets are spherical) and an induction (that given the preponderance of bodies that are and strive to be circular, it is reasonable to conclude that the cosmos follows the general rule). B is incorrect because the passage makes no reference to ancient textual authority. C is incorrect because the passage

makes no reference to experimentation. D is incorrect because the argument is inductive rather than deductive.

9. **C.** Copernicus's willingness to question the traditional notion that the Earth was stationary is evidence that he was working in the skeptical tradition. A is incorrect because the passage offers evidence of Copernicus's willingness to question the traditional, Aristotelian notion that the Earth was stationary. B is incorrect because nothing in the passage suggests that Copernicus was working in a tradition that believed in nature's "hidden powers." Though it is true that Copernicus is understood to have worked in the Platonic/Pythagorean tradition of searching for the underlying mathematical laws of the universe, D is incorrect because there is nothing in the passage that could be used as evidence for such an assertion.

10. **A.** The passage makes it clear that the group met outside of, and independent from, traditional institutions like universities, courts, and the Church. B is incorrect because the passage makes it clear that the group was not part of a royal court. C is incorrect because it is evident from the passage that the group was not part of an effort to form a new university. D is incorrect because the passage makes it clear that the group was not under the auspices of any church.

11. **C.** The passage states that the goal of the group was to know "the state of these studies, as then cultivated at home and abroad" and indicates that members helped to make this knowledge more readily available. A is incorrect because the passage makes no reference the goal of undermining the traditional worldview. B is incorrect because the passage says that the group avoided issues of religion, but not that it was dedicated to challenging the Church. D is incorrect because the passage makes no reference to an attempt to regulate knowledge.

12. **B.** The passage explicitly states that "this power has its original only from compact, and agreement, and the mutual consent of those who make up the community." A is incorrect because the passage does not refer to divine right, a concept that Locke wished to discredit. C is incorrect because the word Locke chooses is *consent*,

which implies the possible withdrawal, rather than Hobbes's word—*covenant*—which implied permanency. D is incorrect because the passage does not refer to conquest.

13. **C.** Locke's expression of the preservation of the "lives, liberties, and possessions" of society's members, of the limited nature of properly derived political power, and of the consent of the members of society as the origin of properly derived political power are all key concepts of constitutionalism. A is incorrect because the passage does not argue in favor of divine right monarchy. B is incorrect because the passage explicitly argues that properly derived political power cannot be arbitrary. D is incorrect because Locke's emphasis on the protection of the property and possessions of society members is more in line with liberal constitutionalism than socialism.

14. **D.** The passage states that a government [legislature] forfeits its legitimacy when it "endeavor[s] to grasp themselves, or put into the hands of any other, an absolute power over the lives, liberties, and estates of the people." A is incorrect because the passage does not state that a government loses legitimacy in moments of weakness. B is incorrect because the passage does not say that a government loses its legitimacy any time the people wish to make a change. C is incorrect because the passage does not say that instances of corruption equate to illegitimacy, only that corruption can be one motivation for a government seeking to exercise absolute power.

15. **C.** The illustration demands that people have access to the commons (common land), a custom that was being denied them through the enclosure of land. While the illustration dates from the era of the English Civil War, A and B are incorrect because the illustration does not indicate that Winstanley and the Diggers supported any particular faction. D is incorrect because the illustration does not refer to a three-field agricultural system.

16. **B.** The illustration shows the military force being used to expel Winstanley and the Diggers from the commons. A, C, and D are incorrect because the illustration shows the military force expelling Winstanley and the Diggers and not supporting them, awarding them lands, or showing indifference, respectively.

17. **A.** The passage expresses the atheist view that "men have no need of theology, of revelation, or of gods." B is incorrect because a deist theology holds that God is necessary. C and D are incorrect because both Protestant and Catholic theologies begin with a belief in a necessary God.

18. **D.** Both the date of the passage and its advocacy of atheism locate it in the later, radical phase of the Enlightenment. A is incorrect because the date of the passage and its atheistic stance show that it is not a passage from the later stages of the Protestant reformation. B is incorrect because the passage offers a critique of religion, not political ideas. C is incorrect because the passage offers a critique of religion, not an argument for the need for an enlightened sovereign.

19. **B.** The passage affirms the core Enlightenment ideals of reason and freedom of thought by arguing for a rational critique of religious belief. A is incorrect because not all of the Enlightenment's thought on religion and faith was atheistic. C is incorrect because the passage does not offer rational proof of the existence of God. D is incorrect because the passage is not satirical.

20. **B.** The passage indicates that the clergy of France are to be elected by the people of France, and that these clergy are to "be loyal to the nation." A is incorrect because the passage makes no reference to Protestant theological reforms. C is incorrect because the passage refers to the election of clergy and their loyalty to the nation, not their complete abolishment. D is incorrect because the passage forbids the French people from recognizing clergy appointed by anyone foreign to France (which includes the pope) and because it commands French clergy to be loyal to the nation.

21. **C.** The existing archbishops owed their position to their contacts in Rome and ultimately to the pope. A is incorrect because the document expresses the will of the National Assembly that the clergy be brought under the auspices of the French state. B is incorrect because the document states that, henceforth, the clergy must be loyal to "the nation, the law, and the king," and because a large number of the king's supporters believed the independent power and wealth of the clergy needed to be curbed and brought under the authority of the state. D is incorrect because some simple parish priests sided with the National Assembly on this issue, believing that simple people would be given greater attention and care under a clergy that was elected and loyal to the French nation.

22. **D.** The document proclaimed that, by law, "all Frenchmen are in permanent requisition for the service of the armies." A is incorrect because the French Republic was proclaimed to exist on September 22, 1792, nearly a year prior to the publication of the *Levée en Masse*. B is incorrect because the Committee of Public Safety was created in March 1793 by the National Convention and then restructured in July 1793; it was the Committee of Public Safety that authored the *Levée en Masse*. C is incorrect because France had declared war on the Habsburg monarchy of Austria on April 20, 1792, and the kingdom of Prussia joined the Austrian side a few weeks later. The *Levée en Masse* was a response to the needs of France in the face of war with the First Coalition, not a declaration of it.

23. **B.** The *Levée en Masse* is a good example of the way in which the Committee of Public Safety successfully harnessed the human resources of the new French Republic; it succeeded in training an army of about eight hundred thousand soldiers in less than a year, turning the tide of the War of the First Coalition in France's favor. A is incorrect because the *Levée en Masse* does not deal with efforts to reform the economy of the new French Republic. C is incorrect because the *Levée en Masse* does not deal with efforts to reform the religious rituals of the Church. D is incorrect because the *Levée en Masse*, and the military success it brought, actually increased the popularity of the Committee of Public Safety.

24. **D.** It can be reasonably argued that the *Levée en Masse* was the first instance in modern European warfare where all elements of the population and all the reserves of the state were committed to a war effort. A is incorrect because the *Levée en Masse* did not introduce weaponry produced by large-scale industrialization. B is incorrect because the *Levée en Masse*

did not advocate the total extinction of France's enemies. C is incorrect because the War of the First Coalition continued to be run by French generals; the *Levée en Masse* simply increased the size and improved the training of the soldiers available to them.

25. **A.** The passage describes the effects on workers who spun thread in their homes for the textile trade as the mode of production shifted to more mechanized labor in a mill system. B is incorrect because the passage does not describe the effects of shifting from agricultural work to industrial manufacturing. C is incorrect because the passage does not discuss shifts in the textile markets, but rather in the mode of production. D is incorrect because the passage does not describe the effects of trade unions.

26. **C.** The passage indicates that there is an initial investment of "A wooden wheel costing 2 s[hillings] for each person, with one reel costing 3 s[hillings] set up the family," while a wife and four children could add six or seven shillings *a week* "by their wheels." A is incorrect because the passage does not indicate that spinning took very little time. B is incorrect because the passage indicates that spinning done by the wife and children supplemented the husband/father's income rather than replaced it. D is incorrect because the passage indicates that spinning as a cottage industry was done by a wife and all the household children; it was in the mill system that it was done almost exclusively by girls.

27. **D.** The passage indicates the author's concern for the moral effects of taking young girls and "herding them together" with unmarried men and boys. A is incorrect because the passage does not refer to a lack of religious instruction in the mills. B is incorrect because the passage does not refer to theft on the part of workers. C is incorrect because the women and girls were already employed in the spinning trade before the shift to the mill system.

28. **B.** The passage states Chadwick's belief that "the various forms of epidemic, endemic, and other disease [are] caused . . . by atmospheric impurities . . . , by damp and filth, and close and overcrowded dwellings." A is incorrect because the passage does not refer to the diet of the poor. C is incorrect because the passage does not refer to the Black Death. D is incorrect because the passage does not refer to the working conditions of the poor.

29. **C.** Chadwick reported that "the ravages of epidemics and other diseases . . . tend to increase the pressure of population." A is incorrect because Chadwick reported that "the ravages of epidemics and other diseases do not diminish but tend to increase the pressure of population pressure." B and D are incorrect because Chadwick reported that "the ravages of epidemics and other diseases . . . tend to *increase* the pressure of population."

30. **A.** The passage indicates a belief that unsanitary living conditions produce a population that "is less susceptible of moral influences" and therefore "improvident, reckless, and intemperate, and with habitual avidity for sensual gratifications." B is incorrect because the passage indicates that unsanitary living conditions had the effect of producing a population that is "improvident, reckless, and intemperate." C is incorrect because the passage does not examine the physical effects of poor sanitation, but rather the moral effects. D is incorrect because the passage indicates that unsanitary living conditions produce a population that is "improvident, reckless, and intemperate," not one with improved morals.

31. **B.** The title ("History of Swing"), the reputed authorship ("Kent Rick-Burner"); and the burning hayrick in the background all refer to the Swing Riots, the widespread uprising by agricultural workers in response to the use of labor-displacing threshing machines and the threatening notes, usually left at the scene of the crimes, signed "Captain Swing." A is incorrect because the images contain no reference to the English monarchy. C is incorrect because the image contains no references to the July Revolution in France. D is incorrect because the image contains no references to the Irish Potato Famine, and because 1830 is too early for such images.

32. **D.** The image depicts a horse-mounted landlord pointing to his burning hayrick and an agricultural laborer pointing to his starving family because their income has been reduced by the use of threshing machines. A is incorrect because the image does not depict a factory setting. B is incorrect because the image does not depict a naval setting. C is incorrect because the image does not depict any industrial setting or interests.

33. **B.** The passage states that "nationality ought only to be . . . a human group called by its geographical position, its traditions, and its language." A is incorrect because the passage does not argue that a nation must be a kingdom or have long-standing borders. C is incorrect because the passage does not say that a nation is only a nation if its people are strong enough to avoid foreign domination. D is incorrect because the passage does not argue that a nation must be made up of people with a unified political ideology.

34. **C.** The passage reflects Mazzini's nationalist desire for a united Italy and his romantic sense that a united Italy is a "natural" entity and a moral imperative of history. A is incorrect because Mazzini's desire for a new nation of Italy goes against mid-nineteenth-century nationalists' emphasis on tradition, stability, and legitimacy. B is incorrect because there are no expressions of socialist ideas in the passage. D is incorrect because there are no expressions of either anarchism or socialism in the passage.

35. **D.** Bismarck, the conservative chancellor of Germany, is portraying his conservative government as the natural caretaker of the nation and its working people, in contrast to the Social Democrats, whom he depicts as doing the bidding of bourgeois capitalists and splitting the nation by looking to exploit and dominate the working classes. A is incorrect because the passage does not address constitutionalism, an ideology born in seventeenth-century Europe. B is incorrect because Bismarck is a conservative delivering a conservative national message. C is incorrect because popular nationalism came into being in the first half of the nineteenth century.

36. **A.** Bismarck says that the purpose of government "is to serve the people," and that as the governing party, the conservatives "want to serve the people." In contrast, he depicts the Social Democrats as a party whose "mission is to lead, to rule." B is incorrect because Bismarck depicts his government as servants of the people, not as absolute rulers who should lead without opposition. C is incorrect because it is the Social Democrats whom Bismarck characterizes as believing that they are "leaders" who should be followed. D is incorrect because Bismarck is the leader of the governing party in Germany, not the loyal opposition.

37. **D.** The passage says that "there are objectives that only the state in its totality can fulfill," and that fulfilling them is a "responsibility of the state from which the state will not be able to withdraw." A is incorrect because the passage states that it "would be madness for a corporate body or a collectivity to take charge of those objectives that the individual can accomplish." B is incorrect because the passage says that "there are objectives that only the state in its totality can fulfill," and that fulfilling them is a "responsibility of the state," not that of private individuals. C is incorrect because the passage does not say that the state must fulfill any objective demanded by the people.

38. **C.** The cartoonist depicts Garibaldi as one of two men responsible for the unification of Italy, allowing one to infer that the cartoonist believed Garibaldi to have had a significant, if subservient, role in that accomplishment. A and B are incorrect because the cartoon offers no clues as to whether the cartoonist approved or disapproved of Italian unification. D is incorrect because Count Cavour's absence from the cartoon disallows a reliable inference as to his importance.

39. **C.** Garibaldi surrendered the southern lands of the Italian Peninsula to Victor Emmanuel II on the bridge of Teano on October 26, 1860. A and B are incorrect because 1848 is well before Garibaldi's campaign in Italy, which occurred in 1860. D is incorrect because Garibaldi would not have been depicted as aiding Victor Emmanuel II until after he surrendered the

southern lands of the Italian Peninsula to him in October 1860.

40. **A.** The cartoon depicts Garibaldi fitting the entire boot of Italy onto the leg of King Victor Emmanuel II, allowing the inference that the cartoonist viewed the unification of Italy as progressing. B is incorrect because fitting the entire boot suggests that the cartoonist viewed the unification of Italy as progressing, not doubtful. C and D are incorrect because nothing in the cartoon allows an inference as to whether the cartoonist viewed the unification of Italy as either a positive or negative development.

41. **B.** The telegram represents Germany's response, as a fellow member of the Triple Alliance, to Austria-Hungary concerning the scope of action open to them in dealing with the Balkan situation, which came to a head with the assassination of Crown Prince Franz Ferdinand on June 28, 1914. A is incorrect because the telegram was not sent during the process of German unification, which occurred from roughly 1866 to 1871. C is incorrect because the telegram was not sent during Germany's rearmament in violation of the Treaty of Paris, which occurred in the 1930s. D is incorrect because the telegram was not sent during 1882 when the Triple Alliance was created.

42. **B.** Bethmann-Hollweg's telegram is often referred to as Germany's "blank check" because it was understood to give Austria an unlimited scope of response to the assassination of Franz Ferdinand, to Serbia, and Pan-Slavism within the Austro-Hungarian Empire. A is incorrect because the telegram did not pledge Germany to join the Triple Alliance, which was previously created in 1882. C is incorrect because Franz Joseph was already emperor of Austria-Hungary; Franz Ferdinand had been his heir. D is incorrect because the telegram was understood to give Austria an unlimited scope of response.

43. **D.** The passage discusses social changes that were occurring during World War I, which broke out in 1914 and would continue to rage until 1918. A is incorrect because the essay was written in 1916, and World War II did not begin until 1939. B is incorrect because World War I

had only been going on for two years in 1916. C is incorrect because the so-called Inter-War Years were between 1918 and 1939.

44. **C.** The passage states that "[b]ecause it will obviously be impossible for all to find work quickly . . . there is almost certain to be an outcry for . . . women [to go] 'Back to the Home!'" A is incorrect because the passage says that forcing women back into the home would be unjust; it does not say that women would never be able to adjust. B is incorrect because the passage does not refer to an outright revolt of the nation's women. D is incorrect because the passage indicates that women could be seen as a cheaper alternative labor source by some employers; it does not say that they would be better paid than men.

45. **A.** The passage states that "conscienceless employers may regard women's labor as preferable, owing to its cheapness and its docility." B is incorrect because the passage does not refer to women being corrupted by the workplace. C is incorrect because the passage does not refer to women in the context of military service. D is incorrect because the passage does not refer to women working alongside men.

46. **A.** The Bolshevik government of Russia agreed to the punitive nature of the treaty with Germany and its allies because of Russia needed to end the war effort to consolidate its revolutionary gains. B is incorrect because the treaty was not a result of corruption or of collaboration between Bolsheviks and Russian business interests. C is incorrect because the dissolution of the Triple Entente alliance of Britain, France, and Russia was a *result* of the Treaty of Brest-Litovsk. D is incorrect because French and British aid being given to the so-called White Russians who opposed the Bolshevik government *resulted* from the Treaty of Brest-Litovsk.

47. **D.** In Article III of the treaty, Russia surrendered the eastern part of its empire (Poland, Ukraine, Finland, and the Baltic Provinces) to Germany. A and B are incorrect because, in Article III of the treaty, Russia ceded territory to the German Empire, not the other way around.

C is incorrect because, in Article III of the treaty, Russia surrendered of the *eastern* part of its empire (Poland, Ukraine, Finland, and the Baltic Provinces) to Germany.

48. **C.** The passage indicates that Morris had dedicated himself to his "hope of [modern civilization's] destruction" and "its supplanting by Socialism." A is incorrect because the passage does not refer to a dedication to the spread of mechanical power in industry. B is incorrect because the passage does not refer to transforming Britain into a commonwealth. D is incorrect because the passage does not refer to the spread of liberal democracy.

49. **A.** The passage indicates that Morris turned to socialism because he was deeply disturbed by modern civilization's "waste of mechanical power" and "its stupendous organization—for the misery of life!" B is incorrect because the passage makes no reference to Marx's arguments. C is incorrect because the passage indicates that Morris thought it was the past "struggles of mankind," not socialism, that had produced "nothing but this sordid, aimless, ugly confusion." D is incorrect because the passage indicates that his "deep love of the earth and the life on it" was one reason that he chose to embrace socialism, not reject it.

50. **D.** The passage calls for the removal by force of Alexander Kerensky's provisional government, which was the initial act of the October Revolution in Russia in 1917. A is incorrect because Russia had entered World War I in 1914. B is incorrect because the February Revolution in Russia led to the *establishment* of Kerensky's provisional government, not its fall from power. C is incorrect because Russia withdrew from World War I only after Lenin's Bolsheviks had replaced Kerensky's provisional government.

51. **C.** The passage asserts that the Bolsheviks had to seize power immediately from Kerensky and the provisional government. A is incorrect because the passage makes no reference to a new military offensive. B is incorrect because the passage asserts that the Bolsheviks had to seize power immediately from Kerensky and the provisional government, not that Kerensky had to move against the Bolsheviks. D is incorrect because the passage

makes no reference to military rule and because the concept of military rule was antithetical to Lenin's political beliefs.

52. **C.** The passage asserts that life has a physical basis; that is, it possesses "no properties but those of ordinary matter." A is incorrect because the passage states that "the conception of life as a something which works through matter" is a commonly held but incorrect view. B is incorrect because the passage makes no reference to life as a philosophical notion. D is incorrect because the passage asserts that life has a "physical basis," not a supernatural one.

53. **B.** Huxley's view that life has a physical (that is, a material) basis is representative of the nineteenth-century ideology of materialism, which held that nothing exists except matter. A is incorrect because the passage does not represent the nineteenth-century ideology of anarchism, a political ideology that advocated stateless societies. C is incorrect because the passage also does not represent conservatism, a political ideology that advocated respect for tradition in the face of external forces for change. D is incorrect because the passage does not represent romanticism, which urged the cultivation of sentiment and emotion by reconnecting with nature and the past.

54. **B.** Weisel asserts that his German audience was "responsible, not for the past, but for the way it remembers the past." A is incorrect because the passage indicates that Weisel "never believed in collective guilt." C is incorrect because in the passage Weisel asserts that his German audience was *not* responsible for the past. D is incorrect because Weisel asserts that his German audience *was* responsible "for the way it remembers the past."

55. **A.** The passage asserts that remembering the Holocaust is necessary for "coming to terms" with and finding "redemption" for Germany's past. B is incorrect because the passage intimates that remembering the Holocaust would promote healing among the German people, not hinder it. C is incorrect because the passage does not assert that remembering the Holocaust could ensure that it never happened again. D is incorrect, because the passage does not mention Jewish forgiveness of the German people.

Strategies and Suggestions for Responses to the Short-Answer Questions

Strategies

Step 1. Compose a topic sentence that responds to the question and gives you something specific to support and illustrate.

Step 2. Support and illustrate your assertion in the topic sentence with specific examples.

Suggested Responses

1. Briefly explain TWO ways in which the economy of Europe changed from a system of locally and agriculturally based economies to a system of more interconnected economies based on capital.

   Topic sentence for first part of answer: One way in which the economy of Europe changed from a system of locally and agriculturally based economies to a system of more interconnected economies based on capital was through the enclosure movement.

   Body of paragraph for first part of answer: For example, the enclosure of what had formerly been commons land had a two-prong effect. First, it gave landowners access to liquid capital by freeing up land for the planting of cash crops such as wheat, which could then be sold to the highest bidder. Second, it deprived serfs of their traditional rights to subsistence farming, forcing them, at great hardship, to seek various kinds of work for wages, another form of liquid capital.

   Topic sentence for second part of answer: A second way in which the economy of Europe changed from a system of locally and agriculturally based economies to a system of more interconnected economies based on capital was through the development of cottage industries.

   Body of paragraph for second part of answer: As the population of Europe rose in the eighteenth century, merchants needed to circumvent the guild system for supply to meet the new demand for goods. Their solution was to create cottage industries. For example, the spinning and weaving of wool cloth was done by peasants in the countryside, supplied with machinery and raw material by the merchants. This furthered the shift to a capital-based economy by providing liquid capital to a significant portion of the population that previously had no access to it.

2. Answer Parts A and B.
   A) Briefly give TWO possible explanations for the rise of the New Imperialism at the end of the nineteenth century.

   First topic sentence for Part A: One explanation often given for the rise of the New Imperialism at the end of the nineteenth century is the need for new markets to sell European manufactured goods and invest newly created capital.

   Body of first paragraph for Part A: This explanation argues that the increase in the production of goods and capital in nineteenth-century European economies forced European states and private investors to look outside Europe for new markets in which to sell their goods and for new economies in which to invest their capital. That, in turn, caused European states to push into Asia and South America with the greater intensity that characterized the New Imperialism at the end of the nineteenth century.

   Second topic sentence for Part A: A second explanation often given for the rise of the New Imperialism at the end of the nineteenth century is the need for competing European political elites to win the support of the newly politicized and enfranchised masses.

   Body of second paragraph for Part A: This explanation notes that the greater intensity that characterized the New Imperialism at the end of the nineteenth century followed closely on the heels of an increase in the percentage of the population that was eligible to vote, particularly in Britain and France, the two countries that were at the forefront of the New Imperialism. This explanation argues that the imperial conquests heightened enthusiasm for and confidence in the parties and candidates that promoted the New Imperialism.

   B) Briefly explain which of the possible explanations (given in A) is more plausible.

   Topic sentence for Part B: The explanation that argues the New Imperialism was due to the need for competing European political elites to win the support of the newly politicized and enfranchised masses is the more plausible of the two.

Body of paragraph for Part B: The logic of this argument is sound and is supported by the evidence. For example, in Britain at the end of the nineteenth century, both the Liberal and Conservative parties initiated new imperial policies and conquests, even though the leader of the Liberal party, William Gladstone, was personally opposed to them. Conversely, while the logic of the explanation that the New Imperialism is best explained by the need for new markets in which to sell European manufactured goods and invest newly created capital is sound, it is not borne out by all the evidence. There is a fair amount of data showing that the increase in sales and capital investment going into imperial projects was greater *before* the New Imperialism at the end of the nineteenth century.

3. Answer Parts A and B.

A) Briefly explain TWO effects of the development of separate sphere ideology on women in the nineteenth century.

Topic sentence for first Part of A: One effect that the development of separate sphere ideology had on women in the nineteenth century was to make any activity outside the home suspect and, therefore, dangerous to a woman's reputation.

Body of paragraph for first Part of A: The best example of this can be seen in the logic and enforcement of Britain's Contagious Disease Act, first passed in 1864. The act, originally intended to curb the spread of venereal disease in towns with naval ports, allowed police to detain any woman suspected of prostitution and force her to have a gynecological exam. In practice, the act was enforced over much of Britain, and any woman caught alone on the streets at night was subject to arrest and the forced exam because the assumption, enforced by separate sphere ideology, was that the only woman who would be out alone after dark was a prostitute.

Topic sentence for second Part of A: Conversely, the development of a separate sphere ideology in the nineteenth century gave women more power within the household.

Body of paragraph for first Part of A: The existence of this effect is more controversial among historians, but one school of thinking argues that the restriction of women's sphere of action to the home actually increased their power within that sphere, giving them almost total control over their children's education, domestic servants, and certain parts of the household budget.

B) Briefly explain ONE reason for the emergence of separate sphere ideology in the nineteenth century.

Topic sentence for Part B: One reason that historians almost always cite for the emergence of a separate sphere ideology in the nineteenth century is the competition for jobs created by the second phase of industrialization.

Body paragraph for Part B: The initial phases of industrialization, occurring in the late eighteenth and early nineteenth centuries, had been labor-intensive, drawing large numbers of men, women, and children into the factories and mills. But in the second half of the nineteenth century, complex machinery began to make much of that labor unnecessary, creating unemployment and intense competition for jobs. Initially men lost their jobs because women and children were cheaper labor. Hence, men reacted by creating a separate sphere ideology that asserted it was unhealthy and unnatural for women to work outside the home.

Question 4 is based on the following passage:

Détente does not and cannot abolish the class struggle. No one can expect that under conditions of détente the communists will reconcile themselves to capitalist exploitation or that the monopolists will become revolutionaries. Thus the strict observance of the principle of non-interference in the affairs of other states, respect for their independence and sovereignty—this is the indispensable condition for détente.

We do not hide the fact that we see in détente the road to the creation of more favorable conditions of peaceful socialist and communist construction. This only goes to show that socialism and peace are inseparable.

Leonid Brezhnev, excerpts from a speech at the CPSU Congress, February 29, 1976

4. Answer Parts A and B.

A) Briefly explain ONE reason why the passage can be identified with developments in the Cold War.

Topic Sentence for Part A: The passage can be identified with developments in the Cold War because of frequent references to détente.

Body of paragraph for Part A: The word *détente* denotes an era of relaxing tensions, especially between the United States and the Soviet Union during the Cold War. When used by Leonid Brezhnev, general secretary of the Central Committee of the Communist Party of the Soviet Union from 1964 to 1982, détente can only refer to the era of the Cold War that was characterized by a number of nuclear test-ban treaties and arms-limitation talks between the two superpowers, the Soviet Union and the United States.

B) Briefly describe TWO factors that explain Brezhnev's willingness to cultivate an atmosphere of détente with the United States during this period.

Topic Sentence for first Part of B: One reason that explains Brezhnev's willingness to cultivate an atmosphere of détente with the United States during this period is the rethinking of U.S. and Soviet foreign policy that followed the Cuban Missile Crisis in 1962.

Body of paragraph for first Part of B: After this event, which brought the two superpowers to the brink of nuclear war, a rethinking of positions occurred in which both sides acknowledged that more direct and open communication was necessary to avert such brushes with disaster in the future. Détente was essentially an extension of that notion.

Topic Sentence for second Part of B: Another reason that explains Brezhnev's willingness to cultivate an atmosphere of détente with the United States during this period was the economic strain that the nuclear arms race put on the Soviet Union.

Body of paragraph for second Part of B: The constant need to keep its country's nuclear arms arsenal more advanced than its opponent's made great demands on both the U.S. and the Soviet economies. The effects of these demands were felt more acutely in the Soviet Union whose economy was less productive than that of the United States. The cost savings gained from the signing of treaties such as SALT I, SALT II, and the Helsinki Accords, which limited the number of nuclear weapons in each superpower's arsenal, provided a great incentive for Brezhnev to cultivate an atmosphere of détente.

Strategies and Outline for Response to the Document-Based Question

Strategies

Remember the five steps to a short history essay of high quality:

Step 1. As you read the documents, decide how you are going to group them.

Step 2. Compose a thesis that explains why the documents should be grouped in the way you have chosen.

Step 3. Compose your topic sentences and make sure they logically present your thesis.

Step 4. Support and illustrate your thesis with specific examples that contextualize the documents.

Step 5. *If you have time,* compose a one-paragraph conclusion that restates your thesis. This question asks you to compare and contrast views of empire offered over time. Begin by identifying their similarities and differences (ask what the authors agree and disagree about) and then see if any trends develop over time.

Outline

A possible outline to the answer for this question looks like this:

Thesis: The documents illustrate arguments over the value of colonies to the colonizing nations and illustrate a tendency over time for arguments of political and strategic necessity to replace arguments of economic profitability and moral duty.

Topic Sentence A: Documents 1 and 3 both make arguments that colonies are unnecessary and undesirable because they are economically unprofitable; document 3 makes the further argument that colonies damage the moral standing of the colonizing nation.

Specific Examples: In #1, Gregg (1851) states that colonies have been rendered economically unprofitable (and therefore unnecessary) by the rise of a system of free trade. In #3, Gladstone (1878) says that colonies are unprofitable in both the material and moral sense, as they must be held by military means against the wishes of those who hold them.

Topic Sentence B: Documents 2 and 4–7 make arguments for the economic, moral, and strategic necessity of colonies.

Specific Examples: In #2, Disraeli (1872) argues that colonies are desired by "more primitive civilizations" and necessary for a nation to retain international influence and prestige. In #4, Paton (1883) maintains that colonies are morally profitable and necessary for moral reasons—that is, civilizing and Christianizing missions. In #5, Ferry (1884) states that colonies are economically, morally, and strategically necessary due to the need for economic outlets, to fulfill a Christian civilizing mission, and to establish military defense bases. The 1890 German newspaper advertisement in #6 claims that colonies are necessary for reasons of both economic interest and national honor. Finally, in #7, Lugard (1893) reasons that colonies are economically necessary for new markets and for the "development" of the colonizing nation—to prevent the nation from "falling behind."

Topic Sentence C: Read in chronological order, the documents illustrate a trend over time for arguments of economic and strategic necessity replacing arguments of economic profitability and moral duty.

Specific Examples: No documents in the set argue directly for the economic profitability of colonies (though some argue for their economic necessity); the only evidence of that arguments for profitability exist is the need to refute them shown in documents 1 and 3. The dominant chord of argument in all documents after 1884 (documents 5–7) is necessity—economic, political, and strategic. There is no reference to moral duty after 1890 (documents 6 and 7).

Strategies and Outline for Response to the Long Essay Question

Strategies

Choose the question for which you can quickly write a clear thesis and three topic sentences that you can illustrate and support with several specific examples. Then follow the five-step formula to constructing a history essay of high quality:

Step 1. Find the action words in the question and determine what it wants you to do.

Step 2. Compose a thesis that responds to the question and gives you something specific to support and illustrate.

Step 3. Compose your topic sentences and make sure they logically present your thesis.

Step 4. Support and illustrate your thesis with specific examples.

Step 5. *If you have time*, compose a one-paragraph conclusion that restates your thesis.

And remember the traps to avoid:

- **Long sentences with multiple clauses.** Your goal is to write the clearest sentence possible; most often the clearest sentence is a relatively short one.
- **Digressions.** No matter how fascinating or insightful you find some idea or fact, if it doesn't directly support or illustrate your thesis, don't put it in.
- **Mystery.** Don't ask a lot of rhetorical questions, and don't go for a surprise ending. The readers are looking for your thesis, your argument, and your evidence; give these points to them in a clear, straightforward manner.

Outlines

Question 1: Compare the political effects of nationalism on European civilization from 1789 to 1848 with the political effects of nationalism on European civilization from 1866 to 1945.

Thesis: From 1789 to 1848, nationalism tended to support the liberal notion that political sovereignty resided with the people, helping to fuel popular uprisings against traditional governments. From 1866 to 1945, nationalism tended to support the conservative belief in the value of historical traditions, helping to fuel movements of national unification under traditional, conservative monarchies and the rise of totalitarian parties with ultranationalist ideologies.

Topic Sentence A: From 1789 to 1848, nationalism was opposed by conservative forces, and nationalists made common cause with liberal reformers.

Specific Examples:

- The "Representatives of the Nation" rhetoric of the French Revolution from 1789 to 1799
- The wave of Liberal Nationalist revolutions from 1820 to 1848, including Spain (1820–1823), Sicily and Piedmont (1821), Greece (1829), Belgium (1830), France (1830), and all of Europe in 1848

Topic Sentence B: From 1866 to 1945, the conservative tendencies of nationalism came to the fore and beliefs in the value of historical traditions and heavily mythologized dreams of past national glories fueled conservative-led movements of national unification and empire building.

Specific Examples:

- The unification of Italy under Cavour and King Victor Emmanuel II
- The unification of Germany under Bismarck and Kaiser Wilhelm I of Prussia
- The rise of fascist movements in the 1920s and 1930s
- The NSDAP's rise to power in Germany and the popularity of Hitler's ultranationalist rhetoric

Question 2: Compare the context in which scientific work was done in the seventeenth century with the context in which scientific work was done in the nineteenth century.

Thesis: In the seventeenth century, scientific work was done in the context of both the Church and new, secular institutions that were just beginning to offer greater intellectual freedom. In the nineteenth century, scientific work was done almost exclusively in secular institutions that tended to foster materialist theories.

Topic Sentence A1: In the seventeenth century, scientific work was done in both the traditional Church-related institution and in new secular institutions.

Specific Examples:

Science in Church institutions:

- Jesuit astronomers in Italian universities
- Isaac Newton in Cambridge

Science in new secular institutions:

- Royal courts, such as the Court of Cosimo de Medici in Florence
- Royal societies and academies, such as the Royal Society of London
- Smaller, independent academies, such as the Neoplatonic Academy in Florence

Topic Sentence A2: The kind of scientific work (or natural philosophy, as it was termed in the seventeenth century) that was produced in the tension between Church and secular institutions tended to be a blend of traditional thinking in terms of God's purpose and newer thinking that emphasized natural laws and quantifiable, mechanical forces.

Specific Examples:

- Galileo's retention of the traditional, Aristotelian concept of uniform circular motion, combined with his emphasis on direct observation of heavenly bodies and the quantification of their orbits.
- Newton's introduction of the concept of force and his quantification of the force of universal gravitation, together with his retention of a belief in an active God in the universe.

Topic Sentence B1: In the nineteenth century, scientific work was done almost exclusively in secular institutions.

Specific Examples:

- Secular universities, such as the University of Edinburgh and the University of London replaced Cambridge and Oxford as hubs of science in Britain.
- The British Association for the Advancement of Science displaced the Royal Society of London.

Topic Sentence B2: In the new secular context of the nineteenth century, materialist theories replaced more orthodox theories of divine forces and plans.

Specific Examples:

- Darwin's theory of evolution by natural selection replaced Paley's theory of natural theology and divine design.
- Huxley's *Physical Basis of Life* supplanted vital force theories theories.